D0075680

The Early Modern Englishwoman:
A Facsimile Library of Essential Works

Series II

Printed Writings, 1641–1700: Part 1

Volume 6

Almanacs

Advisory Board:

Margaret J.M. Ezell
Texas A & M University

Elaine Hobby
Loughborough University

Suzanne W. Hull
The Huntington Library

Barbara K. Lewalski
Harvard University

Stephen Orgel
Stanford University

Ellen Rosand
Yale University

Mary Beth Rose
University of Illinois, Chicago

Hilda L. Smith
University of Cincinnati

Retha M. Warnicke
Arizona State University

Georgianna Ziegler
The Folger Shakespeare Library

The Early Modern Englishwoman:
A Facsimile Library of Essential Works

Series II

Printed Writings, 1641–1700: Part 1

Volume 6

Almanacs

Selected and Introduced by
Alan S. Weber

General Editors
Betty S. Travitsky and Patrick Cullen

Ashgate

Aldershot • Burlington USA • Singapore • Sydney

The Introductory Note copyright © Alan S. Weber 2002

All rights reserved. No part of this publication may be reproduced, stored in a retrieval system, or transmitted in any form or by any means, electronic, mechanical, photocopying, recording, or otherwise without the prior permission of the publisher.

Published by
Ashgate Publishing Limited
Gower House
Croft Road
Aldershot
Hants GU11 3HR
England

Ashgate Publishing Company
131 Main Street
Burlington, VT 05401–5600 USA

Ashgate website: http://www.ashgate.com

PR121
.E A2
2000,
pt. 1
vol. 6
~07546021SX

British Library Cataloguing-in-Publication Data
The early modern Englishwoman : a facsimile library of
   essential works
   Part 1: Printed writings, 1641–1700: Vol. 6:
   Almanacs
   1. English literature – Early modern, 1500–1700   2. English
   literature – Women authors   3. Women – England – History –
   Modern period, 1600 – – Sources   4. Women – Literary
   collections
   I. Weber, Alan S.
   820.8'09287

Library of Congress Cataloging-in-Publication Data
The early modern Englishwoman: a facsimile library of essential works. Part 1. Printed Writings 1641–1700 / general editors, Betty S. Travitsky and Patrick Cullen.

See page vi for complete CIP Block 00–64299

The image reproduced on the title page and on the case is taken from the frontispiece portrait in *Poems. By the Most Deservedly Admired Mrs. Katherine Philips* (1667). Reproduced by permission of the Folger Shakespeare Library, Washington, DC.

ISBN 0 7546 0215 X

Printed in Great Britain by Antony Rowe Ltd, Chippenham, Wiltshire

CONTENTS

Library of Congress Cataloging-in-Publication Data

Almanacs / selected and introduced by Alan S. Weber.

    p. cm. – (The early modern Englishwoman. Printed writings, 1641–1700. Part 1 ; v. 6)
    Includes bibliographical references.

    Contents: An almanack or prognostication for the year of our Lord, 1658 / by Sarah Jinner – An almanack and prognostication for the year of our Lord, 1659 / by Sarah Jinner – An almanack for the year of our Lord God 1664 / by Sarah Jinner – The womans almanack for the year of our Lord, 1688 / by Mary Holden – The womans almanack: or, an ephemerides for the year of our Lord, 1689 / by Mary Holden – The woman's almanack, for the year 1694 / by Dorothy Partridge – The prophesie of Mother Shipton in the raigne of King Henry, the Eighth / Mother Shipton – The honest Welch-cobler / by Shinkin ap Shone – Shinkin ap Shone her prognostication for the ensuing year, 1654 / Shinkin ap Shone – The womans almanack: or, Prognostication for ever/ by Sarah Ginnor.

    ISBN 0-7546-0215-X

    1. Almanacs, English.   I. Weber, Alan S. II. Jinner, Sarah, fl. 1658–1664. Almanack or prognostication for the year of our Lord, 1658. III. Jinner, Sarah, fl. 1658–1664. Almanack and prognostication for the year of our Lord, 1659. IV. Jinner, Sarah, fl. 1658–1664. Almanack for the year of our Lord God, 1664. V. Holden, Mary. Womans almanack for the year of our Lord, 1688. VI. Holden, Mary. Womans almanack. VII. Partridge, Dorothy. Womans almanack for the year 1694. VIII. Shipton, Mother (Ursula). Prophesie of Mother Shipton in the raigne of King Henry, the Eighth. IX. Shinkin ap Shone. Honest Welch-cobler. X. Shinkin ap Shone. Shinkin ap Shone her prognostication for the ensuing year, 1654. XI. Ginnor, Sarah. Womans almanack. XII. Title: Almanack or prognostication for the year of our Lord, 1658. XIII. Almanack and prognostication for the year of our Lord, 1659. XIV. Title: Almanack for the year of our Lord God, 1664. XV. Title: Womans almanack for the year of our Lord, 1688. XVI. Title: Womans almanack. XVII. Title: Woman's almanack for the year, 1694. XVIII. Title: Prophesie of Mother Shipton in the raigne of King Henry, the Eighth. XIX. Title: Honest Welch-cobler. XX. Title: Shinkin ap Shone her prognostication for the ensuing year, 1654. XXI. Title: Womans almanack: or, prognostication for ever.
AY750.C58
031.02–dc21

00–64299

PREFACE
BY THE GENERAL EDITORS

Until very recently, scholars of the early modern period have assumed that there were no Judith Shakespeares in early modern England. Much of the energy of the current generation of scholars has been devoted to constructing a history of early modern England that takes into account what women actually wrote, what women actually read, and what women actually did. In so doing the masculinist representation of early modern women, both in their own time and ours, is deconstructed. The study of early modern women has thus become one of the most important—indeed perhaps the most important—means for the rewriting of early modern history.

The Early Modern Englishwoman: A Facsimile Library of Essential Works is one of the developments of this energetic reappraisal of the period. As the names on our advisory board and our list of editors testify, it has been the beneficiary of scholarship in the field, and we hope it will also be an essential part of that scholarship's continuing momentum.

The Early Modern Englishwoman is designed to make available a comprehensive and focused collection of writings in English from 1500 to 1750, both by women and for and about them. The three series of *Printed Writings* (1500–1640, 1641–1700, and 1701–1750) provide a comprehensive if not entirely complete collection of the separately published writings by women. In reprinting these writings we intend to remedy one of the major obstacles to the advancement of feminist criticism of the early modern period, namely the limited availability of the very texts upon which the field is based. The volumes in the facsimile library reproduce carefully chosen copies of these texts, incorporating significant variants (usually in appendices). Each text is preceded by a short introduction providing an overview of the life and work of a writer along with a survey of important scholarship. These works, we strongly believe, deserve a large readership—of historians, literary critics, feminist critics, and non-specialist readers.

The Early Modern Englishwoman also includes separate facsimile series of *Essential Works for the Study of Early Modern Women* and of *Manuscript Writings*. These facsimile series are complemented by *The Early Modern Englishwoman 1500–1750: Contemporary Editions*. Also under our general editorship, this series will include both old-spelling and modernized editions of works by and about women and gender in early modern England.

New York City
2002

INTRODUCTORY NOTE

[It is in the nature of ephemera that they become difficult to read over the centuries. A 'Key to Difficult-to-Read Passages' has been provided by Dr. Weber in Appendix B, to assist the reader. In a departure from our usual practice, we included modern page numbers at the foot of each page of text for the ease of readers consulting Appendix B. — The General Editors]

The almanacs reproduced in this volume contribute to our understanding of women's participation in popular culture, astrology, medicine and prophecy. As the most inexpensive form of printed matter in the early modern period, and due to their practical use as a calendar, literary miscellany, guide to the weather, advertising medium, and source book, almanacs exerted a tremendous influence on popular opinion throughout the early modern period.

By the sixteenth century, the almanac had stabilized into the two-part structure found in the examples in this volume, with part one composed of the ephemeris (astronomical tables) listing the risings and settings of the sun and moon, times of the eclipses, and the aspects of the planets. This information was used in astrological calculations to predict future events, to forecast the weather, to determine the best times for administering medicines and performing phlebotomy, and to cast horoscopes predicting a child's future temperament and development. The second part of the almanac typically contained astrological prognostications or prophecies for the coming year, which could be political, scientific, or medical in nature.

The appearance of the medical and prophetic advice in Sarah Jinner's and Mary Holden's works was partially due to several larger trends, including an increase of women's literacy and an explosion of female authorship after the 1640s. Following the example of the female medieval medical authorities Trotula of Salerno and Hildegard of Bingen, women in the seventeenth century began publishing in increasing numbers on medical matters in a variety of genres: for example, Elizabeth Grey's *Choice Manual of Rare and Select Secrets in Physick and Chyrurgery* (1653), Jane Sharp's *Midwives Book* (1671), Queen Henrietta Maria's *The Queen's Closet Opened* (1655), Alethea Talbot's *Natura Exenterata* (1655) and works by Hannah Wolley.

The picture that emerges when historically situating the work of Holden and Jinner within early modern English medicine is that an increasingly literate readership of women, spurred by Nicholas Culpeper's English translations of Galen and the London dispensatory, were gaining better access to classically-based medical knowledge. A small handful of women, educated through self-study, practical experience or apprenticeship to male relatives, attempted to raise the standards of female-administered health care, through the publication of their own works and by challenging the male medical hierarchy itself by proposing formal education of midwives by midwives.

Holden was forced to defend astrology in her almanac as an ancient and venerable religious practice. I suspect that this apology for astrology and the uneasiness with political prophetic utterance in both Jinner and Holden represents a conscious effort to distance themselves from other female religious prophets of the period by relying on the status of astrology as a rational science. In sharp contrast, the ecstatic female prophets of the sixteenth and seventeenth centuries in establishing their right to prophesy would oftentimes draw on their stereotypical female passivity and irrationality, and argue that instead of intellectually interpreting scripture, they were merely serving as conduits of the *vox Dei*. Jinner and Holden, on the other hand, would probably both argue that they were natural philosophers, investigating the 'book of nature' through astrological calculation.

Sarah Jinner

Bernard Capp has discovered that a Captain Henry Herbert in 1673 made reference to a Sarah Jinner as a well-known practising London astrologer. Jinner may have also been practising medicine, judging from the medical receipts published in her almanac; medical advice books and almanacs were commonly printed (as we will see later in the case of Mary Holden) as advertisements for an individual's medical practice. Legally, Jinner could have been charging fees for dispensing internal medicines only if she had obtained a licence from the local bishop, as the London College of Physicians prosecuted irregular practitioners and women healers who infringed upon its rights. It is interesting that Jinner's *floruit* coincides exactly with one of the lowest incidences of College prosecutions for *mala praxis* in its entire history. The College of Physicians' inability or unwillingness to harass and restrict non-Collegiate practitioners during the interregnum may have emboldened Jinner to set her own medical and prophetic views in print.

An Almanack or Prognostication for the year of our Lord 1658

Jinner's first surviving almanac sets the pattern for her subsequent work. This work includes the following standard items: the chart of differences between Julian and Gregorian calendar dating, dates of the terms, the zodiacal man (illustrating which astrological houses govern which part of the body), a legend of symbols, monthly ephemeris tables, prognostications for each month, and 'Physical Observations' on medicine. Many of Jinner's medical recipes are reprinted in her later almanacs. In 'To the Reader', Jinner dismisses Aristotle's claim that women are only imperfect men (B1r), and argues against women's exclusion from the educational system, by pointing out that women possess intellective souls. She also lists the historical achievements of such female worthies as Semiramis, Elizabeth I, Katherine Philips, and Maria Cunitia, author of an epitome of Kepler. Thus Jinner provides a brief yet important defence of women's writing and a critique of a society that excluded women from serious intellectual endeavour. The copy used here is held by the Guildhall Library, London. Two other copies are housed in the Bodleian Library (only the ephemeris tables are extant in this copy), and British Library (this copy was unavailable for reproduction due to binding problems).

In the preface of her next almanac, Jinner discusses the fact that her promulgation of women's secrets (medical advice) in 1658 may have been offensive to some: 'therefore this year, I here present thee with some other of the like nature, avoiding such Language, as may, perhaps be offensive to some, whose tender Ears cannot away with the hearing of what, without scruples they will do' (B1r). That her fears were not unfounded is shown by the satirical almanac by Sarah Ginnor [pseud.?] reprinted in the Appendix to this volume.

For further study on human generation, Jinner recommends Levinus Lemnius's *The Secret Miracles of Nature* (1658) and A. Massarius's *The Woman's Counsellour* (1657), both published by Jinner's own publisher John Streater. Massarius's work is based on standard classical medical authors such as Avicenna, Galen and Hippocrates and several of the female cures listed in Jinner's almanacs are drawn verbatim from *The Woman's Counsellour*. Jinner is therefore working firmly within a learned and written tradition of medicine, not a folk-herbalist or oral body of knowledge as one might expect judging from the popular nature of the almanac. The well-preserved copy reprinted herein is from The Huntington Library; other copies of the 1659 text exist in the Bodleian and British Libraries and another edition by J. Streater can be found in the Balliol Library.

Jinner's 1660 (Wing 1846) almanac unfortunately could not be reproduced for this volume because both surviving copies (located in the British and Yale libraries) were tightly bound with considerable loss of text. Jinner's 1660 almanac begins to take on more overt political overtones when she suggests that her earlier prognostications had foreseen the actions of the kings of Sweden and Denmark; she also claims to have predicted the unhappy undertakings of the people of Cheshire and Lancaster (B1r).

In addition to the traditional astrological observations and advice provided for each month, the bulk of the *The Almanack or Prognostication for the Year of Our Lord 1660* is again filled with medical remedies, with a greater percentage of cosmetic receipts such as 'To Make the Face Fair' and 'To Take Away Hair' (B2v).

These receipts indicate that Jinner was developing a women's medicine concerned with the physical, emotional and psychological needs of her patients. Jinner clandestinely supplies advice on the use of abortifacient and emmenagogic drugs, such as pennyroyal and mugwort (*Artemisia vulgaris*), although like many male gynecological and pharmaceutical writers of the time, she never mentions these drugs in connection with aborting a live foetus.

An Almanack for the Year of our Lord God 1664

Jinner's 1664 almanac continues her 'Physical Observations', again primarily relating to the diseases of women and children, and her prophetic commentary is limited in this work to observations about the weather, planting, husbandry, and suggestions relevant to estate management. This almanac also contains some historical material with a table listing the reigns of the English kings and a chronology of the most remarkable events occurring between 1600–1664 (A2v). Jinner includes several Latin quotations for the first time in her work, undoubtedly added to demonstrate that she is working within a respectable tradition of natural philosophy (astrology). Another interesting feature of this work is the recipe 'For such as *think* themselves bewitched, that they cannot do the act of Venery' (emphasis mine) – here Jinner implies a disbelief in the power of witchcraft. Astrology, prognostication, and witchcraft were often linked in the popular mind. Similarly, Jinner had predicted in 1659 an 'increase and discovery of Witches and Fortune Tellers', in order to distinguish herself from similar kinds of prognosticators whom she believed to be frauds and evil-doers (B3r). The sole surviving copy of this almanac, fortunately in excellent condition, is housed in the Edinburgh University Library.

Mary Holden

No biographical information for Mary Holden has been uncovered, apart from scattered comments in her two published almanacs. The title page of her 1688 almanac describes her as a 'midwife in *Sudbury*, and Student in *Astrology*' and on her 1689 title page she is described as a 'Student in Physick'. On the back pages of both her almanacs, Holden advertises her own medical remedies in order to promote her midwifery and medical practice in Sudbury.

In London, the apothecaries, physicians, surgeons and midwives represented clearly defined groups with well-organized (except in the case of midwives) guild and apprenticeship structures. Outside of London where university-trained physicians were few, however, the bulk of medical care was carried out by mixed practitioners like Holden who combined the skills of the apothecary, surgeon, physician, midwife, and herbalist; this fact is reflected in the provincial mixed-guild structure.

Holden's work can be profitably situated within early modern learned medicine, specifically Elizabeth Cellier's unsuccessful professionalization of female medicine or midwifery along the lines of the London College of Physicians. Cellier addressed a proposal to James II in 1687 for the government incorporation and instruction of midwives. (For a discussion of Cellier, see Volume Four of this series, *Writings on Medicine*.)

The period of activity of Cellier and Holden again coincides with a sharp decline (1689–90) in College of Physicians' prosecutions for irregular practice; after the political uncertainties of the Glorious Revolution and continuing attacks by the apothecaries, Paracelsians, and Royal Society virtuosi, the College of Physicians' influence over medical affairs declined precipitously.

The Womans Almanack for the Year of our Lord, 1688

Holden's advertisements in her 1688 almanac indicate that she probably practiced apothecary and compounded electuaries (compound medicaments) specifically for women. It was technically legal for a woman outside the seven-mile London jurisdiction of the College of Physicians to practice medicine and prescribe drugs with a license from the local Bishop. Midwives, although not legally incorporated anywhere in England, were licensed in ecclesiastical courts. Thus, Holden should be viewed as a fully professionalized practitioner, possibly belonging to a guild and practicing as an apothecary and physician, and probably well-trained in obstetrics through the midwives' informal system of apprenticeship. In both her almanacs, Holden displays a general knowledge of Hippocrates, a central authority in male professional medicine.

Reflecting increased scepticism towards astrology at the close of the seventeenth century, Holden defends the prognostic art against the frequent criticism of its pagan origins: 'For as much as some do think that Astrology was invented by the Heathens, I shall endeavour to prove that it was from the beginning of the World, devised by the Sons of *Seth* ... .' (A5r). She provides biblical quotations to demonstrate the ancient origins of knowledge of the stars, passed down to modern times as a *prisca theologia*. The excellent copy used for reproduction in this volume is from the Magdalene College, Cambridge Library (Pepys Library), and two other less than perfect copies are housed at the Edinburgh University Library and UCLA. Although the *STC* records another copy at the Library Company of Philadelphia, the library has no record of ever owning the work.

The Womans Almanack: Or, An Ephemerides For the Year of Our Lord, 1689

Holden's second surviving almanac (1689) repeats much of the same kind of information in her earlier work, but also adds such miscellaneous pieces as a table of the high water at London Bridge and some basic astronomy lessons. The planetary system she is describing is Ptolemaic (geocentric) rather than Copernican (helio-centric), which is not surprising in English almanacs even of this late date, since prognosticators normally made their determinations from intermediary precalculated tables, and the actual physical structure of the heavens was of practical indifference to them, except in the matter of greater accuracy. Holden continues to advertise her medical cures for hysteria and other female medical problems: 'I make a rare Electuary, that cureth any Fits, caused by Wind, Vapours, the rising of the Mother, Convulsion: It seldom fails of curing any Fits whatsoever' (B3v). The best surviving copy of this work, reprinted in this volume, is housed at the Folger Library, and one other copy in good condition is housed at the Houghton Library.

Dorothy Partridge

Dorothy Partridge's *The Womans Almanack, For the Year 1694* is probably pseudonymous since publisher Benjamin Harris falsely claimed that Dorothy Partridge was the wife of the celebrated almanac author John Partridge and issued at least one almanac with her name on it in 1712, *Mrs Dorothy Partridge's Speculum for the Year 1712.* Harris was caught distributing unauthorized almanacs under the name of Vincent Wing and making additions to John Partridge's legitimate almanacs (Capp 241). He was undoubtedly capitalizing on the famous name of Partridge, as well as attempting to create a new market (female readers) with the ruse of female authorship. It is possible, however, that the Dorothy Partridge of the 1694 almanac printed for J.S. was a real midwife and astrologer not directly related to the famous Partridge almanac family. Whether by a male or female author, the almanac was clearly directed at a female audience, although most women readers would have probably found the humour offensive.

The Woman's Almanack, For the Year 1694

Authorship of Partridge's 1694 almanac, 'Containing many choice, useful, pleasant, and most necessary Observations, adapted to the Capacity of the Female Sex', (A1r) is attributed to a 'Dorothy Partridge, Midwife, Student in Astrology'. This work, which was printed without the usual standard ephemeris tables, contains 'Monthly Observations in Goodhousewifery', (A1v *et seq.*) primarily dealing with gardening. Separately paginated ephemeris tables may have accompanied this almanac, but they have not survived. As with the other female-authored almanacs and according to astrological theory – in which human behaviour was controlled by the stars – Partridge recommends the proper times for her readers to 'use Venus' (A2v). The work also includes several short articles on chiromancy for distinguishing character traits and fortunes by interpreting lines on the hands and wrist.

    This almanac exhibits the same sort of sexual humour found in the Sarah Ginnor [pseud.?] almanac, which marks the work as the likely product of a male pen, such as the chiromantical observation that a certain line of the hand 'denotes and intimates the Woman will kiss in a Corner, or beat her Puff-past with her Neighbour's Rowling-pin' (B2r). In addition, Partridge supplies several cosmetic recipes for colouring the hair red, to cure a red face, and to whiten an old woman's teeth, as well as suggestions on 'How to know whether a Woman be a Maid or no' and 'How to make a Philtre, or Love powder' (B2v). These last concerns were important medical and sexual questions for middle- and lower-class readers who had little access to Latin or vernacular medical works or trained doctors, and who may have been prevented by shame or poverty from enquiring about these problems. The sole surviving copy, in poor condition, is housed in the Bodleian Library.

Appendix A:

Mother Shipton

The secular prophet Mother Shipton of Knaresborough, Yorkshire was reputedly born in 1488 or earlier. William H. Harrison, who investigated the bulk of her prophecies, stated in 1881 'There is no absolute evidence that any one of the details [of Mother Shipton's life] is true, but there may be some foundation for the incident narrated about Cardinal Wolsey' (43).

Further details about Shipton's career appeared in the probably fictional *Life and Death of Mother Shipton* (1684) by the Irish writer Richard Head. Another alleged biography, the anonymous *Strange and Wonderful History of Mother Shipton* (1686) claimed that Shipton had successfully foretold the Great Fire of London and the Plague of 1665. Samuel Pepys noted in his diary that Prince Rupert exclaimed at the outbreak of the Fire of London: 'now Shipton's prophecy was out' (*DNB*, 'Mother Shipton', XIX:119).

Although the events foretold by Shipton – Cardinal Wolsey's journey and death, the destruction of Trinity steeple and Ouse Bridge, and Thomas Cromwell's beheading – took place during or after the reign of Henry VIII, no written record of her existence can be uncovered before the edition of Richard Lownd's *The Prophesie of Mother Shipton* (1641), reprinted below. Given that these sorts of prophecies were often reinterpreted in the seventeenth century to suit the particular political climate, one suspects that the story of Thomas Cromwell told by Mother Shipton may have been reissued (or first written) for political reasons surrounding the rise of Oliver Cromwell. In addition to reprints in 1642, 1644, 1648, 1651, 1663, 1678, 1682, and 1685 by various printers, astrologer and almanack maker William Lilly also included Mother Shipton's prophecy in his *A Collection of Ancient and Moderne Prophesies* (1645), and a comedy entitled *Life of Mother Shipton: A New Comedy* written by the 'Poor Plagiary' Thomas Thompson appeared in 1668. A Dutch version entitled *Moeder Schiptons prophecyen van Engelandt* was published in 1667. These prophecies were taken very seriously by both statesmen and ordinary citizens: Lilly's surviving printer's bill indicates that 4,500 copies of his *Collection of Ancient and Moderne Prophesies* were printed (Thomas 412–13).

The iconography of Mother Shipton on the various reprint editions demonstrates the public ambivalence towards female secular prophecy, as sometimes Shipton appears as an unremarkable woman in middle-class dress, and in other images with the unmistakable physiognomy of the witch, with wart, bedraggled hair and crooked nose and chin. Richard Head noted: 'though she was generally believed to be a Witch, yet all persons what ever, that either saw, or heard of her, had her in great esteem' (30). The copy printed in this volume, one of the best preserved examples, is in the Thomason Tracts collection at The British Library, and other copies can be found at the Bodleian Library (Fairfax), Canterbury Cathedral, and the Library Company of Philadelphia. Most surviving examples of Shipton's prophecies are heavily worn and well thumbed indicating her widespread use and readership.

Shinkin ap Shone

The two satirical works of Shinkin ap Shone reprinted in the appendix – *The honest Welch-Cobler* (1647) and *Shinkin ap Shone Her Prognostication for the ensuing Year, 1654* – satirize the Welsh people and language. In the text itself, the prognosticator is male. (He has a wife, children, and cuckold's horns.) The pseudo-Welsh dialect with its insistently repeated 'her', however, creates such satirical gender confusion, if only temporarily, that the texts are worth reprinting here. On the title page of *The honest Welch-Cobler*, Shinkin is designated one of the 'Shentlemen in Wales' and speaks of 'herself' as a 'man of valour' (4). Shinkin's dialogue parodies Welsh dialect throughout, with many of the same orthographic features found in Shakespeare's Fluellen. According to Heather Rose Jones at Berkeley, Welsh has no neuter third person singular pronoun, and Welsh speakers speaking English may have frequently substituted 'her', leading to the stereotype among English speakers that the Welsh used 'her' indiscriminately as a feature of their dialect.

The honest Welch-Cobler

In the opening of this work, Shinkin declares her intention to demonstrate 'the candour of her ententions, and the excellencie of her inventions' (2), but since many of the long-winded sentences often trail off into nonsense, Shinkin's Welsh 'sharpenesse of wit' is obviously being called into question by the author of this pamphlet. Repeated jokes about running away in battle are also made. Contemporary figures in this work serve as the butt of jokes: the Marquis of Newcastle, Prince Maurice, Lord Littleton 'that ran away with the Creat Seale', and Lord Hopton. The copy reprinted is from The British Library Thomason Tracts, and other copies in very good condition exist at the Boston Public Library, New York Public Library, and Yale University; the surprisingly good condition of all copies of these ephemeral pamphlets indicates that they may not have been read extensively.

This work further reinforces stereotypical English anti-Celtic views of Welsh foibles – their rashness, idleness, promiscuity, untrustworthiness and love of leeks, for example. Shinkin provides a insulting explanation of the origin of the Welsh people, based on a linguistic misunderstanding (which propels much of the satire and legitimates the past political and military violence against the Welsh, i.e., as an inferior and irrational race since they are unable to speak 'intelligibly'): misunderstanding a letter from the King of Cornwall requesting French *oars*, the King of France instead sends a shipload of half-naked French *whores* to Cornwall. The enraged Cornish King then sends to Ireland for Irish *rugs* to clothe the whores, but misunderstanding the Cornish tongue, the King of Ireland sends over a shipload of Irish *rogues*. The Cornish King disposes of the whores and rogues by sending them into unpopulated Wales from whence springs the Welsh race (4–5). The astrological art is also satirized in this work through Shinkin's interpretation of the *Stella nova* seen in London on February 22–23, 1654, which portends '(if any thing at all) either peace or war, or both…' (8). The best preserved copy, reprinted here, can be found in The British Library Thomason Tracts, and one other copy exists in the Bodleian Library.

Sarah Ginnor

Sarah Jinner's fears expressed in her 1659 almanac that her writings describing female medical problems might unwittingly provide titillating material for salacious readers were not unfounded, as a satirical almanac signed Sarah Ginnor entitled *The Womans Almanack: Or, Prognostication for ever* appeared in 1659 published by a J.J. Similar concerns appear in European midwife manuals by both men and women. Sarah Ginnor is probably a pseudonym for a male writer. Since female health in classical medical texts was often reduced to complaints concerning the womb (suffocation or dislocation of the matrix or mother, a catch-all disease known as hysteria), and such cures as marriage or masturbating female patients to expel corrupted humours were prescribed in medieval and Renaissance medical manuals, the equation between sexuality and female disease was an easy one for the early modern mind to take.

The Womans Almanack: Or, Prognostication for ever

The Sarah Ginnor fraud is immediately apparent, as the crude and frivolous portrait on the cover of the 'Ginnor' almanac contrasts sharply with the elegant engraving of Jinner which accompanies all of her legitimate almanacs. The numerous sexual quips in the work portray women as wanton and sexually deceitful, such as the joke when Venus appears in the 12th house in exaltation, it 'denoteth that women will be more free than usual in bestowing the P– on their Clients' (A2v). In addition to parodic weather predictions, sexual humour runs throughout the work with jokes such as 'if a man be fortified strongly with the Scepter of Mars, it denotes a fit time for Venus to lye down, that mirth may be produced by the Turks entrance into Constantinople' (A8v). The Ginnor almanac thus provides important evidence for the reception of Jinner's legitimate work, as the Ginnor author obviously felt that Jinner's medical advice to women was in some sense sexual in nature, and therefore a fit object for pornographic humour. The sole surviving copy of this work, reproduced in this volume, can be found in the Thomason Tracts in The British Library.

Acknowledgements

The editor would like to thank the following individuals who provided invaluable assistance in locating texts and advice on the best possible base texts for reproduction in this volume: Jean Archibald (Edinburgh Library), Vivian Bradley (Bodleian), Lynn Braunsdorfer (Beinecke Library), Bernard Capp (Warwick), Lisa Forman Cody (Claremont McKenna College), David S. Cousins (Canterbury), William Falcon (Boston Public Library), A. Fitzsimons (Magdalene College, Cambridge University), Susan Harris (Bodleian), R.M. Harvey (Guildhall Library, London), Sarah Hutton (University of Hertfordshire), Clive Hurst

(Bodleian), Alan Jutzi (Huntington Library), Dr. Luckett (Pepys Library, Cambridge), Giles Mandelbrote (British Library), Mary E. Morrison (United Microfilms Incorporated), Jessy Randall (Library Company of Philadelphia), Stephen Tabor (Clark Library, UCLA), Ted Teodoro (New York Public Library), Goldie Zarnoch (United Microfilms Incorporated), Georgianna Ziegler (Folger), Roberta Zonghi (Boston Public Library). This volume could not have appeared without the guidance and advice of Betty S. Travitsky and Patrick Cullen. The Pennsylvania State University, Faculty Grants Committee, provided grant support for this project as well as a related website on Early English Almanacs, and Charles Burroughs of CEMERS at the State University of New York, Binghamton, has also provided valuable assistance. The editor would also like to thank Jonas Pontusson, Susan Tarrow, and Pat Wasyliw of the Institute for European Studies at Cornell University for supporting his research fellowship for 1999–2000.

References

Aveling, James Hobson (1872; Reprint, 1967), *English Midwives: Their History and Prospects*, London: Hugh K. Elliott Ltd.

Blank, Paula (1996), *Broken English: Dialects and the Politics of Language in Renaissance Writings*, London: Routledge

Bosanquet, Eustace F. (1930), 'English Seventeenth-Century Almanacks', *The Library* 10, no. 4: 361–97

Camden, Jr., Carroll (1931–32), 'Elizabethan Almanacs and Prognostications', *The Library* 12: 83–207

Capp, Bernard (1979), *English Almanacs 1500–1800: Astrology and the Popular Press*, Ithaca: Cornell University Press

Easton, Jon (1998), *Mother Shipton, The Prophecies of Ursula Sontheil* Chester: Fenris Press

Furst, Lilian R. (ed.) (1997), *Women Healers and Physicians: Climbing a Long Hill*, Lexington: University Press of Kentucky

Geneva, Ann (1995), *Astrology and the Seventeenth-Century Mind: William Lilly and the Language of the Stars*, Manchester: Manchester University Press

Harrison, William H. (1881), *Mother Shipton Investigated*, London: William H. Harrison

Hunter, Lynette and Sarah Hutton (eds.) (1997), *Women, Science and Medicine 1500–1700: Mothers and Sisters of the Royal Society*, Thrupp: Sutton Publishing Limited

Hurd-Mead, Kate Campbell (1938), *A History of Women in Medicine from the Earliest Times to the Beginning of the Nineteenth Century*, Haddam, Conn.: Haddam Press

The Life and Prophecies of Ursula Sontheil, Better Known as Mother Shipton; Carefully Collected and Compiled (1967), Knaresborough, Yorks: Dropping Well Estate

Mack, Phyllis (1992), *Visionary Women: Ecstatic Prophecy in Seventeenth-Century England*, Berkeley: University of California Press

Marland, Hilary (ed.) (1993), *The Art of Midwifery: Early Modern Midwives in Europe*, London: Routledge

Tester, S.J. (1987), *A History of Western Astrology*, Woodbridge: The Boydell Press

Thomas, Keith (1971), *Religion and the Decline of Magic*, New York: Charles Scribner's Sons

Towler, Jean and Joan Bramall (eds.) (1986), *Midwives in History and Society*, London: Croom Helm

Watt, Diane (1997), *Secretaries of God: Women Prophets in Late Medieval and Early Modern England*, Cambridge: D.S. Brewer

Weber, A.S. (forthcoming), 'English Women's Early Modern Medical Almanacs in Historical Context', *ELR*

ALAN S. WEBER

Sarah Jinner's *An Almanack or Prognostication for the year of our Lord 1658* (Wing 1844) is reprinted from the copy at the Guildhall Library (Shelfmark S. Pamphlet 173). The text block of the Guildhall copy is 71 × 114 mm. Page A2r–v, missing in the Guildhall edition, is supplied from the incomplete copy in the Bodleian Library.

For passages that are blotched, please consult Appendix B, 'A Key to Difficult-to-Read Passages'.

ALMANACK

OR

PRÓGNOSTICATION for the year of our
LORD 1658, Being the second after Biſſextile or
Leap year. Calculated for the Meridian of London,
and may indifferently ſerve for England, Scotland,
and Ireland.

ʙʏ SARAH JINNER. Student in Aſtrology.

London, Printed by I. Streeter for the Company

Common notes for the year 1 6 5 8.
according to the

Julian, English or old Account.	} {		Gregorian Forreign or New Account.
6	The Golden Number		6
15	The Circle of the Sun.		15
Œ	The Dominicall Letter		F
11	The Roman Indiction.		11
6	The Epact.		16
21	The Number of Direction.		24

Old Acount,	Moveable Feasts according to the	New Account.
February 7	Septuageſſima.	17 February.
February 24	Aſhwedneſday.	6 March
April 11	Eaſter-day	21 April.
May 16	Rogation Sunday	26 May.
May 20	Aſcenſion day.	30 May.
May 30	Whitſunday	9 June
June 6	Trinity Sunday.	16 June
Novemb. 28	Advent Sunday.	1 December.

A Table of the four Terms and their Returns
for the year 1658.

Hillary Term begins Jaunary 23, ends February 12, and hath four Returns.

| Octab.Hil. January 20. | Craſt.Purif. February 3 |
| Quind.Hil. January 27. | Octab.Purif. February 9 |

Eaſter Term begins April 28, ends May 24 and hath five Returns.

Quind.Paſch.Ap. 26	Quinq; paſch. May 17
Tres Paſch. May 3	
Menſ. Paſch. May 10	Craſt. Aſcen. May 21

Trinity Term begins *June* 11 ends *June* 30 and hath four Returns.

| Craſt. Trin. June 7 | Quind. Trin. June 21. |
| Octab. Trin. June 14 | Tres Trin. June 15. |

Michaelmas Term begins Octob. 23, ends November 29 and hath ſix Returns.

Tres Mich. October 20.	Craſt. Mart. Novemb. 11
Menſe Mich. October 27.	Octab. Mar. Novemb. 18.
Craſt. anim. November 3.	Quind. Mar. Novemb. 25

The Characters and Names of the twelve Signes, with their Dominion in Man's Body.

The Names and Characters of the 7 Planets.

♄ ♃ ♂ ☉ ♀ ☿ ☽

Saturn, Jupiter, Mars, Sol, Venus, Mercury, Luna

The Characters and Names of the Aspects.

☌ ☍ ✱ ☐ △

Conjunction, Opposition, Sextile, Quadrate, Trine.

January hath XXXI Dayes.

☽ First quarter 1 day, 1 hour after noon.
○ Full moon 9 day, 56 min. past 10 in the morning.
☾ Last quarter 16 day 52 min. past 10 in the Morning.
● New Moon 23 day 45 min. past 10 in the morning.
☽ First quarter 31 day, 45 min past 10 in the morning.

1	a	New years day	21 ♑ 42	♈	8 2	
2	b		22 43	♉	8 0	☌☉☿ 6 m. cold
3	c		23 44	♉	7 58	winds driving
4	d	Telesphorus	24 45	♉	7 57	snow or rain,
5	e	Simeon	25 46	♊	7 56	more temperate
6	f	Epiphanie	27 48	♊	7 55	☍♃♀ o.
7	g	Julian	28 49	♋	7 54	⚹♃♂ 11 n.
8	a		29 50	♋	7 53	clearing winds
9	b		0 ♒ 51	♌	7 52	with frost.
10	C	1 Sun. af. Epip.	1 52	♌	7 50	inclinable to
11	d		2 53	♌	7 49	moisture, cloudy
12	e		3 55	♍	7 47	and dark most
13	f	Hilary	4 56	♍	7 46	part of the quar-
14	g	Felix	5 57	♎	7 45	ter, not very cold
15	a		6 58	♎	7 44	warm & temperat
16	b	*Marcellus*	7 59	♏	7 42	□☉♂ 6 n.
17	C	2 Sun. af. Eph.	8 0	♏	7 41	△☿♄ 9 m. cold
18	d		9 1	♐	7 39	□♄♀ 8 n. winds
19	e		10 2	♐	7 38	bring moisture.
20	f	Octab. Hilary	11 3	♑	7 36	
21	g	Agnes	12 4	♑	7 34	much snow or
22	a	Vincentius	13 5	♒	7 32	cold rain falls.
23	b	Term begins	14 6	♒	7 31	
24	C	3 Sun. af. Epi.	15 6	♒	7 30	△♃☿ 4 n. clea-
25	d	Conve. of Paul	16 7	♓	7 28	ring winds and
26	e	Polycarpus	17 8	♓	7 26	more temperate,
27	f	Quind. Hilary	18 9	♈	7 25	△☉♄ 5 n. cold
28	g		19 9	♈	7 23	and close, cloudy
29	a		20 10	♈	7 21	in some place a-
30	b	Adelgunda	21 11	♉	7 20	rain.
31	C	4 Sun. af. Epi.	22 12	♉	7 18	

◉ Full moon 7 day 57 min. paſt 11 at night.
☽ Laſt quarter 14 day 6 min. paſt 11 at night.
☽ New moon 22 day 22 min. paſt 2 in the morning.

1	d		23 ♋	12	♊	7	17	This Month be=
2	e	Puriſ. Mary	24	13	♊	7	16	ginneth as the
3	f	Blaſius	25	13	♊	7	14	other ended.
4	g		26	14	♋	7	13	More ſerene and
5	a	Agathe	27	15	♋	7	11	temperate,
6	b	Dorothea	28	15	♌	7	10	
7	c	Septuageſſima	29	16	♌	7	8	
8	d		♒	16	♍	7	6	△ ◯ ♃ 5 n.
9	e	Octab ., Puriſ.	1	16	♍	7	4	ſerene temperate
10	f	Scholaſtica	2	17	♎	7	2	with wholſome
11	g		3	17	♎	6	59	froſts, cold rain
12	a	Termends	4	17	♏	6	58	△ ♄ ♀ 10 m.
13	b		5	18	♏	6	56	or ſnow.
14	c	Sex. Valentine	6	18	♐	6	55	
15	d	Fauſtinus	7	18	♐	6	54	wind drives ſnow
16	e	Julianus	8	18	♑	6	53	☌ ◯ ♀ 6. n.
17	f		9	18	♑	6	51	or rain.
18	g		10	19	♑	6	49	□ ♂ ♀ 7 n.
19	a		11	19	♒	6	46	Much ſnow or
20	b		12	19	♒	6	44	cold rain falls in
21	c	Quinquageſſi.	13	19	♓	6	42	many places.
22	d		14	19	♓	6	40	
23	e	Shrovetueſday	15	19	♈	6	38	☌ ♀ ♀ ♃: more
24	f	Mathias Aſh.	16	19	♈	6	35	rain or ſnow.
25	g		17	18	♉	6	32	△ ♃ ♀ 6. n. with
26	a	Victor	18	18	♉	6	30	□ ♂ ♀ 4 n. high
27	b	Leand.	19	18	♉	6	27	winds to the end
28	c	1 Sun. in Lent	20	18	♊	6	24	of the Month.

March hath XXXI Dayes.

☽ First quarter 2 day 36 min. past 6 in the morning.
● Full moon 9 day, 44 min: past 10 in the morning:
☾ Last quarter 16 day, at 2 in the morning:
● New moon 23 day 53 min. past 6 at night.
☽ First quarter the 31 day, 23 min. past 10 at night

1	d	David	21 ♓	17	♊	6	23	☽☋ Cloudy,
2	e	Simplicius	22	17	♊	6	20	
3	f		23	17	♋	6	18	clearing
4	g	Adrianus	24	16	♋	6	16	
5	a		25	16	♌	6	14	
6	b	Fridelinus	26	16	♌	6	11	the wind high dri-
7	C	2 Sun. in Lent	27	15	♍	6	9	△♃☿ 1 a. veth
8	d		28	15	♍	6	7	hail and rain,
9	e		29	14	♎	6	5	
10	f	Alexander	0 ♈	13	♎	6	3	
11	g	Days & N.eq.	1	13	♏	6	0	□☉♃ 8 n. clea-
12	a	Gregory	2	12	♏	5	50	ring & temperate,
13	b	Euphrasia:	3	11	♏	5	57	
14	C	3 Sun. in Lent	4	11	♐	5	56	☽☋
15	d		5	10	♐	5	54	
16	e	Cyriacus	6	9	♑	5	52	
17	f		7	8	♑	5	50	
18	g		8	7	♒	5	48	a kind & pleasant
19	a	Josephus	9	6	♒	5	46	season with
20	b		10	5	♓	5	44	□♃♀ 5 *m.* some
21	C	4 Sun. in Lent	11	4	♓	5	42	□♂☿ 5 n.
22	d		12	3	♓	5	40	seasonable showres
23	e		13	2	♈	5	39	
24	f		14	1	♈	5	37	close cloudy and
25	g	Ann. of Mary	15	0	♉	5	36	☍☉♄ 3. wet.
26	a	Castulus	15	59	♉	5	34	
27	b		16	58	♉	5	32	
28	C	5 Sun. in Lent	17	56	♊	5	30	storms with rain
29	d		18	55	♊	5	28	☍☉♂ 0. hail or
30	e	Guido	19	54	♋	5	26	☍♄♀ 6 *m.* snow,
31	f		20	52	♋	5	24	

☉ Full Moon the 7 day, 5 min. past 7 at night.
☾ Last quarter 14 day, at noon.
☽ New Moon 22 day, 53 min. before noon.
First quarter 30 day 49 44 min. past 10 in the morn.

1	g		22	♈51	♋	5	20	
2	A	Mary Ægyp.	23	50	♌	5	18	
3	b		24	48	♌	5	16	
4	C	Palm Sunday	25	47	♍	5	14	□ ♃ ♀ 8 n. winds
5	D		25	45	♍	5	12	and some moisture
6	E		26	44	♎	5	10	✶ ♂ ♀ 3 m.
7	f	Egisippus	27	42	♎	5	7	
8	g		28	40	♏	5	4	
9	A		29	39	♏	5	2	☌ ♄ ♃ 11 b.
10	b		0	♉32	♐	5	0	very cold winds
11	C	Easter-day	1	35	♐	4	58	
12	D	Julius	2	34	♑	4	57	
13	E	Justinus	3	32	♑	4	45	
14	f	Tiburtius	4	30	♒	4	53	
15	g	Olympias.	5	28	♒	4	52	✶ ♂ ♃ 12 n. serene
16	A		6	26	♓	4	50	✶ ♃ ♀ p. and very
17	b		7	24	♓	4	48	temperate with
18	C	Low sunday.	8	22	♓	4	46	☌ ☉ ♀ 5 m. windy
19	D		9	20	♈	4	44	and dry
20	E		10	18	♈	4	42	
21	f		11	16	♉	4	40	✶ ♃ ♀ 11 n.
22	g		12	14	♉	4	39	
23	A	S. George	13	12	♉	4	37	
24	b	Albertus	14	10	♊	4	35	
25	C	Mark Evang.	15	8	♊	4	32	☌ ☉ ♀ 10 n.
26	D	Quæsid Pasch	16	6	♊	4	31	the winds high
27	E	Anastasius	17	4	♋	4	29	with some
28	f	Terme begins	18	2	♋	4	27	☌ ♀ ♀ 7 m. moisture
29	g		19	59	♌	4	25	
30	A		20	57	♌	4	23	

Full Moon 7 day, 47 min. past 3 in the morning.
Last quarter 13 day 44 min. past 11 at night.
New Moon 22 day 57 min. past 2 in the morning.
First quarter 39 day, 19 min. past 7 at night.

1	b	Phil. & Jacob	21	55	♍	4	22	☌♃♂ 4 n.
2	C	Jubilate	22	52	♍	4	21	Great heat with
3	D	Invent. Cru.	23	50	♎	4	20	storms of thunder
4	E	Florianus	24	48	♎	4	19	and fiery corrup-
5	f	Gothardus	24	45	♏	4	17	tations for many
6	g	Joh. Port. Lat.	25	43	♏	4	15	daies.
7	a		26	41	♐	4	13	□♄♂ 4 n.
8	b	Stanislaus	27	38	♐	4	12	△♄☿ 10 n.
9	C	Cantate	28	36	♑	4	11	blustring stor ns
10	D	Menle Pasch.	29	33	♑	4	10	of wind.
11	E	Mamert.	30	31	♒	4	9	
12	f	Pancratius	1	28	♒	4	7	
13	g	Servatius	2	25	♒	4	6	
14	a		3	25	♓	4	5	
15	b	Sophia	4	20	♓	4	3	△♄☿ 6 n. in Tome
16	C	Rogation	5	18	♈	4	2	places showres of
17	D	Quinq. Pasch.	6	15	♈	4	1	rain,
18	E		7	13	♈	3	5	△♄♃ 6 n. expect
19	f		8	10	♉	3	58	a very turbulent
20	g	Ascention	9	7	♉	3	56	air thunder and
21	a	Craft. Ascen.	10	5	♊	3	55	rain,
22	b		11	2	♊	3	54	
23	C	Exaudi	12	59	♊	3	53	△☉♄ o.
24	D	Term ends	13	56	♋	3	53	more cool and
25	E	Vrbanus	14	54	♋	3	52	dark clouds and
26	f	Beda	15	51	♌	3	52	some rain,
27	g		16	48	♌	3	52	
28	a		16	45	♍	3	51	with □♄☿ 1 a.
29	b		17	43	♍	3	5 n	
30	C	Whitsunday	18	40	♍	3	58	great storms of
31	D	Petronella	19	37	♎	3	50	wind.

June hath XXX Dayes.

Full moon the 4 day, 18 min. past 10 in the morn.
First quarter 12 day, at 23 min. past 1 afternoon.
New moon 20 day, 19 min. past 5 afternoon.
Last quarter 28 day, 31 min. past 1 in the morning.

1	e		20	♊ 34	♎	3	50	
2	f	Marcellus	21	31	♏	3	49	
3	g	Erasmus	22	29	♏	3	49	☌♃☿ 8 m. winds
4	A		23	26	♐	3	49	with some show-
5	b	Boniface	24	23	♐	3	48	ers,
6	c	Trinity	25	20	♑	3	48	
7	d		26	17	♑	3	48	
8	e	Medardus	27	14	♒	3	47	□♄☿ 12. n. cold
9	f		28	11	♒	3	47	and dark weather
10	g	Onophrius	29	9	♓	3	47	with showers of
11	a	Term begins	0	6	♓	3	47	rain.
12	b		1	3	♈	3	47	☌♃☿ 8 n.
13	c	1 Sun. af. Trin.	2	0	♈	3	47	☌♃☿ 3 n.
14	d	Valerius	3	57	♈	3	47	a wholsome air
15	e	Vitus	4	54	♉	3	48	with some gentle
16	f	Rolandus	5	51	♉	3	48	showres,
17	g		6	48	♉	3	48	
18	a		6	45	♊	3	49	
19	b	Gervasus	7	43	♊	3	49	
20	c	2 Sun. af. Trin.	8	40	♋	3	49	
21	d		9	37	♋	3	50	most of this quar-
22	e	Achatius	10	34	♌	3	50	□♄☿ 11 b. ter
23	f		11	31	♌	3	51	☌☉☿ 0. high
24	g	John Baptist	12	28	♌	3	51	△☉♄ 5 m. winds
25	A		13	25	♍	3	51	✶♄♂ 3 m. rain
26	b		14	22	♍	3	52	thunder with
27	c	3 Sun. af. Trin	15	19	♎	3	53	distempered face
28	d		16	16	♎	3	54	of Heaven.
29	e	Peter Apostle	17	13	♏	3	55	
30	f	Term ends	18	11	♏	3	56	

July hath XXXI Dayes.

🌕 Full moon 4 day, 30 min. past 6 at night.
🌗 Laſt quarter 12 day 39 min. paſt 5 in the morning.
🌑 New moon 20 day, 54 min. paſt 5 in the morning.
🌓 Firſt quarter 27 day, 7 min. paſt 3 in the afternoon.

1	D		19	♋ 8	♐	3	57	Clouds flying in
2	a	Viſit. Mary	20	5	♐	3	57	ſome places a lit.
3	b		21	2	♑	3	58	✳ ♄ ☿ 8 n. the rain
4	c	4 Sun. af. Trin.	22	59	♑	3	59	☌ ☉ ♃ 7 n.
5	D	Anſelmus.	23	57	♒	4	0	
6	e		24	54	♒	4	2	Wholſome blaſts
7	f		25	51	♓	4	3	and ſerene. but
8	g	Chilianus	26	48	♓	4	5	hot and inclmable
9	a	Cyrillus	26	45	♓	4	6	to thunder.
10	b	7 brethren	27	43	♈	4	8	
11	c	5 Sun. af. Trin.	28	41	♈	4	9	great heat
12	D		29	38	♉	4	11	
13	e		0	♌ 34	♉	4	12	☌ ☽ ☿ 1 m.
14	f	Bonaventure	1	32	♉	4	13	☿ in Max. elong.
15	g	Swithin	2	29	♊	4	14	☽ ? ? (a. ☉ e.
16	a		3	26	♊	4	15	□ ♄ ☿ 2 m.
17	b	Alexius	4	23	♋	4	16	high winds and
18	c	6. Sun. af. Trin.	5	21	♋	4	17	ſtorms.
19	D		6	18	♋	4	18	
20	e	Margaret	7	15	♌	4	20	
21	f	Dog-days beg.	8	13	♌	4	21	
22	g	Mary Mag.	9	10	♍	4	23	
23	a	Apollina	10	8	♍	4	25	
24	b	Chriſtiana	11	5	♎	4	27	
25	c	James 7 S. a. T,	12	3	♎	4	29	wind ſtirring,
26	D	Anna	13	0	♏	4	30	☌ ♃ ☿ 2 m.
27	e	Martha	14	58	♏	4	32	drives a little
28	f	Sampſon	15	55	♐	4	34	✳ ☉ ♄ 3 a. moi-
29	g		16	53	♐	4	36	☽ ? ? ſture or
30	a		17	50	♐	4	37	clouds.
31	b	Germanus	17	48	♑	4	38	

August hath XXXI Dayes.

○ Full moon 3 day, 14 min. past 4 in the morning.
☾ Last quarter 10 day, 40 min. past 11 at night.
○ New moon 17 day 55 min. past 2 in the afternoon.
☽ First quarter 25 day, 27 min. past noon.

1	G	Lammas	18	♌ 45	♑	4	39	Seasonable and
2	D		19	43	♒	4	40	good weather,
3	E		20	41	♒	4	43	✶♄ 2 a.
4	f	Aristarchus	21	39	♓	4	44	winds and dry.
5	g	Oswaldus	22	36	♓	4	46	
6	A	Sixtus	23	34	♈	4	48	
7	b		24	31	♈	4	50	dry hot and un-
8	C	9 Sun. af. Tr.	25	29	♈	4	52	♂○☿ 16. whol-
9	D		26	27	♉	4	55	some air,
10	E	Laurentius	27	25	♉	4	56	wind
11	f		28	23	♊	4	58	a more wholsome
12	g		29	20	♊	4	59	✶♃ 4. air and
13	A		0 ♑ 18		♊	5	1	pleasant, in some
14	b	Eusebius	1	16	♋	5	3	places some moi-
15	C	10 Sun. af. Tr.	2	14	♋	5	5	sture,
16	D	Rochus	3	12	♌	5	6	
17	E		4	10	♌	5	8	
18	f	Helena	5	6	♍	5	10	
19	g	Sebaldus	6	4	♍	5	12	storms of hail
20	C	Bernard	7	8	♎	5	14	♂○☿ 2 a. and
21	b		8	3	♎	5	16	thunder in some
22	C	11 Sun. af. Tr.	9	1	♎	5	18	places, yet the
23	D	Zacheus	10	59	♏	5	20	most part fair.
24	E	Bartholomew	11	57	♏	5	22	
25	f	Ludovicus	12	55	♐	5	24	
26	g		13	54	♐	5	26	♂♄ 3 w. a dark
27	A	Dog days end.	14	52	♑	5	28	face of Heaven.
28	b	Augustine,	15	50	♑	5	30	some rain.
29	C	12 Sun. af. Tr.	16	49	♒	5	31	the month ends
30	D	Paulinus	16	48	♒	5	33	✶♃☿ ●, with
31	E		17	46	♓	5	35	fair weather.

September hath XXX Dayes.

Full Moon 1 day 7 min, past 4 after noon.
Last quarter 9 day 14 min, past at night.
New moon 17 day 4 min, past 3 in the morning.
First quarter 23 day 30 min past 7 at night.

1	f	Giles	18	♍ 44	♓	5	37	Most of this quar-
2	g	Veronica	19	42	♓	5	40	ter very good and
3	a		20	41	♈	5	42	pleasant weather.
4	b	Theodosius	21	40	♈	5	44	
5	c	13 Sun. af. Tr.	22	39	♉	5	45	
6	d	Magnus	23	37	♉	5	47	
7	e	Regina	24	36	♊	5	49	
8	f	Nat. Mar.	25	35	♊	5	50	☌♄♃ 12 at night
9	g	Gorgon	26	34	♊	5	51	high winds,
10	a		27	33	♋	5	53	
11	b		28	31	♋	5	55	□♃♀ 1 a, serene
12	c	14 Sun. af. Tr.	29	29	♌	5	58	and good wether
13	d	Day & N. equ.	0	28	♌	6	0	most part of this
14	e	Holy crosse	1	27	♌	6	2	quarter.
15	f	Nicodemus	2	26	♍	6	4	
16	g	Euphem,	3	25	♍	6	6	
17	a	Lampert	4	24	♎	6	8	the wether dry
18	b		5	23	♎	6	10	and fair, most of
19	c	15 Sun. af. Tr.	6	22	♏	6	12	this quarter hot
20	d	Fausta	7	21	♏	6	14	✳♃ ♂ 11 b. and
21	e	Matthew Apo	8	21	♐	6	16	✳ ☉♃ 4 m. trilu-
22	f	Mauricius	9	20	♐	6	18	☌☉ ♂ 6 m. lent.
23	g	Esdra	10	19	♑	6	20	
24	a	Samuel	11	19	♑	6	22	
25	b	Cleophas	12	18	♒	6	24	
26	c	16 Sun. af. Tr.	13	17	♒	6	26	□♃♀ 7 a. high
27	d		14	17	♓	6	28	winds ends this
28	e	Wences	15	19	♓	6	30	Month, in some
29	f	Michael Arch.	16	16	♓	6	34	places some
30	g	Hieronymus	17	15	♈	6	32	flowers.

October hath XXXI Dayes.

🌑 Full Moon 1 day, 31 min. past 6 in the morning.
☾ Last quarter 9 day, 24 min. past noon.
🌑 New Moon 16 day, 57 min. past noon.
☽ First quarter 23 day 59 min. past 4 in the morning,
🌕 Full Moon 30 day, 52 min. past midnight.

1	a			18 ♎	15	♈	6	36	
2	b			19	14	♓	6	38	a dark and cloudy
3	c	17 Sun. af. Tr.	20	14	♉	6	40	
4	d	Franciscus	21	13	♉	6	42	☌ ☉ ♄ 4 a. aire
5	e		22	13	♊	6	44	an appearance
6	f	Faith	23	13	♊	6	46	of much rain
7	g		24	13	♋	6	48	
8	a		25	12	♋	6	50	fairer near the
9	b	Dionysius	26	12	♋	6	52	last quarter,
10	c	18 Sun. af. Tr.	27	12	♌	6	54	▫ ♃ ♀ 5 n. △ ♃ ♀
11	d	Burchard	28	12	♌	6	56	high violent (8 n.
12	e	Coleman	29	12	♍	6	58	☌ ♄ ☌ 3 m. and
13	f		0 ♏	12	♍	7	0	impetuous storm
14	g	Calixtus	1	12	♎	7	2	of wind bringing
15	a	Hedewig.	2	12	♎	7	4	showres of rain in
16	b	Gallus	3	12	♏	7	6	☌ ☉ ♀ 7 n. some
17	c	19 Sun. af. Tr.	4	12	♏	7	8	places, a blustring
18	d	Luke Evang.	5	12	♐	7	10	Lunation.
19	e	Ptolomeus	6	12	♐	7	12	
20	f	Tres Michael	7	13	♑	7	14	
21	g	Ursula	8	13	♑	7	15	☌ ☉ ♀ o. ✶ ♄ ♀ 9 n.
22	a	Cordul.	9	13	♒	7	17	winds and clouds,
23	b	Term ends	10	14	♒	7	19	
24	c	20 Sun. af. Tr.	11	14	♒	7	20	some showres
25	d	Crispinus	12	14	♓	7	22	✶ ♀ ♀ 2 m. ▫ ☉ ♃ o.
26	e	Amandus	13	15	♓	7	24	some clearing, &
27	f	MenteMichael	14	15	♈	7	26	temperate frosty
28	g	Simon & Jud.	15	16	♈	7	28	morning,
29	a		16	16	♈	7	30	
30	b		17	17	♉	7	32	
31	c	21 Sun. af Tr.	18	17	♉	7	33	♀ in max. elonga. ☉

November hath XXX Dayes.

☾ Laſt quarter 8 day 39 min. paſt 3 in the morning.
● New Moon 14 day 9 min. paſt 11 at night.
☽ Firſt quarter 21 day min paſt 5 at night.
○ Full Moon 29 day 27 min, paſt 8 at night.

1	d	All Saints	19 ♏	♊	7	34	
2	e	Animarum	20	♊	7	36	
3	f	Theop. Craſt.	21	♊	7	38	⚹ ♂ ♀ 5 *m.*
4	g	animarum	22	♋	7	39	the air inclinable
5	a	Powder Treaſ	23	♋	7	40	to moiſture,
6	b	Leonard	24	♌	7	42	
7	C	22 Sun. af. Tr.	25	♌	7	43	
8	d		26	♍	7	45	high winds dri-
9	e	Theodorus	27	♍	7	46	ving ſome rain or
10	f		28	♍	7	48	ſnow
11	g	Martine	29	♎	7	49	☌ ♂ ☿ 6 *n* □ ♃ ☿ 8.
12	a	Craſt. Mart.	0 ♐	♎	7	50	but [□ ♃ ♂ 10. n
13	b		1	♏	7	52	changing to ſere-
14	C	23 Sun. af. Tr.	2	♏	7	53	nity,
15	d	Leopaldus	3	♐	7	55	
16	e		4	♐	7	56	
17	f	Hugh (Mart.	5	♑	7	57	
18	g	Gelaſius Oct.	6	♑	7	58	expect rain and
19	a	Elizabetha	7	♒	7	59	⚹ ♀ ☿ 6 *m.* dark
20	b	Amos	8	♒	8	0	air.
21	C	24 Sun. af. Tr.	9	♓	8	1	□ ♄ ♀ 2 a.
22	d	Cæcilia	10	♓	8	2	♀ *elong.* a. ☉e:
23	e	Clemens	11	♈	8	3	
24	f	[Mar.	12	♈	8	4	temperate ſerene,
25	g	Kather. Quin.	13	♈	8	5	△ ☉ ♃ 2 *m.*
26	a	Conradus	14	♉	8	6	and froſt moſt part
27	b		15	♉	8	6	of this quarter.
28	C	Advent Sun.	16	♊	8	7	
29	d	Term ends	17	♊	8	8	
30	e	Andrew Ap.	18	♊	8	9	

⟨ Last quarter 2 day 26 min. past ... at night.
☉ New moon 14 day 48 min. past 9 at night.
☽ First quarter 21 day 9 min. past 10 in the morning.
🌕 Full Moon 29 day 42 min. past 3 in the afternoon.

1	f	Candidus	19	46	♋	8 10 △ ♃ ♈ 2 m.
2	g	Cassianus	20	48	♋	3 9 Winds clear the
3	A	Cassianus	21	49	♌	8 12 air most part of
4	b	Barbara	22	50	♌	8 the quarter tempe-
5	c	2 Advent	23	51	♌	8 13 rate and clear
6	d	Nicolaus	24	53	♍	8 11
7	e		25	54	♍	8
8	f	Concep. of Ma.	26	55	♍	8 13
9	g	Joachimus	27	57	♎	8 11 clouds the wind
10	A	test day	28	58	♏	8 13 ✳ ☉ ♃ ♂ ♌ speed
11	b	Damasus shor	29	59	♏	8 13 ✳ ♄ ♃ 3 m. then
12	c	3 Advent	1	♐	♐	8 13 ♌ ⊙ 9 afternoon
13	d	Lucia	2		♐	8 11 nelly and foul
14	e	Nicasius	3			8
15	f		4		♒	8 23 Mask'd this quar-
16	g				♒	8 22 ter the weather
17	A	Lazarus	6		♓	8
18	b	Christopher	7	8	♓	8
19	c	4 Advent				8
20	d				♈	8
21	e	Thomas Apo.	10	12	♈	8 8
22	f	Theodosus	11		♉	8 8 △ ♃ ⊙
23	g				♉	8 6 inclination consi-
24	A	Adam & Eve	13	16	♊	8 5 dered pleasant
25	b	Nat. of Christ	14	18	♊	8
26	c	Stephen		19	♋	8
27	d	John EV.		20	♋	8
28	e	Innocents	17	22	♌	8
29	f		18	23	♌	8
30	g	David	19	24	♌	8 2 △ ♄ 5 m.
31	A	Silvester	20	25	♋	8 2 cold winds.

To the Reader.

YOu may wonder to see one of our Sex in print especially in the Celestial Sciences: I might urge much in my defence, yea, more then the volume of this Book can contain: in which I am confined, not to exceed ordinary bulk: But, why not women write, I pray? have they not souls as well as men, though some witty Coxcombs strive to put us out of conceit of our selves, as if we were but imperfect pieces, and that Nature intending a man, when the seminal conception proves weak, there issues a woman. But know that Aristotle affirms, that woman doth contribute to formation matter as well as place, Mankind is preferred by woman: many other rare Benefits the world reapeth by women, although it is the policy of men, to keep us from education and schooling, wherein we might give testimony of our parts by improvement: we have as good judgement and memory, and I am sure as good fancy as men, if not better. We will not boast of strength of body, let Horses and Mules do that, What rare things have women done? What Cures in Physick, which great Doctors have left? How many Common-wealths have been managed by woman, as the Amazones? Did not Semiramis set the Babylonian Kingdom in great glory? Tomyris cut off the head of Cyrus, Nay, let me tell you, we have had a Pope of our sex, named Pope Joan, which the best Historians do not deny. When, or what Commonwealth was ever better governed than this by the vertuous Q: Elizabeth? I fear me I shall never see the like again, most of your Princes now a dayes, are like Dunces in comparison of her: either they have not the wit, or the honesty that she had: Somewhat is the matter that things do not lodge so well: well, no more of that. To our business again, What rare Poets of our sex were of old? and now of late the Countess of Newcastle. And, I pray you, what a rare Poem hath one Mistris Katherine Philips near Cardigan writ, it is printed before Cartwrights Poems, who, if her modesty would permit, her wit would put down many men in a Masculine brain. I could tell you of many more, that have been famous in Philosophie and Physick, as the Countess of Kent, and others. And lastly, of

Cunetia a Germane Lady, that lately did set out Tables of the Planets Motion: therefore, why should we suffer our parts so rusty? Let us scowre the rust, by ingenous endeavouring the attaining higher accomplishments? This I say, not to animate our Sex, to assume or usurp the breeches: No, but perhaps if we should shine in the splendor of vertue, it would animate our Husbands to excel us? So by this means we should have an excellent Work.

But now to give you an account of this Book: In the first sheet there are the moveable Feasts, the Terms and returns thereof? also a Table of the Signs of Mans Body, the Planets and Aspects: then in order followeth the twelve Months, in which the fourth Column is the place of the Sun in the Zodiack at noon: the fifth column is the sign that the Moon is in: the sixth is the rising of the Sun. After the Months, the remaining discourse is Astrological Predictions upon the Suns entring Aries, Cancer, Libra, and Capricorn, briefly handled according to the Rules of Art. Also most admirable Medicines tending to the good of mankind in Generation. (More I could have inserted, but for modesties sake I omit, referring you to a most excellent piece of small price, entituled, **The Womans Counsellor,** or, **the Feminine Physician,** a work of no small profit and use.) And lastly short Monthly observations Astrological, and other tending to good Houswifry: It is not my intentions, to advise our Sex to be unprofitable, no, but to be meet helps.

Farewell till next year,

Reader, thou art desired to keep these annuall pieces, for if, life be permitted, it is intended to be a collection of Rules, worth thy view and preserving.

A

A
PROGNOSTICATION
FOR
The year of our LORD.
1658.

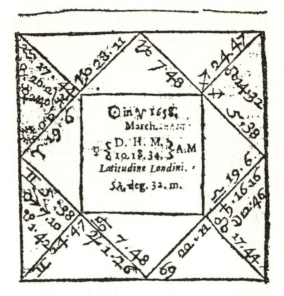

○ in ♐ 1658,
March.
D. H. M.
♀ 10. 18. 34. ♂ A.M
Latitudine Londini.
♌ deg. 32. m.

I Nd this figure and the figure of the præventional full Moon, and postventional new Moon, Saturn, Jupiter, Venus, and Sol, seem to contend for dignities; but by reason all the Angles are moveable, it imports uncertainty, both of Counsel, and Action in the affairs of the world. Venus is Lady of the sign intercepted in the Horoscope, essentially dignified, speaketh kindnesse to the people, and fortifieth their resolutions.

B2   She

She hath good share in the Dominion of the year, but she falling into the sixth House, and being with Saturn, both mischief to the people in Trade, in health, and otherwise, obstructions in their affairs. Saturn being Lord of the tenth House, afflicts the Moon: it denotes servitude, and sickness to attend the people, especially, the West and North-west parts of the world, all such as live upon the ruins of the people, and their disagreement: such be Lawyers and Clarks, Attournies and the like. Mars being in the second House the house of treasury, imports, that the Souldiery will be diving in the publick pocket: something of this nature occasioneth tumults, signifyed by the Dragons tail in Gemini, the sign ascending the Cusp of the second House. Jupiter is near the Cuspof the fourth House, allayeth the influence of Saturn, and somewhat bettereth the condition of the Farmer in his calling, and some few others, by finding of hidden Treasure: so much for what concerns the publick. Now let us inquire of this position of the heavens more particularly of our Sex. And first we find Mercury in a feminine sign, in a feminine House, drawing towards a corporal conjunction with Venus, & therefore we shall allow Mercury a female in this case: The Lawyer is no small servant of ours. Mercury to a quartil of Mars & Pisces and Gemini, giveth some of our sex (that are not poysed with vertue) a rare faculty of scolding, in other some muttness and sulleiness, Venus in the twelvth house, in exultation, but applying to combustion with the Sun, signifyeth that some women will be more apt than ordinary in bestowing the Pox upon their Clients. Luna in going to Saturn in the sixth house in Libra, signifyeth, that many an old covetous gruff will doat after young women, signifyed by Luna full of light. Let me advise you to beware marrying in the Spring, for Scorpio being in the seventh house intercepted, denoteth unseemly wantonness, and lightness in women.

Of the *Suns* entrance into *Cancer*.

Mercury Lord of the Ascendant in Cancer, and the Moon, have signification, that the Commonalty suffer much by their strife, dissention, and heart-burning one against another. Great ones suffer by having the Dragons tail in the tenth house, its fatal to some of the biggest of the City of London. Luna being in the seventh house in Pisces, a double bodyed sign, it noteth frequent marri-

marrying, and it is a pretty lucky Position, for Oyster wives, Fish wenches, and others, whose callings are signified by the sign of Pisces. The Moon and Jupiter being in reception, the Moon in Pisces and Jupiter in Cancer, doth tell me that it is a fortunate time of marrying, that many of our sex shall obtain good rich matches: some of them better than they deserve: Mercury and Venus in Cancer, being in conjunction in the eleventh house, the house of friends: the which considered, to marry a Seaman is fortunate, I advise thee to marry the Trumpeter rather than the Gunner: but have a care of Saturn, he casts a quartil into the fifth house, the house of children, but that may be over by the next quarter, if you chance not to lye down before the quarter ends.

Of the *Suns* entrance into *Libra*.

In the Suns entrance of Libra, which will be Sept. the 12th. 25 min, past 12 at night, the general judgement of this figure I shall passe over briefly, for as much as Jupiter is with the Moon in the first house nigh the Cusp, it signifyeth, that Religion shall passe amongst the people with much credit: that the ministry shall have great power of perswading the people; yet for the most part this Religion is but formall.

Jupiter and the Moon being in Leo upon the ascendant, giveth our sex rampant and fiery spirits; proud and ignorant Dames that understand no better will strive for the mastery: but the Sun being near Mars in Libra, his fall and going towards Saturn, a crooked fellow, he will hamper you, and put the distaffe in your hands and make you spinne.

Venus being in Scorpio, I fear me that the naughty wantons of our sex as well as the other sex, will be peppered with the pox, and if so, wo be to your Noses; it is malignant to catch it at this time.

In this Figure, the Dragons head being in Sagittary denoteth fruitfulnesse to honest women.

Of

Of the Suns entrance into *Capricorne.*

In this figure, ♃ ☊ ♂ as Lord of the Ascendant in the eighth house with the Dragons head ☊ devoured some losse of blood by battel, sore robberies, and inhumane murders, diseases, as coughs, sore eyes, and violent feavers, having Venus in the twelvth house in opposition to Jupiter in the sixt house, and the Moon in the seventh in Scorpio, both foretell many diseases in women. Wast would now faine know, if it be good to marry this quarter: I tell you, No, for Saturn is a Tragical enemy to all comfort that way. You have the Moon Lady of the fifth in Scorpio, your children will dye, neither can I promise you any riches: for Mars is in the second house neer the seventh and consumes it all; but Mercury in the ninth house puts you a jogging to see your friends, and delight in discourse, as gossipings.

Of Eclipses.

There will be two Eclipses, but neyther of them will be visible with us: the first the 2 day of May, the second the fourteenth day of November.

and Ginger rootes, Conserves of Piony, and which conserve of an Apple.

A Syrup to stay the immoderate Flux of the Terms.

Take syrup of Endive, one ounce: syrup of Purflain, half an ounce: the Decoction of Egrimony, and of Plantain four ounces: mix them together, and make them into a syrup, and so take it as you please.

An Electuary for the same.

Take Conserve of Roses, two ounces: of Water Lillies, one ounce: of Pearl prepared, and burnt Hartshorn, each half an ounce: Bole Armonick, Terra Lemnia, each half a scruple: mix them together with syrup of Plantain, a quantity sufficient to make it into an Electuary.

An Electuary for the same.

Take Conserve of Roses, six ounces: Conserve of Burrage, Buglas, Balm, of each an ounce: Bolus prepared, a dram: Pearl prepared a quarter of an ounce of Rubies, Jacinths, Saphir, each a scruple: Cinamon, a dram; mix them together, and make an Electuary thereof.

Another Electuary to stay the Terms.

Take conserve of Roses, three ounces: Marmalade, two ounces and a half: red Coral, a dram: Bolus prepared, half a dram: Blood-stone prepared, two drams; mix them all together with the syrup of Myrtles, and make an Electuary thereof, and take it as you please.

An Electuary to purge the Reins

Take Cassia newly extracted, one ounce: Rhewbarb in powder, one dram: mix them together with syrup of white water Lillies, a sufficient quantity to make it into an Electuary; put this into a penny pot of White-wine

wine, or a little posset drink, which edffe's [...]
hand; stir it well together, till it be all dissolved in
the drink, and so take it in the morning fasting; and go
about your business (if you have any thing to do), above
two hours after, take some broth or posset drink.

This Medicine you may take twice or thrice, as you
see occasion, resting always a day between.

Afterwards, you may take every other day, a drachm of
Troch's de Carabe in Plantane water.

You may also give the Patient, every second or third
day a dram of the filings of Ivory in Plantane water;
it is very good.

Sweating is also much commended in this case,
which may be thus done.

Take Barly water three ounces, strong water three
ounces; give it the Patient very warm, and so let
her sweat.

A Powder to be used in the nature of a Pessary, against the suffocation of the Matrix, or fits of the Mother.

Take red Storax, Lignum Aloes, Cloves, of each a
dram; Musk, Amber, of each half a dram; make them
altogether into a powder, and then wrap it up in a cloth,
in the form of a Pessary, and put it up into the place.

Another for the same.

Take an ounce of Oyl of Lillies, Musk, Saffron,
of each three grains; b use all well together, and make
a Pessary thereof with Wooll, of Cotton and put it up
into the place.

A Fumigation for this Disease.

Take Gallia Moscata, Cassia wood, Cynamon,
Time, of each a like quantity; mix these together, and
make a perfume thereof, and let the smoke be received
up into the Matrix, through a tunnel for that purpose.

If the Patient be a Maid, a husband is the best medicine [...] but to such as cannot [...] then
let

Physical Observations.

A Syrup to Concoct, and prepare the humours, to provoke the Terms.

Take Syrup of Betony, of Mugwort, and Elecampane, of each half an ounce, of the Decoction of Isysop, and Betony, of each four ounces; mix them together, and so take it when you please.

Dangerous things which provoke the Terms are, Cynamon, Cassia Lignea, Costus roots, Muscus, Spica Indie, Spica Romana, Gallia muscata, and such like.

Fumes to be burnt to move the Terms are,

Opppponacum, Goppopita, Frankincense, Lignum Aloes, and the Storax.

Things by nature cool, which move the Terms are,

The seeds of small Endive, of Melons, of Gourds, of Pompeons, Cucumbers and Lettice, of which Pessaries may be made, to use in the Womb; but have a care you put a string to them, to get them out again when you please.

A Syrup to take away the obstructions in the Body which hinder the Terms.

Take Madder, two ounces; of the roots of Lovage, Sperage, Cypers, and grass, each an ounce and a half; Penny mountain and Balm, of each two ounces: Spica Indie, half a dram: Licorice, Currans, Rosemary flowers

flowers, and Seecados, of each an ounce: six ounces of
honey, and nine ounces of Sugar; boyl it into a syrup
and take thereof two ounces at a time.

Another for the same.

Take two ounces of Madder, Sperage roots, Cypers
roots, and the roots of Butchers-broom; of each an
ounce; Valerian Sabine, white water Mints, and
Penny-royal, of each a handful: Balm two handfuls
of Melon seed, one ounce: Licquce and Citralls, each
half an ounce: Honey and Sugar, of each six ounces;
so make it into a syrup, and take thereof about an ounce
and a half at a time.

Common Syrups which remove Obstructions of the Terms, are,

Syrup of Mugwort, of Maiden hair, of Chicory
with Rhubarb, and the syrup of the five roots; these you
may have ready at the Apothecaries.

Another to move the Terms.

Take Mints, Balm, Penny-royal, Marjerom, and
Southernwood, of each an handful; Anniseeds, Fennel and Carraway seeds, of each an ounce: Polipody,
an ounce and an half: Chicory roots, an ounce: cut the
roots and hearbs very small, and boyl them all together
in a quart of water till a third part be consumed; then
strain it, and sweeten it with Sugar to your own like-
ing, and take thereof as you please.

Wines good to provoke the Terms,

Wine of Elecampane roots, of Marjerom gentle,
of the hearb Bennet, of Betony, of Gillow-flowers, and
of Rosemary; these are very good if the Patients Body
be fitting to drink Wine, otherwise discretion may direct you not to use it.

Confections good for this Disease are,

The Confection of Elecampane roots, the Confecti-

let her abſtain from ſtrong wines and fleſh meat, and all ſuch things as increaſe natural ſperme.

And uſe letting blood, ſuch meats and drinks as are cooling; and amongſt the reſt, this Confection following is very good.

A Confection to cauſe fruitfulneſs in Man or Woman.

Take Rapes, Ivory ſhaven, Aſhkeys, Betly, Behen red and white, of each one dram: Cinamon, Doronicum, Mace, Cloves, Galangale, long Pepper, Roſemary flowers, Balſom wood, Blattis, Byzantæ Marito autgentle, Penny-royal of each two ſcruples: Balm, Bugloſs, Citron-pieces, of each one ſcruple: Spica Indie, Amber, Pearls, of each half a ſcruple: Sugar a pound: decoct the Sugar in Malinſey, and the other things; and make them into a Confection, uſe of it a little at a time.

A Powder for the ſame to be ſtrewed on meat.

Take, Nutmegs, Cubebbes, Ginger, of each half a dram: long Pepper, Maſtick, Cinamon, red Behen, white Behen, of each a ſcruple: mix them all together, and make them into fine powder, and ſtrew of it a little upon the parties meat.

Another Confection for the ſame.

Take Honey, three ounces: Linſeed, Grains, Ivory ſhaven, of each one ounce: Borrage, three ounces: Sugar ſ ounces: Musk, Amber, of each half a ſcruple: Cinamon two grains: Cloves, Mace, of each one grain: claſſifie the Honey, then incorporate the other things with it to make a Confection thereof, and take of it as you pleaſe.

A Potion to farther Conception in a Woman.

Take wormwood, Mugwort, of each a handful: boyl them together in a quart of Goats milk, till almoſt half

half be wasted, and let the woman drink thereof first, last, every morning and evening a good draught.

A Confection to further fruitfulness in Men, and Conception in Women.

Take a Boxes stones, Stags pissel shaven small, one ounce, (Bulls pissel, if you cannot get the other, will do as well) Sparrows brains, fifty or sixty, yellow Rape, Eringo root, and Satyrion confected, Ivory shaven, of each three ounces and a half: Cinamon, Dates Indy, Nut Kernels, of each two ounces: Long Pepper, Ginger, Rosemary flowers, of each half an ounce: Hesell, one dram: Nettle-seed, Cloves, Saffron, Mace, Galingale, Cypress roots, Nutmegs Cassia wood, Cucubes, Doronicum, field Mints, Penny-royal, Spica Indie, Musk, Amber, of each one dram: make all these into a Confection with four pounds and an half of white Sugar, refined in Mint water, and take of it as before is directed; and if you cannot easily get all the things, yet refuse not the medicine, but make it with as many as you can come by.

Pills to expel a dead Childe.

Take Trochis of Mirrh, one scruple: Galbanum, half a scruple: make five pills thereof, with Penny-royal water.

A most excellent Plaister to strengthen women with Childe, to wear all the time they be with Childe.

Take oyl Olive, two pound and four ounces: red Lead, one pound: Spanish Sope, twelve ounces: Incorporate them altogether in an earthen pot, and when the Sope cometh upwards, put it upon a small fire of coals: and continue it an hour and a half, stirring it with an iron or stick; then drop a drop of it upon a trencher, if it cleave not, it is enough: spread it on cloths, or lay it on a board till it cools, then make it up into Rolls: it will last twenty years, the older, the better; and

and when you have occaſion to uſe it, for this purpoſe
ſpread a Plaiſter of it, and apply it to the back: and
when you have tryed it, you will give me thanks for it;
It is likewiſe good for the bloody Flux, Running of the
Reins, or any weakneſs in the back; for any bruiſe, to
draw out a Thorn out of the fleſh, and raiſeth Corns, and
is good for a ſtrain, and for the head-ach, being applyed
to the Temples.

Be obſerved, when the woman with childe begins
to draw near her time, then let her uſe ſuch meats and
drinks as nouriſh well, but uſe no exceſs of either; but
eſpecially let her take care to keep her body ſoluble.

An excellent Medicine to procure eaſie delivery in Women.

Take Lupins, cut them in thin ſlices, and fry them
with oyl of ſweet Almonds, and eat thereof in the morning; and at four a clock in the afternoon, uſe it con-
ſtantly, a matter of five or ſix weeks before your time,
till you are brought to bed: and mix ſome oyl of ſweet
Almonds and Sperma ceti together, and anoint the Belly, and Matrix once every day therewith warm, or oftner
if you can conveniently.

A Confection for an exceſſive flood in women lying in Child-bed.

Take Conſerve of Sloes, one ounce; Conſerve of
Roſes, one ounce; Conſerve of Burrage, Buglos,
Balm, of each half an ounce; prepared Bolus, half a
dram; prepared Pearls, one dram; Cynamon, one
dram and a half; mix them all together, and make a
Confection thereof.

Take Bead-Cons, one dram and a half; red Coral,
red pearl, Tormentil, Troches de Gordio, of each half
a dram; ſcraped Ivory, burnt Hartſhorn, of each one
ſcruple; Pearls prepared, four ſcruples; fine Bolus,
ſtone Hamatites, Shepheards purſe, red Sanders, of each

29

&c.ample: Cinamon, one dram, Sugar, six ounces,
wash the Blood-stone in Plantain water, and make
powders or Loranges thereof.

Of the superfluity of Milk, and other accidents happening after the Birth.

Excessive abounding of the Milk, after a woman is
delivered, if it flow more than the Child can grow, there
oftentimes ensues Impostumes, and other Inflammations and distempers, in the Breasts; for Remedies
whereof, use these prescriptions following.

The Patient must eat and drink but moderately, and
avoid all such things as engender much blood, and use
means to dry and take away the superfluous blood, as
Rue and wild Rue, with the seeds Basil, and Krampt together; if one take every day a quarter of an ounce, the
same is very good to dry up the Milk.

To dry up the Milk.

Take Rosen a good quantity, and temper it with
Cream, and lay it luke-warm over the Breasts.

For the same.

Take eight ounces of Honey, and two pints of water,
boyl them well together, and skum it, and dip therein a
threefold cloth, and lay it on the Breasts, and when it is
cold renew it again.

Also for the same, take one dram of Saffron, and eight
ounces of Malmsey, wet a cloth therein, and lay it on
the Breasts as aforesaid.

Also, take Garden Mints, stamp them, and mix them
with Oyl of Roses, and use it as the other.

For a Plaister to dry up the Milk, take Bean-meal,
oyl of Roses, and red Vinegar, a sufficient quantity to
make a Plaister, and apply it to the Breasts.

For clotted or congealed Milk in the Breasts,

Let Women keep sobriety in eating and drinking,
and using moist meats, that may engender subtile Milk;
Pints

Thus Mastique and Cynamon, is good to be used in these meats.

Take grated bread, new milke, and oyl of Roses, of each a like quantity: seethe them together to a pap, and lay it warm upon the Breasts.

For congealed milk and pain in the Breasts.

Take Cork and burn it to ashes, and temper it with oyl of Roses, and a little Vinegar, and therewith anoint the Breasts.

A Salve to dissolve congealed milk in the Breasts.

Take Deeres suet three quarters of an ounce: liquid Syrup, one ounce; Wormwood, Cuminin, Dill-seeds, of each one ounce; oyl of Wormwood, Ducks grease, of each one ounce and an half; Saffron, one scruple, make an ointment or Plaister hereof, and apply it to the Breasts.

A good Plaister to dissolve hard knots in the Breasts.

Take crums of white bread, Barley meal, Mustard-seeds, Fennel, and Holly-hocks roasted under the ashes, of each a like quantity; pound them all well together, and make a plaister thereof, with oyl of Camomile, and apply it warm to the Breasts.

For hardness, and inflammation in the Breasts, through congealed Milk, a Pultis.

Take flowers of Mallows, Violets, Celandine, Daisies, Cinquefoil, of each one handful; boyl them together in two quarts of water, till it come to a pint; then strain it, and mingle it with Wheaten meal, to the thickness of pap, then put to it Hens grease, or Hogs Lard, and boyl it again to a Pultis, spread it on a cloth, about the thickness of a finger, and lay it morning and evening upon the inflamed or sore breast.

A

A Medicine for ſwelling in the breaſts, much profitable and eaſie to be had.

Take a good quantity of Peach leaves, and Rue, and ſtamp them ſmall, and doe them in water to a pultis, and lay it on the grieved place, this will ripen the Impoſtume, and eaſe the pain.

For Cleſts or Chops of the Nipples.

Take Mutton, or Lambs ſuet, as much as you pleaſe, and after it is molten, and clarified, then waſh it in Roſe-water, and therewith anointing the Nipples. And thus much for the Diſeaſes in the Breaſts.

Means and Remedies for thoſe Nurſes that want Milk.

Thoſe women that would increaſe their milk, let let them eat good meats if they can get it, and drink milk wherein Fennell ſeed hath been ſteeped.

If the woman be of a hot nature, and full of Choller, let her drink Barly water and Almond milk, eat Lettice with her meat, Burrage, Spinnage, Goats milk, Cowes milk & Laſid ſodden with Lettice. And avoid too much anger as much as may be: and comfort the ſtomach with Confections of Anniſeeds, Carraway and Cummin ſeeds, and likewiſe uſe drinkſeeds ſotten in water.

If you would have an outward means, uſe this Plaiſter following.

Take half an ounce of Deers ſuet, and as much Paſſy roots, with the hearbs, an ounce and an half of Barly meal, three drams of red Storax, and three ounces of oyl of ſweet Almonds: ſeeth the roots & hearbs well, and beat them to pap, then mingle the other amongſt them, and lay it warm to the Nipples, it increaſeth Milk.

✠✠✠✠✠✠✠✠✠✠✠✠✠✠✠✠✠✠

January *Astrological Observations.*

This season admitteth but of little action, therefore the greater consultations are on foot. The Commonalty every where vexed, endeavour to pry into affairs of State for which they are checked by the frowns of Authority. The Tartar intendeth invasion on his neighbour, it may be the Muscovite; The Irish are not contented. Some great ones decline in their greatness, other inferiors raised by their ruins.

Observations for the good Husbands and good Housewives.

Plow for Pease, fallow such land as you intend shall rest the year following; water your barren Meadows Pasture, and drain arrable ground, especially if you intend to sow Pease, Oats, or Barly the seed time following; allo rub up all rough grounds, trim up your Garden moulds; The weather calm, remove all manner of fruit trees, rear Calves, remove Bees, keep good Dyet.

February, *Astrological Observations.*

We look big upon our neighbours the Dutch: but all is won reconciled, it Discord among the great ones prevent not some underhand dealing in the matter, but peradventure it will be discovered: The Commonalty have the vertues of an Asse willing to bear to the content of the great ones. Private differences and instigation to Law, predominate in people more than ordinary.

Observations for the good Husbands and good Housewives.

Set Beans, Pease, and other pulse in stiff ground, begin the soonest, prepare your garden, prune and trim

your

your fruit trees from Moths, Cankers, and superfluous branches, plash hedges, lay your quickset close, plant Rose, Gooseberry trees, and any other shrub trees, and graft your tender stocks: forbear all phlegmatick meats.

March, Astrological Observations.

SOme triumph, for what I know not. I am sure the Commons are not sharers therein. Discontents for wants of Trade seizeth on them, they still expect better times. No care for taking away the obstructions in Trade. Forreigners play upon us, bereave us of all advantages therein.

Observations for the good Husbands and good Housewives.

Look well to your Ewes, cut up underwood or fewel, transplant all sort of summer flowers, comfort them with good earth, especially the Crown Imperial, Martilius, Tuleps, and Vyacinth, in your barren fruit trees, bore holes and drive hard wedges of Oak, and cover roots of trees close with fat earth that are uncovered; graft fruit trees and sowe Oates, Rye, and Barley. Let your Diet be cold and temperate.

April, Astrological Observations.

NEws of great transactions arrive of the affairs of Europe, the Merchant suffereth exceedingly, the Commons of most Nations are discontented, the most devout complain much. Flanders is much disturbed.

Observations for the good Husbands and good Huswives.

Sowe your Hemp and Flax, sowe and set all sorts of Hearbs, open your Hives, and give your Bees their liberty and let them labour for their living; cut your Oake Timber, the bark is best for the Tanners use. Scowr your ditches, gather your Manure together, in heaps, gather home & prepare hedg-woods, set Osiers and carry home and cast up all decayed fences. For your health use moderate exercise.

May, *Astrological Observations.*

The face of affairs in Europe, seems to change. Matters of great concernment are on foot: the greater ones fear, the lesse being more numerous, which spirit speaks but little safety to them: Lawes and Customes are much slighted, and good manners corrupted.

Observations for good Husbands and good Housewives.

Fold your Sheep, carry forth Manure, and bring home fewel. weed winter Corn, furnish your Dairy, let your Mares go to Horse, eat your dry Kine, and away with them, sowe your tender seeds as Cucumbers, Musmelons, all sweet kind of herbs and flowers. For your health Drink clarified whey.

June, *Astrological Observations.*

Great Forces in the field, great action: a terrible battel fought about this time, great ones dye as well as small, people abroad begin to think of easing their wearied shoulders, wrung by heavy imposed burthens: the sword is drawn, the wronged have the victory Pet. Julii.

Observations for the good Husbands and good Housewives.

Distil all sorts of Plants and Herbs whatever, Cut your rank Meadowes, fetch home fewel, and carry forth Manure, Marle and Lime to mend your Land. Be sure to be chary this Month, whatever you are the rest of the year.

C 2   July.

July, *Astrological Observations.*

Authority seemeth vexed, Subjects not pleased: The Johnsonians in France increase, the Romish faction seek to suppresse that Sect, all to little purpose: The Lawyers are very much discontented at some probable Reformation of the Law: The city of Rome subject to great disasters.

Observations for the good Husbands and good Housewives.

Attend your Hay harvest, shear field sheep: let the hearbs you intend to preserve run to seed: cut off the stalk of your flowers, and cover the roots with new fat earth: sell your Lambs you intended for the shambles. Take no physick, but use in extraordinary cases, restrain surfeit.

August, *Astrologicall Observations.*

A hot and sickly season, about the latter end of this Month somewhat abated. The Austrian family endeavoureth to strengthen it self by Counsell, and Arms. The French seem to be losers. Great abuses of clipping and imbaffing money, the watchful Magistrate ought to be more than ordinarily vigilant in preventing so great and publick abuses. Ancient sports and pastimes (heretofore suppressed) grow again in fashion. Great disputations and controversies in Divinity again revived.

Observations for the good husbands and good Housewives.

Follow diligently your Corn harvest, cut down your wheat and Rye, Mowe Barley and Oats, put off your fat Sheep and Cattel, gather your Plums, Apples, and Pears: make your Summer Perry and Cyder, set raw Slips and Scyons of all sorts of Gilliflowers and other

other flowers; Transplant them that were set in the
Spring, Geld your Lambs, carry Manure from your
Dove-coats put your Swine to the early mast. Refrain
all excess in eating and drinking, drink that which is
cooling.

September, Astrological Observations.

SOme well disposed strive to advance incouragements
for Learning; Divers wish settlement in the Church,
the obstruction lyeth in certain Hereticks that have been
the cause of our misery. Several battels are fought in
several parts of Europe, success is not hereditary.

Observations for the good Husbands and good Housewives.

Cut your Beans, Brank, and all manner of Pulse, in
the Land you intend to sowe Wheat and Rye, bestow the
best manure; gather your Winter fruit, sell your wool,
stocks of Bees, and other commodities you intend to put
off. Search your hive of Bees you intend to keep, and
look that no Mouse, Mice, or other vermin be about
them. Thrash your seed wheat and Rye. Use Physick
moderately, shun the eating of fruit or rotten fruit, avoid
surfeting.

October, Astrologicall Observations.

MEn incline more than ordinary to cruelty, and
Women to crossness. The constellation of Saturn
and Mars this month will produce strange effects, not safe,
nor convenient to be published, let time speak the language that the lines silenceth.

Observations for the good Husbands and good Housewives.

Finish with your Wheat, Rie, plash and lay your
hedges and thickets, scowre your Ditches and Ponds,
transplant

transplant and remove all manner of fruit trees, make
Winter Perry and Cyder, spare your Pastures that fear
upon your corn fields, draw furrows to drain, and
keep dry your new sowen Corn: make Malt, rear all
new falne Calves, all foals that were foaled in the
Spring weaned from the Mares. Sell your sheep that
you do not intend to Winter, and separate Lambs
from the Ewes that you intend to keep. Recreate your
spirits by harmless sports, and take physick by good advice if need be.

November, *Astrological Observations.*

STorms by sea produceth losse to the Marchant.
Storms by Land cause fear and iealousie of the great
ones, who are not a little vexed by the high winds or
minds of the multitude; if any thing break out from
them, it is upon the matter trienstable. Fair words de-
ceive the fond multitude, &c.

Observations for the good Husbands and good. Housewives.

Cut down your Timber for Plows, Carts, Harrows,
Axletrees, Harrows, and other offices about husbandry,
or housewifry: make the last return of grasse feed Cattel,
take your Swine from the mast, and feed them for the
slaughter: Rear all Calves that fall now, break all
Hemp and Flax you intend to spend in the Winter season.
Remove fruit trees, and sow wheat and Rye in hot soyls.
Use spices and Wine moderately.

December, *Astrological Observations.*

The Season admitteth not of action, yet great consultations are on foot, Mony is wanted, foundations for great
attempts are laying against the season of action. Some
malefactors apprehended, if not executed; Robberi
frequent: the best and honestest minded people suffer
most.

Observa-

Observations for the good Husbands and good Houswives.

Put your Sheep to the Peas-reeks, kill your small Porks and large Bacons, lop hedges, save your Timber for building, and lay it to season: plow your ground you intend to sow than Beans on: cover your dainty fruit-trees, drain your corn fields, and water your Meadows: cover your best flowers with rotten horse-litter. Now all sorts of Fowle are in season, keep thy self warm with a wholsome Dyet, and avoid all care that shall trouble the spirit, as a dangerous thing.

FINIS.

Books worth buying, newly printed by *John Streater*, and to be sold by the *Book-sellers* of *London*.

The Vale-Royal of England, being a *Historical & Geographical Description of the County of* Chester. Folio.

The Womans Counsellor, *being a Description of the Diseases incident to that Sex, with the Cures thereof : as also of Barrenness of men or women,* Octavo.

The Refinement of Zion, or the old Orthodox Religion justified and defended. Quarto.

The History of the Wonders of Nature, treating Philosophically and Physically of the Heavens, Elements, Meteors, Minerals, Beasts, Fish, Fowl, Plants, and of Man. Folio.

The

The History of Magick, written in French by G. Naudeus now Englished. A most excellent piece in defence of all the wise men mentioned in the Holy Scriptures, and other Authors.
Octavo.

The Life of Pierescius, written by P. Gassendus, being the sum of his great Attainments in Learning, Philosophy, Physick, Chymistry, Policy, and Antiquity; the like not to be read in any Author.
Octavo.

The History of the Constancy of Nature, proving that the world nor any thing therein, doth not decline or grow worse.
Octavo.

The Protestants Evidence, a most learned work, proving that in the 16. several Centuries since Christ, there hath been eminent and learned men that have professed the Faith as the Church of England doth,
Folio.

Also, A Theological Concordance of the Holy Scriptures, of small price, and performeth as much as many large Volums, very useful for all that desire to attain to Knowledge.
Octavo.

Renadeus his Dispensatory, being the sum of all Physical and Chirurgical operations.
Folio.

Lemnius, Of the secrets of Nature in general, but more especially upon Generation, and the parts thereof, very necessary for all that study Physick, and search into the hidden things of Nature.
Folio.

Oleus Magnus Bishop of Upsal, his History of the Northerne Nations.
Folio.

40

Sarah Jinner's *An Almanack and Prognostication for the year of our Lord 1659* (Wing 1845) is reprinted from the copy at The Huntington Library (Shelfmark 353427). The text block of the Huntington copy is 75 × 135 mm.

For passages that are blotched, please consult Appendix B, 'A Key to Difficult-to-Read Passages'.

AN
ALMANACK
AND
PROGNOSTICATION for the year of our
LORD 1659. Being the third after Biflextile: or
Leap year. Calculated for the Meridian of London
and may indifferently ferve for England ; Scotland,
and Ireland.

By S*RAH JINNER *Student in Aftrology.*
London, Printed by J. S. for the Company of
Stationers.

according to the

Julian, *English*, or old Account.	}{	Gregorian, Forreign, or New Account.
7.	The Golden Number.	7
16	The Cycle of the Sun.	16
	The Dominical Letter.	E
12	The Roman Indiction.	12
17	The Epact.	7
13	The Number of Direction.	16

Old Account,	Moveable Feasts according to the	New Account.
January 30	Septuagesima.	9 February.
February 16	Ashwednesday.	18 February.
April 3	Easter-day.	13 April.
May 8	Rogation Sunday	18 May,
May 12	Ascension day.	22 May.
May 22	Whitsunday,	1 June
May 29	Trinity Sunday.	8 June
Novemb. 27	Advent Sunday.	30 November.

Table of the four Terms and their Returns
for the year 1659.

Hilary Term begins January 24, ends February 12,
and hath four Returns.

| Octab. Hil. January 20. | Craft. Purif. February 3 |
| Quind. Hil. January 27. | Octab. Purif. February 9 |

Easter Term begins April 20, ends May 16 and hath
five Returns.

Quind. Pasch. Ap. 18	
Tres Pasch. Apr. 25	Quinq; pasch. May 9
Mens. Pasch. May 2	Craft. Ascen. May 13

Trinity Term begins June 3, ends June 22, and hath
four Returns.

| Craft. Trin. May 30 | Quind. Trin. June 13. |
| Octab. Trin. June 6 | Tres Trin, June 20. |

Michaelmas Term begins Octob. 24, ends November 28
and hath six Returns.

Tres Mich. October 20.	Craft. Mart. Novemb. 12.
Mens. Mich. October 27.	Octab. Mar. Novemb. 18.
Craft. anim. November 3.	Quind. Mar. Novemb. 25

The Characters and Names of the twelve Signes, with their Dominion in Man's Body.

The Characters and Names of the 7 Planets.

♄   ♃   ♂   ☉   ♀   ☿   ☽

Saturn,   Jupiter,   Mars,   Sol,   Venus,   Mercury,   Luna.

The Characters and Names of the Aspects.

☌   ☍   ✳   □   △

Conjunction,   Opposition,   Sextile,   Quadrate,   Trine.

January hath XXXI Daies.

☾ Laſt quarter 6 day 20 min. paſt 4 in the Morning.
● New Moon 12 day 9 min. paſt 9 at night.
☽ Firſt quarter 20 day, 45 min. paſt 5 in the morning,
● Full moon 28 day, 48 min. paſt 8 in the morning,

1	A	New years day	21	♑	27	♌	8	2	very cold winds
2	b		22		28	♍	8	0	with rain or
3	c		23		29	♍	7	58	ſnow,
4	D	Teleſphorus	24		30	♎	7	57	
5	e	Simeon	25		32	♎	7	56	☍♄♃ 7 m. △ ♄
6	f	Twelfth day	26		33	♏	7	55	(☿ 1 a.
7	g	Julian	27		34	♏	7	54	
8	a		28		35	♏	7	53	much ſnow or
9	b	1 Sun. af.Epip.	29	♒	36	♐	7	52	cold rain.
10	c		●		38	♐	7	50	□⊙♄ s. m. and
11	D	Hyginus	1		39	♑	7	49	thick clouds.
12	e		2		40	♑	7	47	
13	f	Hilary	3		41	♒	7	46	
14	g	Felix	4		42	♒	7	45	more rain and in
15	a	Marcellus	5		43	♓	7	44	ſome parts ſnow.
16	b	2 Sun. af. Eph.	6		44	♓	7	42	△ ♄ ☿ 12 a.
17	c	Antonicus	7		45	♈	7	41	✳ ♂ ☿ 9 m. ✳♄
18	D	Priſca	8		46	♈	7	39	remiſſion (♂ o.
19	e		9		47	♉	7	38	☍⊙♄7 n. of cold
20	f	Fabian	10		48	♉	7	36	and froſt.
21	g	Agnes	11		49	♉	7	34	ſerene with froſt.
22	a	Vincentius	12		50	♊	7	32	
23	b	3 Sun. af. Epi.	13		51	♊	7	31	
24	c	Term begins	14		52	♋	7	30	the winds drive
25	D	Conve. of Paul	15		52	♋	7	28	much ſnow or
26	e	Polycarpus	16		53	♋	7	26	rain.
27	f		17		54	♌	7	25	
28	g		18		55	♌	7	23	
29	a		19		56	♍	7	21	the wind is un-
30	b	Septuageſſima	20		56	♍	7	20	comfortable.
31	c		21		57	♎	7	18	☽⊙☿ 7 m.

☾ Laſt quarter 4 day 25 min. paſt 1 afternoon.
☉ New moon 11 day 8 min. paſt 9 in the morning.
☽ Firſt quarter 19 day, 1 min. paſt 3 in the morning.
☉ Full moon 25 day 2 min. paſt 10 at night.

1	D		22	58	♎	7	17	☌☉☉ 4 a.
2	E	Candlemas	23	58	♎	7	16	a moiſt ſeaſon:
3	F	Blaſius	24	59	♏	7	14	
4	G		25	59	♏	7	13	
5	A	Agathe	27	0	♐	7	11	
6	B	Septuageſſima	28	0	♐	7	10	
7	C		29	0	♑	7	8	
8	D		☽ ♓	0	♑	7	6	△♄☉ 11 a.
9	E	Apollonia.	1	0	♒	7	4	rain or ſnow.
10	F	Scholaſtica	2	0	♒	7	2	
11	G		3	2	♓	6	59	
12	A	Term ends.	4	3	♓	6	58	
13	B	Shrove ſunday	5	3	♈	6	56	
14	C	Valentine	6	3	♈	6	55	
15	D	Shrovetueſday	7	4	♈	6	54	
16	E	Aſhwedneſday	8	4	♉	6	53	
17	F		9	4	♉	6	51	
18	G	Concordia	10	4	♊	6	49	
19	A		11	4	♊	6	46	
20	B	1 Sun. in Len	12	4	♊	6	44	☌☉☿ 5 n. cold
21	C		13	4	♋	6	42	ſhower.
22	D		14	4	♋	6	40	
23	E		15	4	♌	6	38	
24	F	Matthias	16	4	♌	6	35	☿ Stat. SS. ☉.
25	G		17	4	♌	6	32	high, turbulent
26	A	Victor	18	4	♍	6	30	and uncomforta=
27	B	2 Sun. in Lent	19	4	♍	6	27	ble winds.
28	C	Romanus	20	3	♎	6	24	☿ far. diſt. from ☉

March hath XXXI Daies.

☾ Last quarter 5 day, at 57 min. past 8. at night.
● New moon 12 day 17 min. past 10 at night.
☽ First quarter the 20 day, 16 min. past 11 at night.
○ Full moon 28 day, 31 min: past 10 in the morning.

1	d	David	21 ♓	3	♎	6	23	
2	e	Simplicius	22	2	♏	6	20	☍ ♃ ♂ 6 remissi-
3	f		23	2	♏	6	18	on of cold, and a
4	g	Adrianus	24	2	♐	6	16	clear air, with
5	a		25	2	♐	6	14	some frosty mor-
6	B	3 Sun. in Lent	26	1	♑	6	11	nings and cold
7	c	Perpetua	27	1	♑	6	9	winds.
8	d		28	0	♒	6	7	
9	e		29	0	♒	6	5	a pleasant season
10	f	Alexander	29	59	♒	6	3	approaching.
11	g	Days & N. eq.	0 ♈	58	♓	6	0	
12	a	Gregory	1	58	♓	5	50	
13	B	4 Sun. in Lent	2	57	♈	5	57	△ ☉ ♃ 12.
14	c		3	56	♈	5	56	a very good season
15	d		4	56	♉	5	54	for husbandmen
16	e	Cyriacus	5	55	♉	5	52	Gardiners.
17	f		6	54	♉	5	50	
18	g		7	53	♊	5	48	♃ Stat. Dir.
19	a	Josephus	8	52	♊	5	46	
20	B	5 Sun. in Lent	9	51	♋	5	44	
21	c	Benedictus	10	50	♋	5	42	
22	d		11	49	♋	5	40	
23	e		12	48	♌	5	39	△ ♄ ♀ 11. h.
24	f		13	47	♌	5	37	cold rain,
25	g	Lady day	14	46	♍	5	36	
26	a	Castulus	15	45	♍	5	34	
27	B	Palm Sunday	16	44	♎	5	32	△ ♃ ☿ 8 n. bluste-
28	c		17	42	♎	5	30	ring winds drive
29	d	Eustachius.	18	41	♏	5	28	hail in some parts.
30	e	Guido	19	40	♏	5	26	
31	f		20	38	♐	5	24	

April hath XXX Daies.

☾ Last quarter 4 day, 41 min. past 3 in the morning.
🌑 New Moon 11 day, 28 min. past noon.
☽ First quarter 19 day 41 min. past 4 in the afternoon.
🌕 Full Moon the 26 day, 51 min. past 7 at night.

1	g		21 ♈	37	♐	5	20	
2	A	Mary Ægyp.	22	35	♑	5	18	VVinds and
3	b	Easter day	23	34	♑	5	16	△♄♂ 10 n. thun-
4	c	Ambrose	24	33	♑	5	14	der
5	d		25	31	♒	5	12	most of this quar-
6	e		26	30	♒	5	10	ter cold and close
7	f	Egisippus	27	28	♓	5	7	☍☉♄ 7 m. rain
8	g		28	26	♓	5	4	☍♄☿ 7 n. and
9	A		29	25	♈	5	2	high winds.
10	b	Low Sunday	0 ♉	23	♈	5	0	☌☉☿ 3. m.
11	c		1	21	♉	4	58	⚹♂☿ 8 n. □♃☿
12	d	Julius	2	20	♉	4	57	☾ 10 n. ♀ farthest
13	e	Justinus	3	18	♉	4	45	dist. from ☉.
14	f	Tiburtius	4	16	♊	4	53	□♃☉ 6 m.
15	g	Olympias.	5	14	♊	4	52	turbulent winds
16	A		6	12	♋	4	50	and rain, in some
17	b	Miser. Domine	7	10	♋	4	48	parts thunder.
18	c	Valerianus	8	8	♋	4	4[illegible]	
19	d		9	6	♌	4	44	
20	e	Term begins	10	4	♌	4	42	
21	f		11	2	♍	4	40	winds and
22	g		12	0	♍	4	39	⚹☉♂ 2 m.
23	A	Georgius	12	58	♍	4	37	clouds if not rain,
24	b	Jubilate	13	56	♎	4	35	
25	c	Mark Evangel.	14	56	♎	4	32	
26	d	☽ Eclipsed	15	52	♏	4	31	
27	e	Anastasius	16	51	♏	4	29	⚹♃☿ 8 n. the air
28	f	Vitalis	17	48	♐	4	27	warm and dry.
29	g		18	45	♐	4	25	
30	A		19	43	♑	4	23	

Last quarter 3 day 44 min. past 10 in the morning.
New Moon 11 day 40 min. past 3 in the morning.
First quarter 19 day, 42 min. past 6 in the morning.
Full Moon 26 day, 26 min. past 6 in the morning.

1	♌	Phil. & Jacob	20	♉	41	♑	4	22	△♃☿ 11 n.
2	C		21		39	♒	4	21	a wholsome and
3	D	Invent. Cru.	22		36	♒	4	20	fertile air.
4	E	Florianus	23		34	♓	4	19	
5	F	Gothardus	24		31	♓	4	17	
6	G	Joh. Port. Lat.	25		29	♈	4	15	
7	A		26		27	♈	4	13	
8	♌	Rogate.	27		24	♈	4	12	
9	C		28		21	♉	4	11	☿ ☼r. dir. from ☉
10	D		29		19	♉	4	10	
11	E	Mamertius	♊	17	♊	4	9	
12	F	Ascen. Dom,	1	14	♊	4	7	
13	G	Servatius	2	12	♊	4	6	
14	A		3	9	♋	4	5	△♄☿ 3 a. cool
15	♌	Exaudi	4	7	♋	4	3	winds
16	C	Term ends	5	4	♌	4	2	
17	D		6	1	♌	4	1	
18	E		6	59	♌	3	5	
19	F	Bernhardus	7	56	♍	3	58	
20	G		8	53	♍	3	56	the air cloudy, but
21	A		9	51	♎	3	55	wholsome winds,
22	♌	Whitsunday	10	48	♎	3	54	soon clear it again
23	C	Desiderius	11	45	♏	3	53	
24	D		12	43	♏	3	53	
25	E	Vrbanus	13	40	♐	3	52	
26	F	Beda	14	37	♐	3	52	
27	G		15	34	♑	3	51	
28	A		16	32	♑	3	51	
29	♌	Trinity fund.	17	29	♒	3	51	a turbulent air, &
30	C	VVigandus	18	26	♒	3	58	△♄☿ 6n. △♃☉
31	D	Petronella	19	92	♓	3	50	no thunder (10 n.

June hath XXX Daies.

☾ Laſtquarter 1 day, at 20 min. paſt 7 at night.
○ New moon 9 day, 13 min. paſt 7 at night.
☽ Firſt quarter 17 day, 44 min. paſt 5 at night.
○ Full moon the 24 day, 21 min. paſt 10 beforenoon.

1	E		20	♊20	♓	3	50
2	f	Marcellus	21	18	♓	3	49 □♃♀ 9 m. fair &
3	g	Term begin	22	15	♈	3	49 ☌○♀ 0. hot winds
4	A		23	12	♈	3	49 and clouds cool
5	b	1 Sun. af. Trin	24	9	♉	3	48 △○♄ 0. the air:
6	c		25	6	♉	3	48 in ſome parts
7	D		26	3	♊	3	48 ſome ſhowers.
8	e	Medardus	27	0	♊	3	47
9	f		27	58	♊	3	47
10	g	Onophrius	28	55	♋	3	47
11	a		29	52	♋	3	47 ✶♂♀ 10 b. the air
12	b	2 Sun. af. Trin.	0 ♋	49	♌	3	47 generally ſerene
13	c		1	46	♌	3	47 and dry, yet in
14	D	Valerius	2	43	♌	3	47 places ſtorms of
15	e	Vitus	3	40	♍	3	48 thunder.
16	f	Rolandus	4	37	♍	3	48
17	g		5	35	♎	3	48
18	A		6	32	♎	3	49 ☍♄♂ 11 b. a di-
19	b	3 Sun. af. Trin.	6	29	♎	3	49 ſtempered heaven
20	c		7	26	♏	3	49 thunder and fiery
21	D		8	23	♏	3	50 corruſcations.
22	e	Term ends	9	20	♐	3	50
23	f		10	17	♐	3	51
24	g	John Baptiſt	11	14	♑	3	51
25	A		12	11	♑	3	51
26	b	4 Sun. af. Trin.	13	9	♒	3	52 △♄♀ 4 a. winds
27	c	Sep. Dorm.	14	6	♒	3	53
28	D		15	3	♓	3	54
29	e	Peter Apoſt.	16	0	♓	3	55
30	f		17	57	♓	3	56

July hath XXXI Daies.

Last quarter 1 day 39 min. past 6 in the morning.
New moon 9 day, 15 min. past 10 before noon.
First quarter 17 day, 22 min. past 2 in the morning.
Full moon 23 day, 29 min. past 5 in the afternoon.
Last quarter 30 day 54 min. past 8 at night.

1			18	54	♈	3	57	
2		Visit. Mary	19	51	♉	3	57	Serene dry and
3		5 Sun. af. Trin.	20	48	♉	3	58	✱ ♃ ♀ 4 m. seaso
4		Ulrichus	21	46	♉	3	59	nable.
5		Anshelmus	22	43	♊	4	0	✱ ♂ ☿ 12 a. an in
6			23	40	♊	4	2	clination to thun.
7			24	37	♊	4	3	□ ☉ h s m. △ h ♀
8		Chilianus	25	34	♋	4	5	cloudy and (11 n.
9		Cyrillus	26	31	♋	4	6	wet for many days
10		6. Sun. af. Trin.	26	29	♌	4	8	
11		Pius	27	26	♌	4	9	
12			28	23	♍	4	11	
13			29	20	♍	4	12	
14		Bonaventure	0 ♌	18	♍	4	13	
15		Swithin	1	15	♎	4	14	
16			2	12	♎	4	15	□ h ♀ 11 b. wind
17		7 Sun. af. Trin.	3	10	♏	4	16	accompanied with
18		Rosina	4	7	♏	4	17	showers in some
19		Dog days beg	5	4	♐	4	18	parts.
20		Margaret	6	2	♐	4	20	
21			7	59	♑	4	21	
22		Mary Mag.	8	56	♑	4	23	
23		Apollina	9	54	♒	4	25	
24		8 Sun. af. Trin.	10	51	♒	4	27	♂ ☉ ♀ 5 m. high
25		James Apost	11	49	♓	4	29	winds cool the air
26		Anna	12	46	♓	4	30	
27		Martha	13	44	♈	4	32	
28		Sampson	14	41	♈	4	34	□ ♂ ♀ o.
29		Beatrix	15	39	♉	4	36	a turbulent air.
30			16	36	♉	4	37	
31		9 Sun. af. Trin.	17	34	♉	4	38	✱ h ♀ o.

53

August hath XXXI Daies.

○ New moon 8 day 36 min. before 1 in the morning.
☽ First quarter 15 day, 37 min. past 9 in the morning.
☽ Full moon 22 day, 2 min. past 2 in the morning.
☽   29 day, 7 min. past 2 in the afternoon.

1	C	Lammas	18	♌	31	♊	4	39	✳ ☌ ♀ ♃ cloudy
2	D	♃ ☌	19		29	♊	4	40	
3	E		20		27	♋	4	43	□ ♃ ♂ 2 wet and
4	F	Aristarchus	21		24	♋	4	44	turbulent,
5	G	Oswaldus	22		22	♋	4	46	□ ♄ ♀ 3 m. store
6	A	Sixtus	23		20	♌	4	48	of showers,
7	B	10 Sun.af.Tr.	24		17	♌	4	50	
8	C		25		15	♍	4	52	great heat
9	D		26		13	♍	4	55	✳ ☉ ♄ ●.
10	E	Laurentius	27		11	♍	4	56	□ ☉ ♂ 3 m. with
11	F	Eusebius	28		9	♎	4	58	wind or thunder.
12	G	Clara	29		7	♎	4	59	
13	A	Hippolitus	0	♍	3	♏	5	1	
14	B	11 Sun.af.Tr.	1		2	♏	5	3	
15	C		2		0	♐	5	5	
16	D		2		58	♐	5	6	
17	E		3		56	♑	5	8	great heat and fi-
18	F	Helena	4		54	♑	5	10	ery flashings for
19	G	Sebaldus	5		52	♒	5	12	many daies.
20	A	Bernard	6		50	♒	5	14	
21	B	12 Sun.af.Tr.	7		48	♒	5	16	
22	C		8		46	♓	5	18	
23	D	Zacheus	9		45	♓	5	20	✳ ♄ ♃ 2 m. a con
24	E	Bartholomew	10		43	♈	5	22	tinuance of heat
25	F	Ludovicus	11		41	♈	5	24	and an inclinati-
26	G		12		40	♉	5	26	on to thunder.
27	A	Dog daies end	13		38	♉	5	28	
28	B	13 Sun. af. Tr.	14		36	♊	5	30	
29	C	John bap.beh.	15		35	♊	5	31	the air cooler and
30	B		16		33	♊	5	33	inclinable to rain.
31	C	Paulinus	17		31	♋	5	35	✳ ♄ ♀ ●.

September hath XXX Daies.

☽ New moon 6 day 56 min. past 1 after noon.
☽ First quarter 13 day 48 min. past 3 after noon.
○ Full Moon 20 day 49 min. past noon.
☾ Last quarter 28 day 37 min. past 9 in the morning.

1	f	Giles	18 ♍	30 ♋	5	37	☌ ♃ ♀ 11 h.
2	g	Veronica	19	28 ♌	5	40	a fair and plea-
3	a		20	27 ♌	5	42	sant season.
4	b	14 Sun. af. Tr.	21	26 ♌	5	44	
5	c		22	24 ♍	5	45	
6	d	Magnus	23	23 ♍	5	47	
7	e	Regina	24	21 ♎	5	49	☿ far. dist. from ☉
8	f	Nat. Mariæ	25	19 ♎	5	50	
9	g	Gorgon	26	18 ♏	5	51	
10	a		27	17 ♏	5	53	
11	b	15 Sun. af. Tr.	28 ♎	16 ♐	5	55	□ ♂ ♀ 8 n.
12	c		29	15 ♐	5	58	Probably some
13	d		0	14 ♐	6	0	showers.
14	e	Holy crosse	1	13 ♑	6	2	a temperate season
15	f	Nicodemus	2	12 ♑	6	4	to the end of this
16	g	Euphem.	3	11 ♒	6	6	month.
17	a	Lampert	4	10 ♒	6	8	
18	b	16 Sun. af. Tr.	5	9 ♓	6	10	
19	c		6	8 ♓	6	12	
20	d		7	7 ♈	6	14	
21	e	Matthew Apost.	8	6 ♈	6	16	
22	f	Mauricius	9	6 ♉	6	18	
23	g	Esdra.	10	5 ♉	6	20	
24	a	Samuel	11	4 ♉	6	22	
25	b	17 Sun. af. Tr.	12	4 ♊	6	24	
26	c	Cyprian	13	3 ♊	6	26	
27	d		14	2 ♋	6	28	
28	e		15	2 ♊	6	30	
29	f	Michael Arch.	16	1 ♊	6	34	(7 n.
30	g		17	1 ♌	6	32	△ ☉ ♂ 6 n. ☌ ☉ ☿

October hath XXXI Daies.

○ New-Moon 6 day, 57 min. paſt 3 in the morning.
☽ Firſt quarter 12 day 55 min. paſt 10 at night.
○ Full Moon 20 day, 56 min. paſt 2 in the morning.
☾ Laſt quarter 27 day, 57 min. paſt 10 at night.

1	a		18 ♎	0	♌	6	36	
2	b	18 Sun. af. Tr.	19	0	♍	6	38	
3	c		19	59	♍	6	40	
4	d	Franciſcus	20	59	♎	6	42	ſome gentle
5	e		21	59	♎	6	44	☌ ☿ ♀ 9 n. ſhowers.
6	f	Faith	22	58	♎	6	46	
7	g		23	58	♏	6	48	
8	a		24	58	♏	6	50	
9	b	19 Sun. af. Tr.	25	58	♐	6	52	cloudy and an in
10	c	Gideon	26	58	♐	6	54	△ ♂ ♀ 10 n. clina-
11	d	Burchard	27	58	♑	6	56	tion to rain.
12	e	Colman	28	57	♑	6	58	
13	f		29	57	♒	7	0	
14	g	Calixtus	0 ♏	57	♒	7	2	
15	a	Hedewig.	1	57	♓	7	4	
16	b	20 Sun. af. Tr.	2	57	♓	7	6	☌ ☉ ♄ 11 n. cold
17	c		3	58	♈	7	8	☿ far from ☉ cloſe
18	d	Luke Evang.	4	58	♈	7	10	and wet wether.
19	e	Ptolomeus	5	58	♈	7	12	
20	f		6	58	♉	7	14	
21	g	Urſula	7	58	♉	7	15	△ ♂ ☿ 1 m.
22	a	Cordul.	8	59	♊	7	17	winds driving.
23	b	21 Sun. af. Tr.	9	59	♊	7	19	
24	c	Term begins.	10	59	♋	7	20	☌ ♄ ♀ 9 n. rain
25	d	Criſpinus	12	0	♋	7	22	✱ ☉ ♃ 6 m. clears
26	e	Amandus	13	0	♋	7	24	again, froſts.
27	f		14	0	♌	7	26	inclinable to moi-
28	g	Simon & Jude	15	1	♌	7	28	ſture, cold
29	a		16	2	♍	7	30	✱ ♃ ☿ 9 n. winds
30	b	22 Sun. af. Tr.	17	2	♍	7	32	☌ ♄ ☿ 11 n. with
31	c		18		♍	7	33	ſnow or rain.

November hath XXX Daies.

☽ New Moon 4 day 32 min, past 2 in the afternoon.
☽ First quarter 11 day 32 min, past 6 in the morning.
☽ Full Moon 18 day 1 min: past 8 at night.
☾ Last quarter 26 day 35 min, past 12 at night.

1	D	All Saints	19	♏ 3	♎ 7 34			
2	E	Animarum	20	4	♎ 7 36			
3	F	Theophilus	21	4	♏ 7 38	✳ ♃♀ 3 . winds		
4	G		22	5	♏ 7 39	with a probability		
5	A	Powder Treas.	23	6	♐ 7 40	☉ Eclipsed of		
6	✲	23 Sun. af. Tr.	24	6	♐ 7 42	rain,		
7	C	Florent	25	7	♑ 7 43			
8	D		26	8	♑ 7 45			
9	E	Theodorus	27	9	♒ 7 46			
10	F		28	9	♒ 7 48			
11	G	Martine	29	10	♓ 7 49			
12	A		0 ♐	11	♓ 7 50	windy, yet not ve-		
13	✲	24 Sun. af. Tr.	1	12	♓ 7 52	ry cold.		
14	C	Frederick	2	13	♈ 7 53	☐ ♃ ☌ 11 m.		
15	D	Leopaldus	3	14	♈ 7 55	☌ ♀♀ 7 n. incli-		
16	E		4	15	♉ 7 56	nable to moisture.		
17	F		5	16	♉ 7 57			
18	G	Gelasius	6	17	♊ 7 58			
19	A	Elizabetha	7	18	♊ 7 59	the air much		
20	✲	25 Sun. af. Tr.	8	19	♊ 8 0	☍ ♂♀ 12 n. trou-		
21	C		9	20	♋ 8 1	☍ ♃♀ 8 n. bled		
22	D		10	21	♋ 8 2	☍ ☉♀ 4 m. for		
23	E	Clemens	11	22	♌ 8 3	☐ ♃♀ 6 m. many		
24	F		12	23	♌ 8 4	days, and inclina-		
25	G	Catharine	13	25	♌ 8 5	☐ ☉♃ 6 m. ble to		
26	A		14	26	♍ 8 6	moisture, serene		
27	✲	1 Advent	15	27	♍ 8 6	☌ ♀♀ b, and in-		
28	C	Term ends	16	28	♎ 8 7	clinable to free		
29	D		17	29	♎ 8 8	seon altering to		
30	E	Andrew Apost.	18	30	♏ 8 9	cold rain or snow		

December hath XXXI Daies.

○ New moon 4 day 49 min. past 1 in the morning.
☽ First quarter 10 day 18 min. past 5 at night.
☽ Full Moon 18 day 7 min. past 3 in the afternoon.
☾ Last quarter 26 day 17 min. past 5 at night.

1	f		19	32	♏ 8	10	
2	g	Candidus	20	33	♏ 8	11	
3	A	Cassianus	21	34	♐ 8	12	
4	b	2 Advent	22	35	♐ 8	12	
5	c		23	37	♑ 8	13	
6	d	Nicolaus	24	38	♑ 8	13	
7	e		25	39	♒ 8	13	
8	f	Concep. Mary	26	40	♒ 8	13	the air cold, win-
9	g	Joachimus	27	42	♓ 8	13	dy and moist.
10	A		28	43	♓ 8	13	✳ ♄ ☿ 8 n.
11	b	3 Advent	29	44	♈ 8	13	
12	c	Epimachus	0 ♉ 45		♈ 8	13	
13	d	Lucia	1	47	♉ 8	13	△ ♃ ☿ 2 a. winds
14	e	Nicasius	2	48	♉ 8	13	✳ ♄ ☿ 2 a. drive
15	f		3	40	♊ 8	13	snow or rain.
16	g		4	51	♊ 8	12	
17	A	Lazarus	5	52	♊ 8	11	△ ♃ ☿ 11 n. tem-
18	b	4 Advent	6	53	♋ 8	11	perate.
19	c		7	55	♋ 8	10	
20	d		8	56	♋ 8	9	cold, cloudy, and
21	e	Thomas Apoll	9	57	♌ 8	8	✳ ⊙ ♄ 11 n. incli-
22	f	Theodosius	10	59	♌ 8	7	nable to snow, or
23	g		12	0	♍ 8	6	rain more like.
24	A		13	2	♍ 8	5	
25	b	Christs Nativ.	14	3	♍ 8	5	△ ⊙ ☿ ♃ 11 b.
26	c	Stephen	15	4	♎ 8	4	
27	d	John Evang.	16	6	♎ 8	4	the air inclinable
28	e	Innocents	17	7	♏ 8	3	to serenity and
29	f		18	8	♏ 8	3	frost.
30	g	David	19	9	♐ 8	2	
31	A		20	11	♐ 8	2	

To the Reader.

Courteous Reader,

THe laſt year beïng the firſt of my appearing into the world in print, hath encouraged me a-again to ſet Pen to Paper, ſeeing it was ſo well accepted; and finding that it hath don great good in the world. As for the Predictions the laſt year, I dare ſay none fell out more truer; for the Phyſical Cures none were better. Therefore this year, I here preſent thee with ſome other of the like nature, a-voiding ſuch Language, as may, perhaps, be offen-ſive to ſome, whoſe tender Ears cannot away with the bearing of what, without ſcruple they will do. It is not fit the world ſhould be deprived of ſuch helps to Nature; for want of which, many by their Modeſty, ſuffer much: in many of which Caſes, both men and women are very ſhie of acquainting Phyſitians; onely they will carry their water to a Phyſitian, and tell him they have a pain in the bottom of their bellies; and the Phyſitian is ſuch a Dunce, he cannot diſcern the true cauſe of the Di-ſtemper: ſo the party ſuffers. That thoſe parts might be kept in good caſe and ſerve to the mutual comfort of man and woman, I adviſed laſt year my Reader, to buy the book of the Womans

B   Coun-

Councellour, or Feminine Physitian : *and in regard that there be many rare useful and incomparable Directions, much to the benefit of Generation, that are not convenient to be published here,* I
recommend thee to the most excellent piece of Levinus Lemnius, *his secret* Miracles of Nature,
*modestly treating of Generation, and the parts
thereof, and how one may be made fruitful that is
barren ; and, by Art, get a Boy or a Girl, which
they desire most. It also treateth of all manner
of Secrets and Rarities of Nature whatever : with
Rules for a vertuous life. The reason why I commend this piece, is, that our Sex may be furnished
with knowledge : if they knew better, they would do
better. It is better that they should exercise
their parts, in that which appertaineth to a vertuous life, and be made a useful adornment to the
Age wherein they live ; which is the onely Design
of*

S. J.

————————————————————

A

A
PROGNOSTICATION
FOR
the Year of our Lord,
1 6 5 9.

The Sun entreth Aries at 2 min. past 1 in the After-noon the 12th Day of March 1659. at which time I finde Sol or the Sun Lord of the Ascendant, for that Leo is upon the Cusp of the Ascendant 7 deg. and 4. min. Iupiter being up the Ascendant newly ascended the horizon. Our next enquiry of this Position, is to finde how the rest of the Planets are posited: And first, we finde Mercury

turn in the 4th house, in 23 deg. 6 min. of Libra. he being retrograde the head of the Dragon in the same house in 26 deg. and 4 min. of Scorpio being intercepted, Mars and Venus in Aquarius, in the 7th house, Mars in 9 deg. 10 min. and Venus in 19 deg. 52 min. the Moon in :6 min. of Pisces, the Sun Lord of the Ascendant in Aries, upon the cusp of the 10th house : the tail of the Dragon, & Taurus intercepted in the 10th house : the Sun being Lord of the first, house, or Ascendant, and Mars of the 2d, and placed nigh the Cusp of the 10th house, Denoteth and prognosticateth to us, that Governors and Princes are very powerful in their Councels and Resolutions, and are very much apded by this Position, in their putting in execution their Arbytrary commands, to the detriment of the people: but forasmuch as the Sun is Lord of the Ascendant also, the people receive some ayd from his influence ; in regard the Ascendant hath particular regard to the people, their cattle, corn, and other commodities of the people shall much increase. The Undertakings of the people shall have very great success. Most of the children that are born this year shall be of more noble and generous dispositions then ordinary, more fit for Magistracy and publike Trust, more apt to gain Estates, and more ingenuous, fitter to be made Councellors, and to study the Sciences, then those that have been born for many years last past ; Saturn being in the 4th house by Day, argue, that many shall be excessive covetous, gasping and raking together, and out of all measure envious and malicious. Mars being in the 7th house, Denoteth most miserable and Wicked murder and cruelties that shall be committed, Diseases of the belly, trouble of mind, Shipracks, Tempests, and Thievery not a few. Venus being in the 7th house also prognosticateth terrible Adulteries and Fornications, the loss of abundance of Maiden-heads, and the desire of old women to young men. As for the whole year throughout, there will not be much excess of intemperate weather.

Of

Of the Eclipses *this present Year of our Lord, 1659.*

ON the 26 of April, at 34 min. 7 seconds past 6 in the Evening, it continueth more or less eclipsed, untill 9 of the clock : the Duration thereof will be two hours, 51 minutes, and 54 seconds : In this Eclipse we find Mars Lord of the Ascendant, Scorpio being upon the Cusp of the 11th House, or Ascendant, the Moon being eclipsed in that sign of one of the houses of Mars, it doth denote much honour to the Herorck Sea-man, great successe in their undertakings in the Naval Wars. Some are born now that shall be great Generals and famous Captains at Sea, they shall much honour the English Nation : I advise such Sea-men that are of any repute and credit, that intend Wedlock, not to look so low as the blew A-pron, but have higher thoughts, I assure them good suc-cesse in their amorous Courtings. I cannot promise too much honesty of our Sex, but something more then ordinary this year ; for all the Angles are possessed with fixed Signs also. I think that those Knaves that at-tempt the chastity of those that are not professed Whores, will find it a difficult matter to attain their ends : but Mars being in the 4th house, denoteth, that many villanies shall be acted by the scum of Mankind, I mean com-mon souldiers , who shall be ready to put in execution many villainous commands, let them be never so vile and wicked, Venus being in the same house (in Aries, pro-miseth little lesse then Widow-hood to many Women, the Sun being in the Cusp of the 7th House in Taurus, the tayl of the Dragon being in the seventh house prognosti-cateth Ruptures and Impostumes, sore Throates, and such Diseases as flow from the Humours, Jupiter being in the 9th house, denoteth terrible Dreams and Visions, un-quietness of the Mind in sleep, increase and discovery of Witches and Fortune-Tellers. Saturn being in the 11th house, prognosticateth, that Youth under 30. will be gi-ven to excesse in expences, and desire of women. Water shall do much hurt by over-flowing and breaches of Banks.

B 3   Another

A Prognostication,

Another Eclipse of the Moon, is on the 20 of *October*, at 40 min. past one in the morning.

I Shall take little notice of this Eclipse, the Effects of it will principally be seen upon corn and cattle: It will be of some advantage to those that trade in Merchandize, and it fore telleth, of several Upstarts that shall pretend to Divine Revelations and Visions. Likewise the death of several Witches.

One Eclipse of the Sun, visible on the 4th of *November*; it beginneth at 5 1 minutes, 48 seconds, 1 afternoon: it endeth at 13 min. past 4. Continueth 2 hours, 22 min. and 2 seconds.

THe Heavens appear with a notable face at the time of this Eclipse, the Sun, Moon, Venus, Mercury, and Saturn, are all in the 7th house. Much Sicknesse, Hypocrisie, Treason, and secret Plots and Contrivances, which will occasion the fall of some eminent great Stirs by Law-suits, many of which are occasioned by the unruly Tongues of our Sex for which their husbands must suffer; the Lawyers will have too much employment; the Eclipse hath a malevolent influence on the Aged, shrinketh their Sinews and Nerves, and contracteth the parts, which will cause stopping, and cause many to be vexed with Piles and Hemorrhoids, and all sorts of Distempers that flow from the weakness of the back. Several, especially of our Sex, suffer much disgrace by venerous act on. More Maids, then do, would adventure upon it, were it not for fear of the rising of the Apron, which usually deters such actions. Mercury being in the 7th house also with Venus, and the rest of the Planets aforementioned, argueth, that the gift of mens patience is to be exercised by frequent Curtain-Lectures from their Wives. And lastly, many strong Holds that have been long besieged now surrender: And many Ladies that have been besieged by Suitors, do also surrender.

(Physical

Physical Observations.

Of Raptures.

The general kind of Ruptures are three, Aquosa or Watery: this is usual in Dropsies, when much water is descended into the Cods, which causeth them to swell. Uentosa, or a windy Rupture, that is when great store of wind is gathered into the Purse of the Testicles. And Carnosa, or a fleshy Rupture, which is caused either by the Excremental growing of flesh in the Cods, or by the falling of the intestines into the Cods, the film or skin that should keep them up being broken.

Hernia, or Burstness, is also thus defined.

Hernia, or a Rupture, is properly said to be, when any tumor appears in the purse of the Testicles, proceeding either from something descending into the Cods, or from some matter growing there, and causing the same to swel.

The cure of a watery Rupture.

The cure of a watery Rupture requires a two-fold intention, one is to take away the Antecedent cause, which is a flegmatick watry matter, springing from the Liver by reason of indigestion. The second intention is to dissolve that Aquosity, which is in the Cods, or to draw it out by perforation. The first intention is performed by abating the matter digesting and eradicating it.

Digestive Pills.

Take Pill Aggregative, Pill de Rhabarb Milne, of each one scruple, form thereof 5 Pills with syrup of Endive.

Others if it Proceed from the Head.

Take Pill.Chochiæ, Aureæ, of each one scruple, make Pills thereof, and let the Patient take them going to bed.

A

A Digestive, when the watry Humour proceeds from the debility of the digestive vertue of the Liver.

Take syrup of Endive, syrup of Agrimony, Honey of Roses, of each half an ounce: Water of Wormwood, of Agrimony and Endive, of each one ounce, mix them, and take them at a draught.

If the Flegmatick matter proceed from the Head give this digestive,

Take syrup of Stechas, without species, honey of roses, oximel simple, of each half an ounce, waters of Betony, Wormwood, Endive, of each one ounce, mix them, and use them as the former. The matter being digested, give of the Pills of Rhabarb before prescribed, but in a greater Dose, and order them thus, Take Pill Aggregative two scruples, pill of rhabarb one scruple; make thereof 7 Pills, with syrup of stechas, and give them an hour before day, Let the rule of Diet intend to hot and dry, as we have spoken concerning the Dropsie.

The second Intention.

The second Intention is performed by dissolving the water, either sensibly, or insensibly or by drawing it out by perforation, and by restraining it, that it flow no more to the Cods. It is first insensibly to be dissolved with fomentations, Unctions, and applying of Plaisters.

A Fomentation for the Cods may be made thus.

Take Origanum, Calamint, Peny-royal, Camomile, Dill, Anti-seed, of each M. 1. Caraway, Aniles, seeds of Agnus Castus, of each half an ounce, bruise them grosly, and boil them in a sufficient quantity of spring water, till half be consumed: Then dip a spunge in the said decoction, and therewith foment the Cods, repeating it often.

The

*Then when the place is fomented and dryed,
anoint it with this following
Unction.*

Take Oyl of Castor, of Rue and Lillies, of each 8 ounces, infuse therein a Linnen cloth, and apply it to the
cods.

A Resolutive Plaister for the same.

Take Mints, Balsamint, Origanum, Calamint, Cha-
medreos, Cameppes, Camomil, each one handful: Meal of
Fenugreek, Beans, and Lin-seed, of each one ounce, Anni-
sed and Comin seed, of each half an ounce: let the herbs be
subtilly bruised and boiled in a sufficient quantity of Water, to a perfect decoction: then add the seeds in powder and
the meal, and incorporate them well together with Oyl of
Rue: and apply it plaister-wise to the cods; it insensibly
dissolves the water which is included in the purse of the
testicles. But when these Administrations have been u-
sed, and the water cannot thereby be evacuated, it must
then sensibly be drawn out by incision. Let an Orifice be
made with a Lancet on the lower part of the cod; so as
the water may pass out: but if the Patient be weak, then
it is not so convenient to draw it all out at one time, but
reiterate it often, and if the Orifice be closed up, then make
a new one in another place.

The Cure of a Windy Rupture.

The first Intention is performed after the same manner, as the Hernia Aquosa, that is, by evacuating the matter
from whence the windiness proceeds. The second Intention, which hath respect unto the continue cause, is thus
performed: First, by fomenting the purse with such things
as dissolve wind: to which purpose, use such a fomentation
as follows.

A Fomentation for a watry Rupture.

Take Origanum, calamint savin, sage, betony, rue, camomile, of each one handful, seeds of Annis, Fenel, Comin, caraway, Ameos, of each half an ounce, bruise them all
grosly, and boil them in equal parts of Wine and water,
till a third part be consumed: and with a spunge infused
in that decoction, foment the parts affected.

After-

After the Fomentation, and the place is dryed, let this Unction be used.

Take oyl of Castor, Euphorbium, and Elder, of each drams, mix them and anoint the place therewith hot. And afterwards that plaister is convenient to be used, which is before mentioned in Hernia Aquosa.

Wines good to provoke the Terms.

Wine of Eleeampane roots, of Marjerome gentle, of the heard Bennet, of Betony, of Gillow-flowers, and of Rosemary, these are very good if the Patients Body be fitting to drink Wine, otherwise Discretion may direct you not to use it.

Confections good for this Disease are,

The Confection of Eleeampane roots, the Confection of Eringo roots, Conserves of Piony, and Mirrh roasted in Apple.

A Syrup to stay the immoderate Flux of the Terms.

Take syrup of Endive, one ounce: syrup of Purslain, half an ounce: the Decoction of Egrimony, and of Plaintain four ounces: mix them together, and make them into a syrup, and so take it as you please.

An Electuary for the same.

Take Conserve of Roses, two ounces: of Water Lillies, one ounce: of Pearl prepared, and burnt Hartshorn, each half an ounce: Bole Armonick, Terra Lemnia, each half a scruple: mix them together with syrup of Plantain, a quantity sufficient to make it into an Electuary.

An Electuary for the same.

Take Conserve of Roses, six ounces: Conserve of Burrage, Buglis, Valm, of each an ounce: Bolus prepared, a dram: Pearl prepared a quarter of an ounce of Rubies, Jacinths, Saphir, each a scruple: Cinamon, a dram; mix them together, and make an Electuary thereof.

An

An Oyl good to bring down the Tearms.

Take Oyl of sweet Almonds 2 ounces, of white Lillies one ounce, Oyl of Aniseed two drams, mix them, and therewith anoint &c. it is very effectual for infirmities in those parts.

Another Electuary to stay the Terms.

Take conserve of Roses, three ounces: Marmalade two ounces and a half: red Coral, a dram: Bolus prepared, half a dram: Blood-stone prepared, two drams; mix them all together with the syrup of Myrtles, and make an Electuary thereof, and take it as you please.

Common Syrups which remove Obstructions of the Terms, are,

Syrup of Mugwort, of Maiden hair, of Chicory with Rhubarb, and the syrup of the five roots; these you may have ready at the Apothecaries.

Another to move the Terms.

Take Mints, Balm, Penny-royal, Marjerom and Southernwood, of each an handful: Aniseeds, Fennel and Carraway seeds, of each an ounce: Polipody, an ounce and an half: Cicory roots, an ounce: cut the roots and hearbs very small, and boyl them all together in a quart of water till a third part be consumed; then strain it, and sweeten it with Sugar to your own liking, and take thereof as you please.

An Electuary to purge the Reins

Take Cassia newly extracted, one ounce: Rhebarb in powder, one dram: mix them together with syrup of white water Lillies, a sufficient quantity to make it into an Electuary; put this into a penny pot of White-wine, or a little posset drink, which comes first to hand; stir it well together, till it be all dissolved in the drink, and so take it in the morning fasting, and go about your business (if you have any thing to do) about two hours after, take some broth or posset drink.

This

This Medicine you may take twice or thrice, as you see occasion, resting alwayes a day between.

Afterwards, you may take every other day, a dram of Trochis de Carabe in Plantane water.

You may also give the Patient, every second or third day, a dram of the filings of Ivory in Plantane water; it is very good.

Sweating is also much commended in this case, which may be thus done.

Take Barley water, three ounces: strong Wine three ounces: give it the Patient very warm, and so let her sweat.

Afterwards prepare a Clyster in this manner.

A Clyster for the Whites, through Heat or running of the Reins.

Take Beets, Violet leaves, and Night-shade, of each one handful, seeth them well together, & take 12 ounces of the decoction, or boiled liquor, which you please to call it, and to it add, sugar one ounce and a half, yolks of eggs, Oyl of Water-lillies, Oyl of Roses, of each two ounces, salt a dram and a half: Give this Clyster in the Afternoon a little before meat.

Another for the Whites.

Take the seeds of Arch-Angel, or dead Nettles in powder, about a dram at a time in red wine. Candied Aniseeds is also very good for this Disease: and not improperly may be given in either case this following.

Another for the same, or Reds.

Take 4 spoonfuls of red-rose water, a new laid egge, a peny worth of white sugar-candy in powder, and a Nutmeg grated: incorporate all these, and beat them wel together, and drink it last at night going to bed. You may also, if the Issue be sharp, so as to cause pain & soreness, use an Injection or Pessary.

A

A Pessary for the Whites in Women.

Take some whites of eggs, and beat them well in red rose water, and make it into a Pessary, with some cotten or linnen cloaths wet in it, and so put it up into the Matrix, always remembring to tie a string to it, to pull it out again when you please. If the whites flow from abundance of superfluous humor, it will not be unnecessary to endeavour to evacuate the same through the skin, by using often frictions, or rubbing of the whole body, first gently, and then more hard, by which means the humors may be purged through the skin.

Of the Fits of the Mother, or suffocation, or drawing up of the Matrix.

This happens to women through several causes. Oftentimes when there is an obstruction, or stoppage of the Terms, which do burthen the Brain and Matrix with bad humors. Sometimes by reason of the retention of their natural Seed, as in Widows, and old Maids; for this retention causeth wind to ascend, and ill vapours from the Matrix.

But to proceed to remedies when this Disease cometh suddenly, speedily cast cold water on her face, and give her cold water to drink.

A Powder to be used in the nature of a Pessary, against the suffocation of the Matrix, or fits of the Mother.

Take red Storax, Lignum Aloes, Cloves, of each a dram: Musk, Amber, of each half a dram: make them altogether into a powder, and then bind it up in a cloth in the form of a Pessary, and put it up into the Matrix.

A Fumigation for this Disease.

Take Gallia Moscata, Cassia wood, Cynamon, Time, of each a like quantity: mix these together, and make a perfume thereof, and let the smoke be received up into the Matrix, through a tunnel for that purpose. If the Patient be a Maid, a husband is the best medicine, if she can get one: but in case that cannot be, then let her abstain from strong wines and flesh meat, and all such things as increase natural sperme.

And use letting blood, such meats and drinks as are cooling; and amongst the rest, this Confection following is very good.

Another for the same.

Take an ounce of Oyl of Lillies, Musk Saffron, of each three grains; bruise all well together, and make a Pessary thereof with Wooll, or Cotton, and put it up into the place.

A Fume for the falling down of the Womb.

Take Tormentil, Bistort, juyce of soles; of each three drams: Pomegranate pills, the blossoms thereof, of each a quarter of an ounce: Assa fœtida an ounce: Mastick, Frankincense, Galbanum, of each two drams and a half: Cypress Nuts, Galls, Myrtle seed, of each 3 drams: stamp and mix all these together, and strew thereof upon a red hot brick and let the Patient receive the fume thereof beneath. Let it not come at her Nose; but in the mean time let her smell to Musk, Amber, Violets, and such sweet smells, which draw up the Mother, and cause it so ascend again.

An Oyntment for the falling down of the Womb.

Take the Oyntment of Holly hocks, which is called at the Apothecaries, unguent de Althea, mix therewith some marrow of an Ox, or other beast, the grease of a hen or capon, and some oyl: and herewith anoint the neck of the Matrix, and all the parts about it when you go to bed: you may also make a plaister hereof, and apply it all night as before.

To prevent Miscarriages.

Take Carraway seed one dram, Ameos, Ginger, Beaver cod, of each one scruple: Keep the Carraway seed in Vinegar

Uinegar, and dry it again, and beat it to powder : then mixe, with the rest, and give a dram thereof in Wine, every Morning for certain days together.

A Confection to cause fruitfulness in Man or Woman.

Take Rapes, Ivory shaven, Askeys, Sesily, Behen red and white, of each one dram : Cinamon, Doronicum, Mace, Cloves, Galingale, long Pepper, Rosemary flowers, Balsom wood, Blattis, Byzantie Marjoram gentle, Penny-royal, of each two scruples : Balm, Buglas, Citron pieces, of each one scruple : Spica Indie, Amber, Pearls, of each half a scruple : Sugar a pound : decoct the Sugar in Malmsey, and the other things ; and make them into a Confection, use of it a little at a time.

A Powder for the same to be strewed on meat.

Take, Nutmegs, Cubebbes, Ginger, of each half a dram : long Pepper, Mastick, Cinamon, red Behen, white Behen, of each a scruple : mix them all together, and make them into fine powder, and strew of it a little upon the parties meat.

Another Confection for the same.

Take Honey, three ounces : Linseed, Grains, Ivory shaven, of each one ounce : Borage, three ounces : Sugar 24 ounces : Musk, Amber, of each half a scruple : Cinamon, two grains : Cloves, Mace, of each one grain : clarifie the Honey, then incorporate the other things with it to make a Confection thereof, and take of it as you please.

A Potion to further Conception in a Woman.

Take Wormwood, Mugwort, of each a handful : boyl them together in a quart of Goats milk, til almost half be wasted, and let the Woman drink thereof first & last, every morning and evening a good draught.

A Plaister to remedy the corrupt Humors.

Take Roses, Cypres Nuts, burnt Ivory, sandaraca, of each one dram, Rozen 3 ounces : boil the Rozen in red Uinegar

Vinegar, till the vinegar be consumed: then mix the other things with it, and make two plaisters of it, and apply one to the back, and the other to the womb.

Another excellent good Plaister to strengthen Women with Child, that do not use to go out half their times.

Take oyl of Quinces, oyl of Roses, oyl of Mints; of each one ounce and a half, Comphrey, Blood-stone, red-coral, Sanbaraca, Date stones burnt : of each one dram: mix it with a sufficient quantity of wax to make a salve thereof: and with this anoint the Kidneys and Mother.

Pills to expel a dead Child.

Take Trochies of Mirrh 1 scruple, Galbanum half a scruple: make 5 pills thereof with peny-royal water.

A Fume to expel the dead Child.

Take some shavings of an Asses hoof, or of a Horses, if you cannot get the other; and make a Fume thereof, & let the woman sit over it.

A Confection for an excessive flood in women lying in Child-bed.

Take Conserve of Piony, one ounce ; Conserve of Roses, one ounce , Conserve of Burrage, Buglos, Balm, of each half an ounce ; prepared Bolus, half a dram ; prepared Pearls, one dram ; Cynamon, one dram and a half ; mix them all together, and make a Confection thereof.

Lozinges very effectual for the same.

Take Blood-stone, one dram and a half : red Coral, one dram : Tormentil, Trochis de Sodio, of each half a dram : scraped Ivory, burnt Harts-horn, of each one scruple : Pearls prepared, four scruples : fine Bolus, two scruples : Shepyeards purse, red Sanders, of each a scruple ; Cynamon, one dram : Sugar, six ounces : wash the Blood-stone in Plantain water, and make a powder, or Lozinges thereof.

Janu=

January *Aſtrological Obſervations.*

The Seaſon is not more turbulent and unconſtant then the Affairs of State, at this preſent beginning of the Year: Divers eminent Perſons are reduced to private condition, or worſe: Impriſonment the deſerts of others, and death of ſome, I ſhould have ſaid, rather their chance: For it falleth out ſometimes in ſo depraved an Age as this, that the moſt honeſt ſuffer moſt: Trade will not abound, the Treaſure of the Common-wealth is much exhauſted: pray to be delivered.

Obſervations for the good Husbands and good Houſewives.

Plow for Peaſe, fallow ſuch land as you intend ſhall reſt the year following; water your barren Meadows Paſture, and drain arrable ground, eſpecially if you inten d to ſowe Peaſe, Oats, or Barly the ſeed time following: alſo ſtub up all rough grounds, trim up your Garden moulds; The weather calm, remove all manner of fruit trees, rear Calves, remove Bees, keep good Dyet. --

February, *Aſtrological Obſervations.*

This Moneth will be Epidemicall to many Women with child, and of evil conſequence to others, not ſo far gone with child. Many now breeding, endure almoſt alike torture to bringing forth. Therefore good women make much of your ſelves, let your Husbands pay for it. I need not exhort ſome, there are many worthy of reproof, for making too much of naught. Nay, I may add, or never be good. Publike Actions, this Moneth do produce but little. Something will be in the North, and North-Eaſt part of the World: private conſpiracies will be hatching, but few take effect, or be brought to light,

C

Obſerva-

A Prognostication,

Observations very useful and profitable.

Set Beans, pease, and other pulse in stiff ground, begin the soonest, prepare your garden, prune and trim your fruit trees from Moths, Cankers, and superfluous branches, plash hedges, lay your quickset close, plant Rose, Gooseberry trees, and any other shrub trees, and graff your tender stocks: forbear all phlegmatick meats.

March, *Astrological Observations.*

PReparations for Martial Undertakings, I wish we had peace with some, pla nce I dare not speak: some kind of probability there is, that the people may have some eminent Champions to assert their Liberties, not onely by Pen, but also by Council and Arms: the Clergy still endeavour to keep the Cart on the Wheels. Now-ce-Lay Pulpitiers begin more and more to decline their impudent and audacious publike bablings: the Sectaries decrease in credit and number.

Observations very useful and profitable.

Look well to your Elves, cut up underwood or fewel, transplant all sort of summer flowers, comfort them with good earth, especially the Crown Imperial, Narcissus, Tuleps, and Hyacinth; in your barren fruit trees, bore holes and drive hard wedges of Oak, and cover roots of trees close with fat earth that are uncovered; graft fruit trees and sowe Oates, Rye, and Barley. Let your Diet be cold and temperate.

April, *Astrological Observations.*

I Advise the National Ministry to preach, by their practise, amendment of life, as well as by their tongues: They may, peradventure, reprove me of boldness herein, it mattereth not: I could rather see them busied in converting Publicans and sinners, then in Princes Courts, I find some of them busie themselves too much in matters of civill concernments. Great and extraordinary Actions this Moneth, I will lay a wager upon some heads, if they do not part with their shoulders, they will be Masters.

Obser-

Observations very profitable and useful.

Sowe your Hemp and Flax, sowe and set all sorts of Hearbs, open your Hives, and give your Bees their liberty and let them labour for their living; cut your Oake Timber, the bark is best for the Tanners use. Scowre your ditches, gather your Manure together, in heaps, gather stones, repair high-wayes, set Ozters and willows, and cast up all decayed Fences. For your health, use moderate exercise.

May, Astrological Observations.

The effects of what was begun the last Moneth, lasteth this, and will so do for many years. Though acted with much variety, a perfidious Army cleaveth. Those who have been once false, will never be true: A juster reward cannot be. Several Retainers to the Law, receive Additions of honour to their parts. It would be well that they had also one graine or two of honesty by more added, to each of those Worthies of the Long-Robe, for which their Clyents would be no whit sorry.

Observations very profitable and useful.

Fold your Sheep, carry forth Manure, and bring home fewel: weed Winter Corn, furnish your Dairy, let your Mares go to Horse, fat your dry Kine, and away with them: sowe your tender seeds as Cucumbers, Muskmillions, all sweet kind of herbs and flowers. For your health drink clarified whey.

June, Astrological Observations.

Some small amendment of Trade, a good Season, People are disposed to pleasure. Forreign Princes send their Ambassadors to congratulate some new change, or to negotiate some extraordinary Affairs: It will be more then an ordinary mercy, if now we are not in blood: I do not see how without it, such things which we expect, can be brought to pass: the best Title, is power. Other claims, are void.

Observations very profitable and useful.

Distil all sorts of Plants and Hearbs whatever, Cut your rank Meadows, fetch home fewell, and carry forth

C 2

ma.

Manure, Maule, and Lime to mend your Land: Be sure to be chast this Month, what ever you are the rest of the year.

July, *Astrological Observations.*

FRom all parts we hear of desperate and unreconcilable Wars: Germany is not a little concerned: The Turk may adventure upon Transilvania and Hungaria, whilst the Jews may home sily the silver out of our pockets: the people begin to be undeceived, by discerning the abuses frequently administred, and if there be not a Parliament, it is not al together desired, they find that there is great need of one; that although they are bad Food, yet they are good Physick.

Observations very profitable.

Attend your Hay harvest, sheat field sheep: let the hearbs you intend to preserve run to seed; cut off the stalk of your flowers, and cover the roots with new fat earth: sell your Lambs you intended for the shambles. Take no physick, unless in extraordinary cases, refrain venery.

August, *Astrologicall Observations.*

The Catholick Sea bestirreth it self, I mean the Pope by his Councel, and by his Emissaries. Indulgencies, Pardons, and other rare Inventions, are frequent: They would willingly promote their Interest which dieth, and beginneth to decline and wax less. New schism do arise amongst them, much to the detriment of the Church: their extremities increase what they oppose. Murders not a few will be committed this Month.

Observations very useful.

Follow diligently your Corn harvest, cut down your Wheat and Rye, Mowe Barley and Oates, put off your fat Sheep and Cattel, gather your Plums, Apples, and Pears; make your Summer Perry and Cyder, set your slips and Scyons of all sorts of Gillyflowers, and other flowers; Transplant them that were set in the Spring, Geld your Lambs, carry Manure from your Dove-coats put your Swine to the early mast. Refraine all excess in eating and drinking, drink that which is cooling.

Septemb.

September, *Aſtrological Obſervations.*

SOme miſerable diſaſter happeneth in London, I wiſh the evil may be diverted by prayer. Diſtemper of body is very frequent and prevalent; Temperance muſt be your Miſtriſs this ſeaſon, elſe Intemperance will much endanger your health. Plurſies are now frequent, Merchants find the effects thereof to their ſorrow. The Husbandman hath received a great harveſt into his Barn.

Obſervations very uſeful and neceſſary.

Cut your Beans, Peaſe, and all manner of Pulſe; on the Land you intend to ſowe Wheat and Rye, beſtow the beſt manure; gather your Winter fruit, ſell your wool, ſtocks of Bees, and other commodities you intend to put off. Thatch your hive of Bees you intend to keep, and look tha; no Dragns, Mice, or other vermin be about them. Thraſh your ſeed, Wheat and Rye. Uſe Phyſick moderately, ſhun the eating of ſweet or rotten fruit, avoid ſurfeiting.

October, *Aſtrologicall Obſervations.*

FRequent Land-floods and Inundations are threatned, Inconveniencies not a few do abound. The Eminent contend about dividing the ſpoil of the Inſitor, who ſtandeth ſtill the while, A miſery not the laſt, that Mankind is too often caſt into. Arm therefore with Wiſdom and Prudence, to avoid the evil of it, elſe you muſt arm with patience to ſubmit to it, I ſpeak of no other Arms, leſt I ſhould be taken to be a Trumpet to precede Rebellion: howeber, at a venture I will ſay, that a people are not bound to obey well, when Governors do not govern well.

Obſervations very uſeful and profitable.

Finiſh with your Wheat-ſeed, plaſh and lay your hedges and quickſets, ſcowre your Ditches and Ponds, tranſplant and remove all manner of fruit trees, make Winter Perry and Cyder, ſpare your Paſture and feed upon your corn fields: draw furrows to drain: and keep dry your new ſowen Corn; make Malt, rear all new falne Calves, all foals that were foaled in the Spring weanto from the Mares, Sell your ſheep that you do not intend to Winter, and ſeparate Lamb, from the Ewes that you intend to keep. Recreate your ſpirits by harmleſs ſports, and take phyſick by good advice if need be.

C 3   Novem.

A Prognostication,

November, *Astrolgical Observations.*

Come let us all amend, the world is bad enough : the King of Spain after his long and tedious war seeketh peace every where: the French are high and campant. The Dutch are privately huging all advantages possible that may tend to the increasing of Trade. They account it their principal strength to enrich the people. London, not without the Nation, ware-makers of discontent. The great Ones are jealous of their condition, and much question their safety, which hath no other Foundation then the Humour of the people.

Observations for the good Husbands and good Housewives.

Cut down your Timber for Plows, Carts, Naves, Axeltrees, Harrows, and other offices about husbandry, or housewifry; make the last return of grass-fed Cattel, take your Swine from the mast, and feed them for the slaughter: Rear all Calves that fall now, break all Hemp and Flax you intend to spend in the Winter season. Remove fruit-trees, and sow Wheat and Rye in hot soyls; Use spices and wine, moderately.

December, *Astrological Observatiions.*

This Month produceth little of Actions, more then Robberies, Pyracies, and Diseases incident to the Season. Pride, Oppression, Extortion, Injustice, doth not end with this year, nor case to be still over-ruling, and bearing dominion over Mankind.

Observations for the good Husbands and good Housewives.

Put your Sheep to the Peas reeks, kill your small Porks and large Bacons, lop hedges, saw your Timber for building, and lay it to season: plow your ground you intend to sow clean Beans on: cover your dainty fruit trees, drain your corn fields, and water your Meidows: cover your best flowers with rotten horse-litter. Now all sorts of Fowle are in season, keep thy self warm with a wholsome Dyet, and avoid all care that shall trouble thy spirit, as a dangerous thing.

FINIS.

Books worth buying, newly printed and
to be sold by the *Book-sellers* of *London.*

The Vale-Royal of England, *being a Historical & Geographical Description of the County of* Chester.   Folio.

A Treatise of Spectres, *or, an History of Appalitions, Oracles, Prophecies, and Predictions, with Dreams, Visions, and Revelations, and the cunning Delusions of the Devil, to strengthen Idolatry, and the Worshipping of Saints departed; with the doctrine of Purgatory.* by Tho. Bromhall. *Whereunto is annexed a Treatise confuting the Sadduces, denying the appearing of Angels and Devils.*   fol.

A Commentary *an* Antoninus's Itinera y of the Roman Empire, *so far as it concerneth* Brittain: *wherein the Foundation of our Cities, Lawes, and Government, according to the Roman Policy, are clearly discovered.* by Wil. Burton *Batchelor of Lawes. are sold by* H. Twyford Middle-Temple.

The History of Magick, *written in* Fench *by* G. Naudeus *now Englished. A most excellent piece in defence of all the wise men mentioned in the Holy Scripture, and other Authors.*   Octavo.

Κυκνειον ασμα, Cygnea Cantio. *Autore* J. Lelando, *Antiquario. Vaeneunt apud* Octavianum Pulleyn *ad insigne Rosae in Caemiterio.* D. Pauli. 1658.   Octavo.

The Refinement of Zion, *or the old Orthodox Religion justified and defended.*   Quarto.

The History of the Wonders of Nature, *treating Philosophically and Physically of the Heavens, Elements, Meteors, Minerals, Beasts, Fish, Fowl, Plants, and of Man.*   Folio.

A Compendious History of the Swedes, Goths, and Vandals, *and other Northern Nations, being the actions of their famous Heroes, their strange Eccentrick Customs, Fashions, Attire, Sports, Battels, Feasts, Marriages, Religion, and Trades. Together with the horrid Apparitions of Devils, the antick Prestigations of Conjurers, and Magical Inchantments. Fol. the sum of his great Attainments in Learning, Philosophy, Physick, Chymistry, Policy, and Antiquity; the like not to be read in any Author.*   Octavo.

The History *of the* Constancy *of* Nature, *proving that the world nor any thing therein, doth not decline or grow worse.* · Octavo.

The Protestants Evidence, *a most learned work, proving that in the 16. several Centuries since Christ, there hath been eminent and learned men that have professed the Faith of the Church of England* Folio.

Also, A Theological Concordance *of the Holy Scriptures, of small price, and performeth as much as many large Volums, very useful for all that desire to attain to Knowledge.* Octavo.

Renodeus *his Dispensatory, being the sum of all Physical and Chirurgical operations.* Folio

A new Treatise *proving a Multiplicity of worlds, That the Planets are Regions inhabited, & the Earth a Star.* 12.

The Cabinet Council, *containing the chief Arts of Empire, and Mysteries of State; Dicabineted in political and polemical Adhorisms grounded by Authority and Experience, and illustrated with the choicest Axamples and Historical Observations. By the ever-renowned Knight, Sir Walter Raleigh, published by* J. Milton, *Esq. Sold by* T. Johnson, *at the sign of the Key in St. Pauls Church-yard, near the West end.*

An History *of the World from the Creation to this present year* 1658. *Written by* Dionysius Petavius *and others.* Folio

There is now published An excellent Treatise of Physick by Mr. John Tanner. · Octavo

---

The highly approved Pectoral Lozenges, being an effectual Cure of all Diseases incident to the Lungs, as Coughs, Consumptions, Catharrs, Hoarsness, and an Antidote against the Plague, and all other contagious Diseases. and Obstructions of the Stomach; made by Mr. Edward Buckworth, *to be had only at his house in St. Katherines street near the Tower, and at* Mr. Rich. Lownds *Bookseller at the White Lyon near the little North door of St. Pauls Church.*

353427

Sarah Jinner's *An Almanack for the Year of our Lord God 1664* (Wing 1847) is reprinted from the copy at the Edinburgh University Library (Shelfmark M.18.35/18). The text block of the Edinburgh copy is 75 × 135 mm.

For passages that are blotched, please consult Appendix B, 'A Key to Difficult-to-Read Passages'.

18

AN
ALMANACK
FOR

The Year of our LORD GOD, 1664. being Bissextile
or Leap-Year.

Calculated for the Meridian of London, and may indifferently serve for all EUROPE.

By Sara Jinner, *Student in Astrology.*

London, Printed by J. Streater, for the Company
of STATIONERS, 1664.

Julian, or English.		Gregorian, or Forreign.
11	The Golden Number.	12
21	Cycle of the Sun.	21
2	Dominical Letter.	F G
2	Roman Indiction.	2
10	Number or Direction.	16
12	Epact.	2

Febr. 7.	Septuagesima.	Febr. 10.
Febr. 17.	Shrove-Sunday.	Febr. 27.
April 10.	Easter-Day.	April 13.
May 15.	Rogation Sunday.	May 18.
May 19.		May 22.
May 29.	Ascension Day.	Jun. 4.
Nov. 27.	Whitsunday. Advent Sunday.	Nov. 30.

The Characters of the 12. Signs of the Zodiack.

♈   ♉   ♊   ♋   ♌   ♍
Aries, Taurus, Gemini, Cancer, Leo, Virgo,

♎   ♏   ♐   ♑   ♒   ♓
Libra, Scorpio, Sigittarius, Capric. Aquarius, Pisces.

The Characters of the seven Planets

♄   ♃   ♂   ☉   ♀   ☿   ☽
Saturn, Jupiter, Mars, Sol, Venus, Mercury, Luna.

The Characters of the five chief Aspects.

☌   ☍   ✳   ▢   △
Conjunction, Opposition, Sextile, Quartile, Trine.

		January				February	
1	a	New-yeers Day	♊	1	d		♌
2	b		♊	2	e	Purif. Mar.	♌
3	c		♋	3	f	{ Full 1 d. 37	♍
4	D	{ Full, 3 d. 37	♋	4	g	{ m. p. 2. at noon	♍
5	e	{ m. past 3 noon	♌	5	a		♍
6	f	12 day	♌	6	b		♎
7	g		♍	7	c	Septuagef.	♎
8	a	{ L. st q. 10 d.	♍	8	D	☉ in { L. q. 8	♎
9	b	{ 9 h. p. 3 morn	♍	9	e	♓ { c. 31 m. p.	♏
10	c	1 Sun. af. Epiph.	♎	10	f	9. night.	♏
11	D	[☉] in ♎	♏	11	g		♏
12	e		♏	12	a		♐
13	f		♏	13	b		♐
14	g		♐	14	c	Sexagef.	♑
15	a		♐	15	D		♑
16	b		♑	16	e		♓
17	c	Sun. aft. Epiph.	♑	17	f	New 17 d. 10	♓
18	D	New 18 d. 41	♑	18	g	m. past 1 morn.	♈
19	e	m. past 7. morn.	♒	19	a		♈
20	f		♒	20	b		♈
21	g		♓	21	c	Shrove-Sunday.	♉
22	a		♓	22	D		♉
23	b		♈	23	e		♊
24	c	3 Sun. af. Epiph.	♈	24	f	Ashwen.	♊
25	D	Conver. of S. Paul	♈	25	g	Matthias	♋
26	e	First q. 25 d. 46	♉	26	a	First q. 24 day.	♋
27	f	m. past 10 night.	♉	27	b	15 m. p. 7. morn.	♌
28	g		♊	28	c	1 Sun. in Lent.	♌
29	a		♋				
30	b	1. Mar.	♋				
31	c	4 S. af. Epiphany	♋				

1.	B		♏
2	C	☽ Full 2 d. 1	♏
3	D	p. 2 morn.	
4	E		≏
5	F		≏
6	G	2 Sun. in Lent.	♏
7	A		♏
8	B		♐
9	C	☉ in ☽ ☊ L. q	♐
10	D	♈ 9 d. 22	♑
11	E	m. p. noon	♑
12	F		♒
13	G	3 Sun. in Lent.	♒
14	A		♒
15	B		♒
16	C		♓
17	D	☽ New 17 d	♓
18	E	34 m. p. 3 n	♈
19	F		♈
20	G	4 Sun. in Lent	♈
21	A		♉
22	B		♉
23	C	☽ F. q. 24	♊
24	D	38 m. p. 1 a. n	♊
25	E		♊
26	F		♋
27	G	5 Sun. in Lent.	♋
28	A		♋
29	B		♌
30	C	☽ Full 31 d	♌
31	D	18 m. p. 2 a. n	♍

1	E		♍
2	F		♍
3	G		♎
4	A		♎
5	B		♎
6	C		♏
7	D		♏
8	E	☉ ☽ L. q. 8 d.	♐
9	F	♉ in 41 m. n	♐
10	G		♑
11	A		♑
12	B		♒
13	C		♒
14	D		♒
15	E	☽ New 16 d.	♓
16	F	43 m. p. 2. m	♓
17	G		♈
18	A		♈
19	B		♈
20	C		♉
21	D	☽ First q 22	♉
22	E	d. 10 m. p. 8 n	♊
23	F	St. George	♊
24	G	2 Sun at. Easter	♋
25	A		♋
26	B		♋
27	C		♌
28	D		♌
29	E	☽ Full 30 d	♍
30	F	12 m. p. 3 m	♍

1	d			1	g	
2	e			2	f	
3	f			3	g	
4	g			4	a	
5	a			5	b	
6	b	☽ Laſt q. 8 d.		6	c	☽ Laſt q. 6 d.
7	c	23 m. p.6. m.		7	d	at 9 evening
8	d	4 Sun. at Eaſter.		8	e	
9	e			9	f	
10	f	☉ in ♊		10	g	
11	g			11	a	☉ in ♋
12	a			12	b	1 Sun. aft. Trin.
13	b	☽ New 15 d.		13	c	☽ New 13 d
14	c	11 m.p. 11 m.		14	d	at 7 evening.
15	d			15	e	
16	e			16	f	
17	f			17	g	
18	g			18	a	
19	a			19	b	2 Sun. aft. Trin.
20	b			20	c	☽ Firſt quar
21	c	☽ Firſt q. 22		21	d	20 day, 1 m.
22	d	d. 48 m.p.2. m		22	e	
23	e			23	f	
24	f			24	g	
25	g			25	a	
26	a			26	b	3 Sun. aft. Trin
27	b	☽ Full 29 d.		27	c	☽ Full 28 d.
28	c	4 n.p.5 aft.n.		28	d	10 in morn.
29	d			29	e	St. Peter & Paul
30	e			30	f	
31	f					

		July. XXXI. Days.					1604. Days.	
c	G		♓	1	C			♈
d	A		♓	2	D			♈
3	b	4 h. S. aft. Trin.	♓	3	E			♈
e	c		♈	4	f			♈
5	d		♈		G	☾ Laſt quar.		♈
6	E	☾ Laſt q. 6 d.	♈	5	A	6. day 6 even.		♉
7	f	11 in the mor	♈	7	b	9. Sun. af. Trin.		♉
8	G		♈	8	c			♊
9	A		♉	9	D			♊
10	b	5. Sun. af. Trin	♉	10	E			♋
11	c		♉	11	f	☾ N w 11 d.		♏
12	D	☉ ♌	♉	12	G	9 in the mor.		♏
13	E	☾ N w 13 d.	♊	13	A			♏
14	f	2 in the mor.	♊	14	b	10. Sun. af. Trin.		♎
15	G		♋	15	c			♎
16	A		♋	16	D			♎
17	b	6. S. n. af. Trin	♋	17	E			♐
18	c		♌	18	f	☾ Firſt q. 18.		♐
19	D	☾ Firſt q. 19	♌	19	G	d. 10 in m x		♐
20	E	2 a. 9 even.	♌	20	A			♑
21	f		♍	21	b	11. Sun. af. Trin.		♑
22	G		♍	22	c			♒
23	A		♍	23	D			♒
24	b	7. Sun. aft. Trin.	♎	24	E			♒
25	c	James Ap. Ela	♎	25	f			♓
26	D		♏	26	G	☾ Full 26 d.		♓
27	E	☾ Full 27 d.	♏	27	A	3 afternoon.		♓
28	f	11 at Night	♏	28	b	12. Sun. af. Trin.		♈
29	G		♐	29	c			♈
30	A		♐	30	D			♈
31	b	8. Sun. aft. Trin.	♓	31	E			♈

1	f g a	⟨ ☾ Laſt quar. 3		1	a	17 Sun. af. Trin
		⟨ d. in th. m.		2	b	
3	a			3	c d e	⟨ ☾ Laſt quar.
4	b	13 Sun. aft. Trin.		4		⟨ day, 9 in mo.
5	c d e			5	d	
6	d e			6	e f g	
7				7		
8	e f g a			8	g a	
9		⟨ ☾ New 9 day		9		18 Sun. af. Trin
10		⟨ 6 Evening.		10	b	⟨ ☾ New 9 day
11		14 Sun. af. Trin.		11	c d	⟨ 5 in the mor.
12				12	e f	
13	d	☉ in ♎		13		☉ in ♏
14	e			14	g a	
15	f			15		
16		⟨ ☾ Firſt quar.		16	b	19 Sun. af. Trin
17	a	⟨ 17 d. 4 in m.		17	c d e	
18		15 Sun. aft. Trin.		18		
19				19	f	⟨ ☾ Firſt quar.
20	d e			20	g a	⟨ 16 d. at midnight
21		Mathew Apoſtle		21		
22				22	g	
23	f g a			23		20 S. a. T. Terb.
24				24	c	⟨ ☾ Full 24 day
25		16 Sun. af. Trin		25	d e	⟨ 7 at night.
26		⟨ ☾ Full 25 day		26	f	
27	d	⟨ in the morn.		27	g a	
28	e f			28		
29		Mich. Arch.		29	a	
30				30		21 Sun. af. Trin.
				31		☾ L. q. 4 aftern

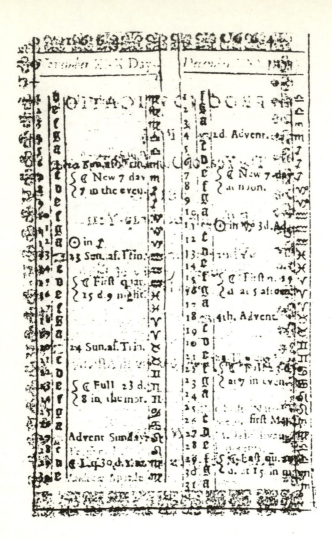

A
PROGNOSTICATION
FOR

The Year of Our LORD, 1664.

BEING

Biſſextile or Leap-Year.

Wherein ſundry Things are
contained, worthy of being
taken Notice of.

By *Sarah Jinner*, Student in Aſtrology.

LONDON,

Printed by *John Streater*, 1664.

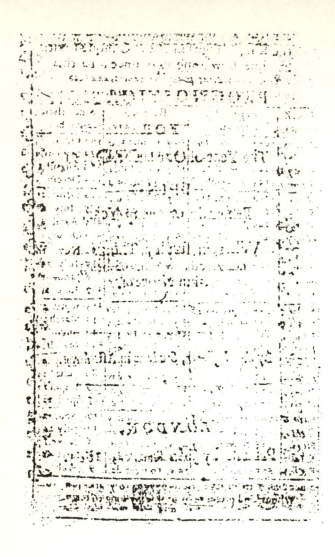

A Table...
... of the Kings, Reigns fince the Conqueſt with
the time how long it is fince, to this
Year, 1664. Being ſit for Scriveners, and ſuch
as are imployed in Law-caſes.

The K. names.	Began his Reign.	Raigned yea: mont: days	Since then Raigns beg:
W. Con.	1066 Octob. 14	20 y. 11 m. 22. d.	598 Octob. 14
W. Ruf.	1087 Septemb. 9	12 y. 11 m. 19 d.	577 Septem. 9
Henry 1	1100 Auguſt 1.	35 y. 4 m. 11 d.	564 Auguſt 1
Stephen	1135 Decemb. 2	18 y. 11 m. 19 d.	529 Decem. 2
Henry 2	1154 Octob. 25.	34 y. 9 m. 2 day	510 Octob. 2.
Rich. 1	1189 July 6	9 y. 9 m. 22 day	475 July 6
K. John	1199 April 6	17 y. 7 m. 6 day	465 April 6
Henry 3	1216 October 19	56 y. 1 Moneth.	448 Octob. 1.
Edw. 1	1272 Novemb. 16	34 y. 8 m. 9 day	392 Nov. 16
Edw. 2	1307 July 7	19 y. 7 m. 6 day	357 July 74
Edw. 3	1326 January 25	50 y. 4 m. 7 day	338 Janua. 2
Rich. 2	1377 June 21	22 y. 3 m. 16 d.	2.7 June 2.
Henry 4	1399 Septemb. 29	13 y. 6 m. 5 day	265 Septe. 2
Henry 5	1412 March 20	9 y. 5 m. 24 day	252 March 20
Henry 6	1422 Auguſt 31	38 y. 6 m. 18 day	242 Auguſt 3
Edw. 4	1460 March 4	22 y. 1 m. 8 day	204 March 4
Edw. 5	1483 April 9	0 y. 2 m. 18 day	181 April 9
Rich. 3	1483 June 22	2 y. 2 mo. 5 day	181 June 22
Henry 7	1485 Auguſt 22	23 y. 8 m. 9 d.	179 Auguſt 22
Henry 8	1509 April 22	37 y. 10 m. 2 d.	155 April 22
Edw. 6	1547 January 28	6 y. 5 m. 19 day	117 Janu. 2.
Q. M.	1553 July 6.	5 y. 4 m. 22 day	111 July 26
Elizab.	1558 Novem. 17	44 y. 4 m. 14 d.	106 Nove. 17
K. James	1602 Marche 4	22 y. 0 m. 3 day	62 March 2.
K. Ch. 1	1625 March 27	24 y. 10 m. 7 da.	39 March 27

Since Charls the 2d. we are to reign, 16 y. are, Jan. 30
Whom God preſerve in proſperity long to reign.

A.2

A succinct Chronology of the most remarkable
Passages which have happened within these his
Majesties Dominions, from the Year 1600.
untill this present Year 1664.

King *Charles* I. born at *Dunferm:* in *Scotl.*   64
Queen *Eliz.* dyed, and *James* proclaimed K. 62
The Powder Treason discovered.   59
The Bible translated by K. *James*'s command. 56
The New Exchange built.   56
Prince *Henry* dyed at St. *James*'s.   52
Prince *Charles* created Prince of *Wales*.   48
Prince *Charles* embarqued for *Spain*, and returned. 41
The marriage with *France* accorded.   40
Amboyna's bloody Cruelty.   40
K. *James* dyed at *Theobalds*, Pr. *Charles* proclaim'd. 39
Duke of *Buckingham* accused of High-Treason. 38
He imbarqued for the Isle of *Rhee*.   40
Parliament began at *Westminster*, wherein the Peti-
tion of Right was granted by the King.   40
London fined for *Lamb*'s death, 6000 l. 36
Duke of *Buckingham* murthered at *Portsmouth.* 35
Prince *Charles* born, baptized, and dyed. 35
Prince *Charles* born and baptized.   34
The Lady *Mary* born.   33
The lamentable fire on *London* Bridge. 32
The Illustrious *James* Duke of *York* born. 31
Charls I. marched against & treated with the *Scots.* 29
Henry Duke of *Gloucester* born.   24
The Long Parliament began.   24
Pr. *Mary* married to the Pr. of *Orange* at *Whitehall.* 23
Earl *Strafford* beheaded.   23
K. *Charles* sentenced to death, and murthered. 16
K *Charles* II. proclaimed in *Scotl.* and *Ireland.* 16
He was Crowned in *Scotland.*   14
Gen. *Monck* marched into *London* with his Army. 13
His Majesty with the Duke of *York* and *Gloucester* ar-
rived at *Whitehall.*   4

Physical Observations.

A Syrup to Concoct, and prepare the humours, to provoke the Terms.

TAke Syrup of Betony, of Mugwort, and Elecampane, of each half an ounce; of the Decoction of Hysop, and Betony, of each four ounces; mix them together, and so take it when you please.

Oustrous things which provoke the Terms are Cynamon, Calisa Lignea, Costus roots, Mascus, Spica Indie, Spica Romana, Galisa muscata, and such like.

Fumes to be burnt to move the Terms are,

Oppoponacum, Soponozia, Frankincense, Lignum Aloes, and red Storax.

Things by nature cool, which move the Terms are,

The seeds of small Endive, of Melons, of Gourds, of Pompions, Cucumbers and Lettice, of which Pessaries may be made, to use in the Womb, but have a care you put a string to them, to get them out again when you please.

Common Syrups which remove Oustructions of the Terms, are,

Syrup of Mugwort, of Maiden-hair, of Chicory with Rhubarb, and the Syrup of the five Roots, this you may have ready at the Apothecaries.

B 2   *Confections*

Physical Observations.

Confections good for this Disesse are,

The Confection of Elecampane root: the Confection of Tango roots, Conserve of Borage and Betty roasted in an Apple.

An Electuary to purge the Reins.

Take Cassia newly extracted, one ounce; Rhubarb in powder, one dram: in writing them with syrup of white water Lillies, a sufficient quantity to make it into an Electuary; put this into a penny pot of white wine, or a little Posset drink, which comes after to hand: stir it well together, till it be all dissolved in the drink, and so take it in the morning early, and go about your business (if you have any thing to do) about two hours after, take some broth or posset drink.

This Medicine you may take twice or thrice, as you see occasion, resting always a day between.

Afterwards, you may take every other day, a dram of Cassia drawn in Pania e water.

You may also give the Patient, every second or third day, a dram or the likings of Ivory in Plantane Water: it is very good.

Sweating is also much commended in this case, which may be thus done.

Take Barley water three ounces: Greek Wine three ounces: give it to the Patient very warm, and so let her sweat.

A Powder to be used in the nature of a Pessary, against the suffocation of the Matrix, or fits of the Mother.

Take red Storax, Lignum Aloes, Cloves, of each a dram: Musk, Amber, of each half a dram: make them altogether into a powder, and then bind it up in a cloth in the form of a Pessary, and put it up into the Matrix.

A

A Confection to cause fruitfulness in Man or Woman.

Take Rapes, Ivory shaven, Ash keys, Geese, Behen, red and white, of each on. dram: Cinamon, Doronicum, Mace, Cloves, Galingale, long Pepper, Rosmary flowers, Balsam wood, Bla tis, Pystadit Marjoram gentle, Penny-royal, of each two scruples: Balm, Bugloss, Citron p lls, of each one scruple: Spica Indie, Amber, Pearls, of each half a scruple: Sugar a pound: bc—e the Sugar in Malmsey and the other things; and make them into a Confection, use of t a litt e at a time.

A Powder for the same to be strewed on meat.

Take Nutmegs, Cubebs, Ginger, of each half a dram: long Pepper, Mastick, Cinamon, red Behen, white Behen, of eic. a scruple: mix them all together, and make th m into a fine powder, and strew of it a little upon the parties meat.

Another Confection for the same.

Take Honey, 3. ounces: Linseed, Grains, Ivory shaven of each one ounce: Borrage, three ounces: Sugar 2 ounce : Musk, Amber, of each half a scruple: Cinamon, two grains: Cloves, Mace, of each one grain: clarifie the Honey, then incorporate the other things with it, to make a Confection thereof, and take of it as you please.

A Potion to further Conception in a Woman.

Take Wormwood, Mugwort, of each a handful, boyl them together in a quart of Goats milk, till almost half be wasted, and let the Woman drink thereof first and last, every morning and evening a good draught.

*A Confection to further fruitfulness in Men, and
Conception in Women.*

Take a Foxes stones, Stags pissel taken small,
one ounce, Bulls pissel, if you cannot get the other,
will do as well, Sparrows brains, fifty or sixty, yellow Rape, Eringo root, and Satyrion confected, Ivory shaven, of each three ounces and a half: Cinamon,
Dates, Indy, Rue Kernels, of each two ounces: Long
Pepper, Ginger, Rosemary flowers, of each half an
ounce: Sesely one dram: Nettle seed, Cloves, Saffron, Mace, Galingale, Cypris roots, Nutmegs,
Cassia wood, Cucubes, Doronicum, field Mints,
Penny royal, Spica Indie, Musk, Amber, of each
one dram: make all these into a Confection with four
pounds and an half of white Sugar, refined in Mint-
water, and take of it as before is directed; and if you
cannot easily get all the things, yet refuse not the
Medicine, but make it with as many as you can
come by.

Pills to expel a dead Child.

Take Trochis of Mirrh, one scruple: Galbanum,
half a scruple: make five Pills thereof, with Penny-
royal water.

A most excellent Plaister to strengthen Women with Childe, to wear all the time they be with Childe.

Take Oyl Olive, two pound and four Ounces, red
Lead, one pound, Spanish Sope, twelve Ounces: Incorporate them all together in an earthen pot, and
when the Sope cometh upwards, put it upon a small
fire of coals: and continue it an hour and a half, stirring it with an Iron or stick; then drop a drop of it
upon a trencher, if it cleave not, it is enough: spread
it on cloths, or lay it on a board till it cools, then
make it up into Rolls: it will last twenty years, the
elder, the better, and when you have occasion to use it
for this purpose, spread a Plaister of it, and apply it
to

to the back: and when you have tryed it, you will give me thanks for it: It is likewise good for the bloody Flux, Running of the Reins, or any weakness in the back, for my self, to draw out a Thorn out of the flesh, and taketh Corns, and is good for a Strain, and for the Headach being applyed to the Temples.

But to proceed, when the woman with childe begins to draw near her time: then let her use such meats and drinks as nourish well, but use no excess of either; but especially let her take care to keep her body soluble.

An excellent Medicine to procure easie delivery in women.

Take Pippins, cut them in thin slices, and fry them with the Oyl of sweet Almonds, and eat thereof in the morning, and at four a clock in the afternoon, use it constantly a matter of five or six weeks before your time, till you are brought to bed, and mix some Oyl of sweet Almonds, and Sperma ceti together, and annoint the Belly and Matrix, once every day therewith warm, or oftener if you can conveniently.

A Confection for an excessive flood in women lying in Child-bed.

Take Conserve of Piony, one ounce: Conserve of Roses, one ounce, Conserve of Burrage, Buglos, Balm, of each half an ounce; prepared Bolus, half a dram, prepared Pearls, one dram; Cynamon, one dram and a half: mix them all together, and make a Confection thereof.

Take Blood stone, one dram and a half: red Coral, one dram: Tormentil, *Trochis de Spodio*, of each half a dram: scraped Ivory, burnt Harts-horn, of each one scruple: Pearls prepared, four scruples: red Bolus, two scruples: Shepheards purse, red Sanders of each a scruple: Cinamon, one dram: Sugar six Ounces: washe

wash the Blood-stone in Plantain water, and make a
Powder, or Lozenges thereof.

Of the super fluity of Milk, and other accidents happen-
ing after the Birth.

Excessive abounding of the Milk, after a Woman
is delivered, if it flow more than the Child can grow
there oftentimes ensue Impostu nes, and other Inflammations and distempers in the Breasts; for Remedies whereof, use these prescriptions following.

The Patient must eat and drink but moderately,
and avoid all such things as engender much blood,
and use means to dry and take away the superfluous
blood, as Rue and wild Rue, with the seeds of Basil,
and stampt together; if one take every day a quarter
of an ounce, the same is very good to dry up the milk.

To dry up the Milk.

Take Rosen a good quantity, and temper it with
Cream, and lay it luke warm over the Breasts.

For clotted or congealed Milk in the Breasts.

Let Women keep sobriety in eating and drinking,
and using moyst meats that may ra t eder subtile
Milk. Mints, Sa ron, and Cinnamon, is good to
be used in their meats:
Take grated Bread, new Milk, and Oyl of Roses,
of each a like quantity: seeth them together to a pap,
and lay it warm upon the Breasts.

For congealed Milk and pain in the Breasts.

Take Cork and burn it to ashes, and temper it
with Oyl of Roses, and a little Vinegar, and therewith
with annoint the Breasts.

A

A Salve to dissolve congealed Milk in the Breasts.

Take Deers Suet three quarters of an ounce; liquid Styrax one ounce; Wormwood, Cummin, Dill seeds, of each one ounce, Oil of Wormwood, Ducks grease, of each one Ounce and an half. Saffron one scruple, make an Oyntment of all these, and apply it to the Breasts.

A good Plaister to dissolve hard knots in the Breasts.

Take crumbs of white Bread, Barley meal, Mustard seeds, Fennel, and Holly-hocks roasted under the ashes, of each a like quantity, pound them all well together, and make a Plaister thereof, with Oyl of Camomile, and apply it warm to the Breasts.

For hardness, and inflammation in the Breasts, through congealed Milk, a Pultis.

Take flowers of Mallows, Violets, Celendine, Daisies, Cinquefoil, of each one handful, boyl them together in two quarts of water, till it come to a pint, then strain it, and mingle it with Wheaten meal, to the like kinds of pap, then put to it Hens grease, or fresh Butter, and boyl it again to a Pultis, spread it on a cloth, about the thickness of a finger, and lay it morning and evening upon an inflamed sore Breast.

A Medicine for swelling in the Breasts, much profitable and easie to be had.

Take a good quantity of Peach leaves, and Rue, and stamp them small, and boyl them in water to a Pultis, and lay it on the grieved place, this will ripen the Impostume, and ease the pain.

For Clefts or Chops of the Nipples.

Take Mutton, or Lambs suet, as much as you please,

please, and after it is molten, and clarified, then wash
it in Rose-water, and therewith annoint the Nipples.
And thus much for the Diseases in the Breasts.

Meanes and Remedies for those Nurses that want Milk.

Those Women that would increase their milk, let
them eat good meats if they can get it, and drink
milk wherein Fennel-seed hath been steeped.

If the Woman be of a hot nature, and full of Choller, let her drink Barly water, and Almond milk, eat
Lettice with her meat, Burrage, Spinnage Goats
milk, Cowes milk, and Lamb sodden with Lettuce.
And avoid sorrow and anger as much as may be: and
comfort the stomach with Confections of Anniseeds,
Carraway and Cominseeds: and likewise use these
seeds sodden in water. If you would have an outward meanes, use this Plaister following.

Take half an ounce of Deers suit, and as much
Barley roots, with the herbs, an ounce and an half of
Barley meal, three drams of red Storar, and three
ounces of Oyl of sweet Almonds: seeth the Roots and
Herbs well, and beat them to pap; and then ming'e
the other amongst them. and lay it warm to the Nipples, it increaseth Milk.

For such as think themselves bewitched, that they can-not do the act of Venery.

Take flying Ants, mixed with the Oyl of Elder,
and annoint the defective Instrument.

To take away the desire of a Woman to the Act of Venery.

Take of a Red Bulls Pizzle, and powder it, and
put in Wine or Broath, the quantity of a Crown
weight of silver, and she will abhor the desire of lying
with a man: this may be a good Medicine for the
Restraining of young Girls throwing themselves a-
way

way upon Wad-cap likewe. The same Ingredient given to men, will provoke Venery in them that are dull and impotent.

To take off the edge of Venery.

Eat Rue and Camphir, it will make a man no better then an Eunuch, and if you lay the seeds under you, it will produce the same: the Matrons of Athens were accustomed to lay Rue leaves under them when they went to Bed.

For prevention of quarrels between Man and Wife.

The heart of a Male Quail carryed by a man about him; and the heart of the female carryed by a woman about her, causeth concord and mutual love, and assured peaceable agreement.

A help to him that desireth to be Chaste, or to be freed from the Plague of Love.

A Turtles heart wrapped in a wolves skin he that carrieth it about him shall be freed from immoderate Love, yea, from loving at all.

When you would have a Woman or Maid discover all that ever she did.

Take the heart of a Pigeon, and the head of a frog, dry them both, and powder them, strew the powder so prepared, upon the brast of her that is asleep, and she will discover what ever she did, and discourse with you, and answer all questions. Albertus Magnus.

To make one appear exceeding fair.

Take whites of Eggs well washed, and grind them upon a Marble stone, as Painters do their Colours;

stones & put water thereunto, let them stand until the
whites sink into the bottom, then take away the water gently, and let the matter that stayeth behind dry
in the Sun; and when you will use it with . . . . . .
means, paring away the yellow as need is
need us, lay it upon a tile as nigh . . . who to night
until it be still above; then next . . . and add
some of the aforesaid Powder, . . This purif-ye this the
face nor teeth as other paintings up a twice do . . .
face is no wise altered by the application of it, & but
it very beautiful to behold. the chiefest of the Venetian
Ladies use this sort of painting . . . .

To colour the Face red.

Take of the Root of Solomons Seal; it is a Plant
common to be had in most Gardens, and rub the face
over with it, and it will make pale, cheeks look red.

To take away Carbuncles, or red Pimples in the Face.

Take four Ounces of Peach Kernels, and Gourd-
Seed blanches, two Ounces, beat them, and press
them strongly, to draw forth an Oily Liquor; with
which, morning and evening, touch the Car-
bunkles, and they will be taken quite away, the red-
ness much abated.

A Water to colour the Face, and causes admirable smoothness:

Let the Whites of Eggs be boiled until they be
hard, then distill water from them, the which is the
like of Rosemary water, Bean-flower water, and the
juice and water of Lemmons.

An Oyl that maketh the Skin fair and shining:

Take white Tartar two pound, Tacun, Salt, of each
half a pound, mingle them, and set them in a Pot-
ters furnace, then put it for fifteen or twenty days
into some bag with a sharp end, and set it in some
moist

moist place free from the Ayr, setting some Vessel
under it to receive the Oyl that runneth from it; the
which use, having first washed your face, and dryed it
well: this is a Medicine that will make you look
young and beautiful beyond measure.

Another of rare quality.

Take Allom bruised, and mixed with whites of
Eggs that are new, being beat and moved continually, will grow thick as an Ointment if you annoint your Face morning and evening therewith, you
will make all the World in love with you; for it
will make you fair, and take all spots out of your
Face.

_____

A Prognostication

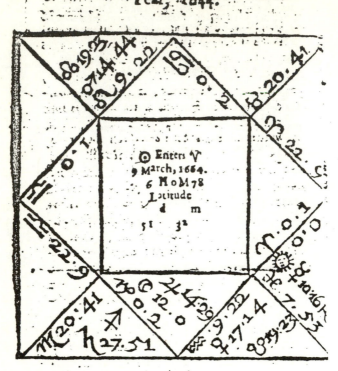

I shall not insist much upon this figure of
the deposition of the Heavens, at the time
of ☉ entering ♈ onely I shall give you some
general Judgments according to Art, we
find all the Planets under the Earth, except
Mars ♂

Mars ♂ and the ☉ Sun himself is partly descended over the Horizon at his first entring ♈ Aries: it being 7 seconds past 6 at night, at which time he equally divideth the dayes and nights throughout the Universe, and runneth his course then in the Meridian, and disperseth the beames of his light impartially: we find ♄ Saturn in the 3d House intercepted in ♐ the day house of ♃ Jupiter, of which he is Lord; the which denoteth, that a very great sluggishness, sloathfulness, and indisposition of Body shall attend many, likewise it will produce much carelesness in Husbandry and Manufactery, the more is the pity: Many Children born this Year, will be foolish, and dull of apprehension; others of a malicious and peevish disposition, and inclined to a sacrilegious temper, and apt to speak evil of Dignities; others will become wasters of their Patrimony, and be theevishly inclined.

This Year many of your Theeves shall have ill success in the r undertakings, they shall be deceived and discovered, to the indangering of their necks: also many Male Children born now, shall live to be stale Batchellors, and contemn Marriage, and Women, and not delight in them for love, but on the contrary, for lust; the which above

C   all

all things, Women ought to beware of, the
☽ Moons being in the 4th House, signifieth
troubles and dangers, not a few that attend
many: together with the peevishness, and
untowardness of Mothers in Law: Also an
insolent humonr raigning in ignoble spirits,
together with many more inconveniencies,
b ut that the ☽ Moons applying her self to
a ♂ Conjunction of ♃ a good Planet, the
evils portended by her possession in the 4th
House, is abated thereby: ♃ being there
posited, denoteth all manner of good to the
Fruits of the Earth, especially of Pastors,
Orchards and Gardens. Likewise the Planet
by his Influence, is a well-willer to the re-
pairer of old Castles, Cathedrals, and Religious and pious Places. Embassadors
are successful in the Service of their Princes,
and old Women have an aking to flatter
young men.

Well, we find ♀ Venus in the 5th House,
in ♒ Aquarius she being in the 17th degree,
and ☋ the Dragons Tail in the 19th degree.
I like her much the worse, otherwise she
would be very fortunate and propidious,
however she is respected by the influence of
the other good Planets: She is a great Friend
to Children, Towns besieged, and all sorts of
Women: Such who have the benefit of this
                                    position

poſition of her in their Nativities, may expect to be famous and eminent; and to be
beloved of Women above meaſure, to advance his Fortune by them in Marriage, and
otherwiſe: The next we find ☿ Mercury
in ♓ Piſes retrograde in the 6th Houſe; denoteth, that Servants will generally be croſs,
vexatious, and intolerable, eſpecially Maid-
ſervants, and that Lawyers will gain much
by the unquietneſs of Women: the truly
Learned will be highly eſteemed, ſeveral of
them will be highly advanced to Dignities.
Shepherds, Goatherds, and Neatheards will
be ſucceſsful: the Sun ☉ upon the Cuſp of
the 7th Houſe, in oppoſition to the Aſcen-
dant, intimateth a ſickly time, and unquiet
turbulent minds, no Planet being in the
10th Houſe. Mars ♂ in the 11th Houſe
in ♌ Leo, the Houſe of the Sun ☉ denoteth
ſucceſs to men at Arms: to Judges, all work-
ers in Furneſſes, Forges, or otherwiſe by
Fire.

Of

There will be 4 Eclipses this present Year, two of the Sun, and two of the Moon, of all which we shall onely see the last, which is a totall Eclipse of the Moon.

The first is an Eclipse of the Sun, upon the 18th of *June*, in the morning, to be seen in the North-East from us.

The second is a great and totall Ectipse of the Moon, on the 1st of *February*, which will be visible to the Eastern parts of the World; where will be seen the whole Body of the Moon, in or near the Meridian, it will be seen in almost all the Eastern parts of *Tartaria*, *China*, *Japan*, and *Philippina*.

The third Eclipse is a small Eclipse of the Sun, upon the 12th of *July*, it will be onely visible to the more remote South parts of the World, unknown to us.

The 4th and last Eclipse of the Moon, will happen the 27 of *July*, it will be visible to us in *England*, at 35 m. 53 2ds past 11 at night.

Observations

Observations for good Husbandry, and good Housewifry.

Januaries Observations.

PLow for Pease, fallow such Land as you intend shall rest the year following; water your barren Meadows, Pasture, and drain arrable ground, especially if you intend to sowe Pease, Oats, or Barley the second time following: also stub up all rough grounds, trim up your Garden moulds; The weather calm, remove all manner of Fruit-trees, rear Calves, remove Bees, keep good Dyet.

Februaries Observations.

Set Beans, Pease, and other pulse in stiff ground, begin the soonest, prepare your Garden, prune and trim your Fruit trees from Moths, Cankers, and superfluous branches, plash Hedges, lay your quickset close, plant Rose, Gooseberry trees, and any other shrub

C 3 trees,

trees, and graft your tender stocks ; forbear all phlegmatick meats.

March's Observations.

Look well to your Ewes , cut up under-wood or Fewel , transplant all sort of Summer flowers , comfort them with good Earth especially the Crown Imperial, Narcissus, Tuleps and Hyacinth ; in your barren Fruit Trees, bore holes, and drive hard wedges of Oak , and cover Roots of Trees close with fat Earth that are uncovered ; graft Fruit Trees, and sowe Oats, Rye, and Barley, let your Diet be cold and tempe-rate.

April's Observations.

Sowe your Hemp and Flax , sowe and set all sorts of Herbs, open your Hives, and give your Bees their liberty, and let them labour for their living ; cut your Oak Timber, the bark is best for the Tanners use. Scower your ditches, gather your Manure together in heaps, gather stones, repair high-wayes, set Oziers and Willows, and cast up all decayed Fences : For your health, use moderate ex-ercise.

Mays

May's Observations.

Fold your Sheep, carry forth Manure, and
bring home Fewel: weed Winter Corn, furnish your Dairy, let your Mares go to Horse,
fat your dry Kine, and away with them: sowe
your tender seeds as Cucumbers, Musmeli-
ons, all sweet kind of Herbs and Flowers.
For your health drink clarified Whey.

June's Observations.

Distil all sorts of Plants and Herbs whatever, cut your rank Meadows, fetch home
sewel, and carry forth Manure, Mause and
Lime to mend your Land: Be sure to be
chast this Month, what ever you are the rest
of the year.

July's Observations.

Attend your Hay-Harvest, shear Field-
sheep: let the Herbs you intend to preserve
run to seed; cut off the stalk of your flowers, and cover the Roots with new fat Earth:
sell your Lambs you intended for the
shambles. Take no Physick, unless in extraordinary Cases, refrain venery.

Augusts Observations.

Follow diligently your Corn Harvest, cut down your Wheat and Rye, mowe Barley and Oats, put off your fat Sheep and Cattel, gather your Plums, Apples, and Pears; make your Summer Perry and Cyder, set your slips and Scyons of all sorts of Gillyflowers, and other flowers; Transplant them that were set in the Spring, geld your Lambs, carry Manure from your Dove-coats, put your Swine to the Early malt. Refrain all excess in eating and drinking, drink that which is cooling.

Septembers Observations.

Cut your Beans, Pease, and all manner of Pulse: on the Land you intend to sowe Wheat and Rye, bestow the best Manure; gather your Winter Fruit, sell your Wooll, stocks of Bees, and other Commodities you intend to put off. Thatch your Hive of Bees you intend to keep and look that no Droans, Mice or other vermin be about them. Thrash your seed, Wheat and Rye. Use Physick moderately. Shun the eating of sweet or rotten Fruit, avoid surfeiting.

Octobers

Octobers Observations.

Finish with your Wheat seed, plash and lay your hedges and quicksets, scowre your Ditches and Ponds, transplant and remove all manner of Fruit Trees, make Winter Perry and Cyder, spare your Pastures, and feed upon your Corn fields; draw furrows to drain, and keep dry your new sown Corn; make Malt, rear all new faln Calves, all Foals that were foaled in the Spring, weaned from the Mares. Sell your Sheep that you do not intend to Winter, and separate Lambs from the Ewes, that you intend to keep. Recreate your spirits by harmless sports, and take Physick by good advice, if need be.

Novembers Observations.

Cut down your Timber for Plows, Carts, Naves, Axeltrees, Harrows, and other Offices about Husbandry, or Housewifry; make the last return of grasse feed Cattel, take your Swine from the mast, and feed them for the slaughter: Rear all Calves that fall now, break all Hemp and Flax you intend to spend in the Winter season. Remove Fruit

Fruit Trees, and sowe Wheat and Rye in hot
Soyls ; Use Spices and Wine, moderately.

Decembers Observations.

Put your Sheep to the Pease Ricks, kill
your small Porks , and large Bacons, top
Hedges, saw your Timber for building, and
lay it to season : plow your ground. you intend to sow clean Beanes on : cover your
dainty Fruit Trees, drain your Corn fields,
and water your Meadows : cover your best
flowers with rotten Horse-litter.   Now all
sorts of Fowl: are in season, keep thy self
warm with a wholsome Dyet, and avoid all
care that shall trouble thy spirit, as a dangerous thing.

Natural Prognosticks for the Judg-
ment of Weather.

THe resounding of the Sea upon the shore,
and the murmur of Winds in the Woods,
with out apparent wind, shew wind to follow:
for such winds breathing chiefly out of the
Earth, are not at the first perceived, except
they be pent by water or wood. And therefore

fore a murmur out of Caves likewise portendeth the same. The obscuring of the smaller Stars is a sign of Tempests following. Also, if the Stars seem to shoot, winds from that quarter the Star came from.

The often changing of the Wind also sheweth Tempests.

If two Rain-bows appear, rain; a Rainbow presently after rain appear, fair Weather.

If the Skie be red in the morning, it is a sure token of Winds or Rain, or both; because those Vapors which cause the rednels, will presently be resolved.

If the Sun or Moon look pale, look for Rain, if fair and bright, fair weather; if red winds as the Verse hath it.

Pallida Luna pluit, rubicunda flat, alba serenat

If a dark Cloud be at Sun-rising, in which the Sun soon after is hid, it will dissolve it, and Rain will follow: if then appear a cloud, and after vapours are seen to ascend up to it, that portendeth Rain.

If the Sun seem greater in the East, then commonly it doth, it is a sign of Rain.

If in the West, about Sun-setting, there appear a black Cloud, it will rain that night, or the day following, because that Cloud shall want heat to disperse it.

Sero.

Sero rubens cœlum tras indicat esse serenum,
Sed si mane rubet venturos indicat imbres.

If Mists come down from the Hills, or descend from the Heavens, and set le in the Vallies, it promiseth fair hot weather ; Mists in the Evening, shew a hot day on the morrow ; the like when w. ite Mists rise from the waters in the Evening.

Water-Fowls (as Sea-gu ls, More-he s &c.) when they flock and fly together from the Sea towards the Shores ; and contrariwise, Land-birds (as Crowes, Swallows &c.) when they fly from the Lands to the Waters, and beat the waters with their wings, do foreshew Rain and Wind.

The Circles that appear about the Sun, if they be red and broken, it portendeth Wind ; if thick and dark, winds, snow, or Rain; which are also presaged by the Circles about the Moon.

Pro die inspice Solem orientem, pro nocte oc-
cidentem.

The Trifoly against Rain swelleth in the stalk, and so standeth more upright ; for by wet stalks do erect, and leaves bow down. There is a small red Flower in the Stubble-fields, which in some Countries is called the Wincopipe, which if it be open in the morning, you may be sure of a fair day to follow.

Even

Even in men, aches, hurts, and corns, do engrieve, either towards Rain, or towards Frost.

Worms, Vermine, &c, do likewise foreshew Rain; for Earth-worms will come forth, and Moles cast up more; Fleas bite more against Rain.

Solid bodies likewise foreshew Rain; as Stones and Wainscot when they sweat.

Prognosticks of Pestilential and unwholesome Years.

It is observed by the Learned, that those Years are Pestilential & unwholesom, when there are great numbers of Frogs, Flies, Locusts, &c. The cause is plain, for that those Creatures being ingendred of putrefaction, when they abound, shew a general disposition of the Year, and constitution of the Air, to Diseases of putrefaction. And the same Prognostick holdeth, if you find Wormes in Oak-apples; for the constitution of the Air appeareth more subtilly, in any of these things, then to the sense of man.

Great and early heats in the Spring (and namely in *May*) without Winds, portend Pestilential Years; and generally so do years with little Wind or Thunder.

Great

Great Droughts in Summer, continuing till towards the end of *August*, and some gentle showres upon them, and then some weather again, do portend a Pestilent Summer th: Year following. For about the end of *August*, all the sweetnes of the Earth, which goeth into Plants and Trees, is exhaled; (and much more if the *August* be dry) so that then nothing can breath forth of the Earth but a gross vapour, which is apt to corrupt the Air; and that vapour, by the first showres, if they be gentle, is released, and cometh forth abundantly. Therefore they that come abroad soon after those showres, are commonly taken with sicknefs. And in *Africk*, no body will stir out of doors after the first showrs. But if the showrs come vehemently, then they rather wash and fill the Earth, then give it leave to breath forth pleasantly. But if dry weather come again, then it fixeth and continueth the corruption upon the Air, upon the first showrs begun, and maketh it of ill influence, even to the next Summer, except a very frosty Winter discharge it, which seldom succeedeth such Drought.

The lesser infection of the small Pocks, Purple-feavers, Agues, in the Summer precedent, and hovering all Winter, do portend a

great

great Pestilence in the Summer following; for putrefaction doth not rise to its height at once.

A dry *March,* and a dry *May,* portend a wholesom Summer, if there be a showring *April* between; but otherwise it is a sign of a Pestilential Year.

Non nobis solum nati sumus, sed partim Patriæ, partim Parentibus, partim amicis debemus.

Furthermore, because the Air according to its scituation doth much alter and change the constitution of Mans body, & may breed pure and wholesom blood, or corrupt & bad blood, and malignant humours. Therefore, that you may know what Air is pure and sound, and what Air corrupt and infectious, I will add some Experiments, which the judicions have observed, whereby you may conjecture how the Ayr is disposed, and that

A sound and pure Ayr is

Made hot presently after Sun rising, and is made cold presently after Sun setting.

Which yieldeth a pleasant smell after rain, clear and not evaporated, open and lightsom where the North Wind bloweth.

Where

Where the East Wind bloweth in the Morning,

A corrupt and infectious Ayr is

Made by the often blowing of the South, or South East Wind, or by the South-West, or West in the Evening, which ingender Sicknesses.

Where the Ayre is cold long after Sunnerising.

Where the Ayre is long hot after Sunne set.

Where the Ayre is long close, cloudy, or thick.

FINIS.

Mary Holden's *The Womans Almanack for the Year of our Lord, 1688* (Wing 1827) is reprinted from the copy at Magdalene College Library (Pepys Library), Cambridge (Shelfmark PL 425 [15]). The text block of the Magdalene College copy is 75 × 135 mm.

For passages that are blotched, please consult Appendix B, 'A Key to Difficult-to-Read Passages'.

The WOMANS
ALMANACK

For the Year of our Lord, 1688.

Being the Bissextile *or* Leap-Year.

Calculated for the Meridian of *London,*
and may indifferently serve for any
part of *ENGLAND:*

By *MARY HOLDEN*
Midwife in *Sudbury,* and Student in *Astrology.*

LONDON,
Printed by *J. Millet,* for the Company of *STA-
TIONERS;* 1688.

this Year 1688. in both Accounts, *viz.*

English.			Forreign.	
	17		17	
	7	The Epact	27	
	17	The Cycle of the Sun	17	
Feb.	25		Febr.	29
April	18		April	18
May	24		May	27
June	3		June	6
June	10		June	13
Decemb.	2		Novemb.	28

♈	*Aries* Head and Face	♎	*Libra* Reins and Loyns
♉	*Taurus* Neck & Throat	♏	*Scorpio* Secret Members
♊	*Gemini* Arms and Shoul.	♐	*Sagitarius* the Thighs
♋	*Cancer* Breast and Stom.	♑	*Capricornus* the Knees
♌	*Leo* Heart and Back	♒	*Aquarius* the Legs
♍	*Virgo* Bowels and Belly	♓	*Pisces* the Feet.

A

begins Janua- 23, and ends February 13, d hath 4 Returns, *viz.*	Octab. Hilar. Jan. 20 Quind. Hilar. Jan. 27 Craft. Purif. Febr. 3 Octab. Purif. Febr. 9
begins May 2. ds May 28, and hath 5 turns, *viz.*	Quind. Pasch. Apr. 30 Tres. Pasch. May 7 Mens. Pasch. May 14 Quind. Pasch. May 21 Craft. Ascen. May 25
begins June 15, ends July 4, and hath 4 turns, *viz.*	Craft. Trin. June 11 Octab. Trin. June 18 Quind. Trin. June 25 Tres. Trin. July 2
begins ober 23, ends November and hath 6 Returns, *viz.*	Tres. Mich. Octob. 20 Mens. Mich. Octob. 27 Craft. Anim. Nov. 3 Craft. Mart. Nov. 12 Octab. Mart. Nov. 19 Quind. Mart. Nov. 26

Note, that the Exchequer openeth 8 days before any
rm. begins, except the Term of Trinity, in which it
neth but 4 days before.

Note also, that the bright Planet *Venus*, will be our
rious Morning Star from the beginning of the year,
the 24 day of *August*; and then making her Con-
ction with the Sun, She becomes Occidental and
r glorious Evening Star to the end of the year.

A. 2   January

Full Moon the 7 day, 13 min. paſt 1 after noon.
Laſt quarter the 15 day, 51 min. paſt 4 after noon.
New Moon the 22 day, 13 min. paſt 10 at night.
Firſt quarter the 29 day, 58 min. paſt noon.

			21	22	Taur.	8	
2	h	Octab. Steph	22	24		21	The month
3	C	Octab. John.	23	25	Gem.	5	begins indif
4	D	Octab. Innoc.	24	26		18	ferently mild
5	E	Simeon	25	27	Canc.	1	conſidering
6	f		26	28		14	the ſeaſon.
7	g	Julian	27	30		26	
8		1 after Epiph.	28	31	Leo	9	
9	h	Agapete	29	32		21	
10	C		0	33	Virgo	4	
11	D	Hyginus	1	34		15	About the
12	E	Satyrius	2	35		27	middle ex-
13	f	Hilary Biſh.	3	36	Libra	9	peer froſt
14	g	Felix	4	37		21	with ſnow.
15		2 after Epiph.	5	38	Scorp.	3	
16	h	Marcellus	6	39		15	
17	C	Anthony	7	41		27	
18	D	Priſca	8	42	Sagit.	10	
19	E	Pontion.	9	42		23	Very, cold
20	f	Octab. Hilar.	10	43	Capr.	7	froſty weather
21	g	Agnes	11	44		22	with much
22		3 after Epiph.	12	45	Aquar.	6	ſnow.
23	h		13	46		21	
24	C	Timothy	14	47	Piſces	6	
25	D		15	48		21	
26	E	Polycarpus	16	49	Aries	6	
27	f	Quind. Hilar.	17	49		20	Cold aba-
28	g	Valerius	18	50	Taur.		ted towards
29		4 after Epiph.	19	51		18	the end.
30	h		20	52	Gem.		
31	C	Virgiſius	21	52		16	

Full Moon the 6 day, 5 min. paſt 7 in the morn.
Laſt quarter the 14 day, 31 min. paſt 10 before noon.
New Moon the 21 day, 25 paſt 8 before noon.
Firſt quarter the 28 day, 40 min. paſt 12 in the morn.

		Feſtival days with Terms.	⊙ place. d. m.		Moons place.		Inclination of the Air.
1	b	Bridget Faſt	22	53	Gem.	28	
2	c		23	54	Canc.	10	Cold weather
3	f	Criſt. Pur.	24	55		23	with much
4	g	Gilbert	25	55	Leo	5	ſnow.
5		5 after Epiph	26	56		18	
6	b		27	56	Virgo	0	
7	c	Zachary	28	57		12	
8	d	Salom	29	57		23	Fine mild
9	e		♓5		Libra	5	weather now
10	f	Scholaſtica	1	58		17	and pleaſant.
11	g	Euphroſina	2	58		29	
12			3	59	Scorp.	11	
13	b		4	59		23	
14	c	Valentine	5	59	Sagit.	6	Very good
15	d	Fauſtine	7	0		19	ſeaſonable
16	e	Julian. Virg.	8	0	Capr.	2	weather
17	f	Polycton	9	0		16	with froſt.
18	g	Concordia	10	0	Aquar.	0	
19			11	0		15	
20	b	Mild ed.	12	0	Piſces	0	
21	c	70 Martyrs	13	1		15	
22	d	Cathedr. Pet	14	1	Aries	0	Towards
23	e	Serenus Faſt	15	1		15	the end, very
24	f		16	1	Taur.	0	windy but
25	e	S. Paul	17	0		14	not very
26			18	0		28	cold.
27	a	Fortuna	19	0	Gem.	12	
28	b	Shrove-Tueſ.	20	0		26	A 3
29	c	Aſh-VVedneſ.	21	0	Canc.	8	

131

Full Moon the 7 day, 59 min. paſt 1 in the morn.
Laſt quarter the 15 day, 15 min. paſt 1 in the morn.
New Moon 21 day, 16 min. paſt 5 after noon.
Firſt quarter the 28 day, 30 min. paſt 2 after noon.

1	b	David Biſh.	22	c	Canc.	20	
2	c	Chad Biſh.	22	55	Leo	2	
3	f	Lucius	23	59		15	Tempeſtuous
4		1 Sun. in Len.	24	55		27	but not much
5	a	Euſebius	25	5	Virgo	9	froſt.
6	b	Frederick	26	58		20	
7	c		27	57	Libr.	2	
8	d	Cyprian	28	5		14	
9	e	40 Martyrs	29	55		26	
10	f		0 ♈ 55		corp.	8	Moiſt and
11		2 Sun. in Len.	1	5		20	not very
12	a	Gregory	2	55	ſagit.	2	cold.
13	b	Erneſtus	3	54		15	
14	c	Eutychus	4	53		28	
15	d	Longinus	5	52	Capr.	11	
16	e	Boniface	6	52		24	
17	f	Gertrude	7	51	Aquar.	9	Windy and
18		3 Sun. in Len.	8	5		23	cold about
19	a	Joſeph	9	49	Piſc.	8	this time.
20	b	Mildred	10	48		23	
21	c	Benedict	11	47	Aries	8	
22	d	Paulinus	12	46		24	
23	e	Theodore	13	45	Taur.	8	
24	f	Quirine Faſt	14	44		23	
25			15	43	Gem.	7	Cloudy dark
26	a	Caſtulus	16	42		21	weather, with
27	b	Archibald	17	40	Canc.	4	rain.
28	c	Gideon	18	39		17	
29	d	Euſtachius	19	38		29	
30	e	Guido	20	37	Leo	11	
31	f	Balbina	21	35		24	

Full Moon the 5 day, 5 min. past 6 at night.
Last quarter the 13 day, 5 min past noon.
New Moon the 20 day, 28 min. past 3 in the morn
First quarter the 27 day, 15 m. past 6 before noon.

1		5 Sun. in Lent	22	34	Virgo	6	
2	a	Mary Egypt	23	33		17	Misty and
3	b	Christian	24	31		29	something
4	c	Ambrose	25	30	Libra	11	cold.
5	D	Vincent	26	28		23	
6	e	Sixtus	27	27	Scorp.	5	
7	f	Celestine	28	25		17	
8			29	23		29	
9	a		0 ♉ 22		Sagit.	12	Windy but
10	b	Ezechiel	1	20		25	warmer,
11	c	Leo P.	2	18	Capr.	7	with gentle
12	D	Julius	3	17		21	showers.
13	e	Good Friday	4	15	Aquar.	4	
14	f	Tiburtius	5	13		18	
15			6	11	Pisces	2	
15	a	Isidore	7	9		17	
17	b	Anicetus	8	8	Aries	2	Very good
18	c	Apollin.	9	6		17	seasonable
19	e	Timothy	10	4	Taur.	2	weather.
20	e	Sulpitius	11	2		17	
21	f	Emmanuel	12	0	Gem.	1	
22			12	58		15	
23	a	S. GEORGE	13	56		29	
24	b	Albertus	14	53	Canc.	13	Windy with
25	c		15	51		25	rain or hail,
26	D	Cletus	16	49	Leo	8	and thunder
27	e	Anastas.	17	34		21	
28	f	Vitalis	18	45	Virg.	2	
29		2 after Easter	19	43		14	
30	a	Quind. Pasch.	20	40		25	

A 4

Full Moon the 5 day, 37 min. past 9 before noon.
Last quarter the 12 day, 57 min. past 6 at night.
New Moon 19 day, 11 min. past 4 in the morn.
First quarter the 26 day, 42 min. past 10 at night.

1	h		21	38	Libr.	8
2	g		22	36		20	Fine tempe-
3	d	Invent. Crucis	23	33	Scorp.	2	rate and se-
4	c	Martian	24	31		14	rene air, with
5	f	Gothard	25	28		27	gentle gales
6		3 after Easter	25	26	Sagit.	9	of wind.
7	a	Tres Pasch.	27	24		21	
8	b	Appar. Mic.	28	21	Capr.	4	
9	c	Hiobe	29	19		18	
10	d		0 II 16	Aquar.	1	
11	e	Anthony	1	13		14	
12	f	Acheley	2	11		28	Cloudy and
13		4 after Easter	3	9	Pisc.	12	warm with
14	a	Mens. Pasch.	4	6		27	some rain.
15	h	Sophia	5	3	Aries	11	
16	g	Peregrin	6	1		26	
17	d	Jodocus	6	58	Taur.	10	
18	e	Bernardine	7	55		25	
19	f	Dunstan	8	53	Gem.	9	Hot weather
20			9	50		24	and windy.
21	a	Quind. Pasch	10	47	Canc.	7	
22	h	Desider. Mar.	11	45		21	
23	c	Transl. Fran.	12	42	Leo	4	
24	d		13	39		16	
25	e	Crast. Ascen.	14	36		28	Towards the
26	f	Edward	15	34	Virgo	10	end tempe-
27		6 after Easter	16	31		22	stuous with
28	a		17	28	Libra	4	thunder.
29	b		18	25		15	
30	c	Wigand	19	22		28	
31	d	Petronel.	20	19	Scorp.	9	

Full Moon the 3 day, 57 min. paſt 9 at night.
Laſt quarter the 10 day, 47 min paſt 5 after noon.
New Moon the 17. day, 6 min. paſt 8 at night.
Firſt quarter the 25 day, 35 min. paſt 3 afternoon.

1	g	Nicomede	21	17	Scorp. 22
2	f	Marcellus	22	14	Sagit. 5	Very hot
3			23	11	18	and dry at
4	a	Petroc. Con.	24	8	Capr. 1	the begin-
5	b	Boniface B.	25	5	14	ning.
6	c		26	2	28	
7	d	Paul Ep.	26	59	Aquar. 11	
8	e	Medard	27	56	25	
9	f	Tranſ.	28	53	Piſces 9	
10			29	51	23	Turbulent
11	a		0♋48	Aries 7	with thun-
12	b	Blandina	1	45	21	der.
13	c	Cyrillus	2	42	Taur. 6	
14	d	Corpus Chriſti	3	39	20	
15	e		4	36	Gem. 4	
16	f	Tr. Richard.	5	33	18	
17		1 after Trin.	6	30	Canc. 2	Windy hot
18	a	Octab. Trin.	7	27	15	Weather with
19	b	Gervaſe	8	24	29	rain.
20	c	Tr. Edward	9	21	Leo 12	
21	d	VValburge. V.	10	18	24	
22	e	Alban	11	15	Virg. 6	
23	f	Baſil. Faſt	12	12	18	
24			13	9	Libra 0	Very good
25	a	Quind. Trin.	14	6	12	ſeaſonable
26	b	Jeremias	15	3	24	VVeather
27	c	7 Sleepers	16	1	Scorp. 6	towards the
28	d	Leo Biſh. Faſt	16	58	18	end.
29	e		17	55	Sagit. 0	
30	f	Com. S. Paul	18	52	13	

135

Full Moon the 3 day, 39 min. paſt 8 in the morn.
Laſt quarter the 10 day, 11 min. paſt 3 in the morn.
New Moon the 17 day, 49 min. paſt 7 in the morn.
Firſt qnarter the 25 day, 35 min. paſt 8 in morn.

1		3 after Trin.	19	49	Sagit.	2
2	a	Ties Trin.	20	46	Capr:	9	Very hot.
3	b	Cornelius	21	43		23	with thun-
4	c		22	40	Aquar.	7	der.
5	d	Anſelm	23	38		21	
6	e	Hector	24	35	Piſces	6	
7	f	Demetrius	25	32		20	
8		4 after Trin.	26	29	Aries	4	
9	a	Cyrillus	27	26		18	Hot ſultry
10	b	7 Ereth. M.	28	23	Taur.	2	weather,
11	c	Pius	29	21		16	with very
12	d		0 ♌ 18		Gem.	0	haſty ſho-
13	e	Margaret	1	15		14	wers.
14	f	Bonavent..	2	12		27	
15		5 after Trin.	3	9	Can.	11	
16	a	Hilarine	4	7		24	
17	b	Alexius	5	4	Leo	7	This month
18	c	Arnulph B.	6	1		20	is generally
19	d		6	59	Virg.	2	hot, inclining
20	e	Margaret	7	56		14	to moiſture.
21	f	Daniel	8	53		26	
22		6 after Trin.	9	51	Libra	8	
23	a	Apolline B.	10	48		20	
24	b	Chriſt. V. F.	11	46	Scorp.	2	
25	c		12	43		14	Toward the
26	d	Anna	13	40		26	end a very
27	e	Martha	14	38	Sagit.	8	turbulent air
28	f	Panthaleon	15	35		21	with thunder
29		7 after Trin.	16	33	Capr.	4	
30	a	Abdon	17	31		17	
31	b	German	18	28	Aquar.	1	

Full Moon the 1 day, 50 min. past 5 afternoon.
Last quarter the 8 day, 45 min. past 8 in the morn.
New Moon the 15 day, 11 min. past 9 at night.
First quarter the 24 day, 35 min. past 12 in the morn
Full Moon the 31 day, 27 min. past 2 in the morn.

1	C	*Lammay day*	19	23	Aqur.	16	
2	D	Stephen M.	20	23	Pisces	0	Good wea-
3	E	Invent. Steph.	21	21		15	ther at the
4	F	Dominick	22	19	Aries	0	beginning
5		8 after Trin.	23	19		14	and tempe-
6	a	Transf. Christi	24	1.		29	rate as to
7	b	Donatus	25	17	Taur.	13	heat.
8	C	Cyracus	26	18		27	
9	D	Romanus	27	7	Gem.	1	
10	E	Laurence	28	5		24	
11	F	Gilbert	29	5	Canc.	7	
12			0	1		20	Windy with
13	a	Hyppolite	0	5	Leo	3	storms of
14	b	Eusebius	1	5		16	hail
15	C	Assump. Mary	2	5		28	
16	D	Roch	3	5	Virgo	10	
17	E	Mammes	4	5		22	
18	F	Helena	5	45	Libra	4	Very hot
19		10 after Trin.	6	47		16	now, and
20	a	Bernard	7	45		28	tempestuous
21	b	Athanasius	8	43	Scorp.	1	with thun-
22	C	Symphor	9	41		22	der.
23	D	Zacheus Fast	10	40	Sagit	4	
24	E		11	38		16	
25	F	Lewis King	12	36		29	
26		11 after Trin.	13	34	Capr.	12	
27	a		14	33		25	Towards the
28	b	Augustine	15	31	Aquar.	10	end hot and
29	E	Decol. J. Bap	16	29		24	dry.
30	g	Felix	17	28	Pisces	9	
31	C	Cuthber. V.	18	26		24	

Laſt quarter the 6 day, 29 min. paſt 4 after noon.
New Moon the 14 day, 50 min. paſt night.
Firſt quarter the 22 day, 4 min. paſt night. noon.
Full Moon the 29 day, 1 min. paſt afternoon. noon.

1	E	Giles Abbot	19	25	Aries		
2		12 after Trin.	20	23			indifferendy
3	a	Euphem.	21	20	Taur.		hot for the
4	b	Theodore	22	21		5	ſeaſon.
5	c	Zachary	23	19	Jem.	7	
6	D	Magnus	24	18		21	
7	e	Regina	25	17	Can.	4	
8	f	Nat. of Mary	26	15		17	
9		13 after Trin.	27	14	Leo	c	High winds
10	a	Soſthenes	28	13		13	and not
11	b	Theobald	29	12		25	much wet.
12	c			11	Virg.	7	
13	D	Amatus	1	10		19	
14	e	Exalt. Crucis	2	9	Libra	1	
15	f	Nicomed.	3	8		13	
16		14 after Trin.	4	7		25	Tempeſtuous
17	a	Lambert	5	6	Scorp.	7	with ſtorm
18	b	Ferriolus	6	5		19	of hail.
19	c		7	4	Sagit.	1	
20	D	Fauſta	8	3		13	
21	e		9	2		25	
22	f	Maurice	10	2	Capr.	7	
23		15 after Trin.	11	1		20	
24	a	Rupert	12	0	Aquar.	4	Very windy
25	b	Cleophas	13	0		18	with rain
26	c	Cyprian	13	59	Piſces	2	and ſome-
27	D	Judith	14	59		17	thing cold.
28	e	Wenceſlaus	15	58	Aries	2	
29	f		16	58		17	
30		16 after Trin.	17	57	Taur.	2	

Laſt quarter the 6 day, 57 min. paſt 4 in the morn.
New Moon the 14 day, 41 min. paſt 6 in the morn.
Firſt quarter the 22 day, at 5 in the morning
Full Moon the 28 day, 13 min. paſt 8 at night.

1	a	Remigius	18	57	Taur.	17	
2	b	Leodegar	19	56	Gem.	2	Cloudy and
3	c	Simplicius	20	56		17	cold at the
4	d	Francis	21	56	Canc.	0	beginning.
5	e	Faith	22	55		14	
6	f	Spes	23	55		27	
7		17 after Trin.	24	55	Leo	10	
8	a	Pelagia	25	55		22	
9	b	Dionyſius	26	55	Virgo	4	
10	c	Gideon	27	55		16	A more clear
11	d	Burchard	28	55		28	air now and
12	e	Wilifride V.	29	55	Libra	10	pleaſant.
13	f		0	55		22	
14			1	55	Scorp.	4	
15	a	Hedwig.	2	55		16	
16	b	Galius	3	55		28	
17	c	Florent.	4	55	Sagit.	10	
18	d		5	55		22	Windy with
19	e	Prideswide	6	55	Capr.	4	cold rain.
20	f	Tres Mich.	7	56		17	
21		19 after Trin.	8	56	Aquar.	0	
22	a	Cordula	9	56		13	
23	b		10	56		27	
24	c	Salome	11	57	Piſces	11	Dark wea-
25	d	Criſpine	12	57		26	ther and
26	e	Amandus	13	58	Aries	10	cold, toward
27	f	Meaſmich. fa	14	58		25	the end
28			15	59	Taur.	11	froſty.
29	a	Narciſſus	16	59		26	
30	b	German	18	0	Gem.	11	
31	c	Wolfgang	19	0		15	

Laſt quarter the 4 day, 52 min. paſt 2 after noon.
New Moon the 13 day, 55 min. paſt 12 in the morn.
Firſt quarter the 20 day, 9 min. paſt 4 after noon.
Full Moon the 27 day, 6 min. paſt 7 in the morn.

1	g		20	1	Canc.	9	
2	A	All Souls	21	1		23	Not very
3	f	Craſt. Anim.	22	2	Leo	6	cold conſi-
4		21 after Trin.	23	3		19	dering the
5	a b		24	4	Virgo	1	ſeaſon.
6	b	Leonard	25	4		13	
7	c	Willibald	26	5		25	
8	d	Claudius	27	6	Libra	7	
9	e	Theodore	28	7		19	
10	f	Triphon	29	8	Scorp.	0	
11			0 f	8		12	Cold incrẽa-
12	a	Craſt. Mart.	1	9		24	ſes now.
13	b	Eugenia	2	10	Sagit.	7	
14	c	Frederic.	3	11		19	
15	d	Leopold	4	12	Capr.	1	
16	e	Edmon. A. B.	5	13		14	
17	f	Hugo	6	14		27	Froſt with
18		23 after Trin	7	15	Aquar.	10	ſnow.
19	a	Octab. Mart.	8	16		24	
20	b	Edmond K.	9	17	Piſces	7	
21	c	Oblat. Mary	10	18		21	
22	d	Cicily Virg.	11	19	Aries	5	
23	e	Clement	12	20		26	Dark, gloomy
24	f	Chriſogon.	13	21	Taur.	4	Weather, and
25		24 after Trin.	14	22		19	Windy, with
26	a	Quind. Mart.	15	24	Gem.	4	cold rain, or
27	b	Agricola	16	25		19	Snow.
28	c		17	26	Canc.	3	
29	d e	Saturnine	18	27		17	
30	e		19	28	Leo	1	

Last quarter the 4 day, 16 min. past 6 at night.
New Moon the 12 day, 59 min. past 6 at night.
First quarter the 20 day, 3 min. past 1 in the morn.
Full Moon the 26 day, 43 min. past 7 at night.

1	f	Longinus	20	29	Leo	14
2			21	31		27	Very good
3	a	Cassianus	22	32	Virgo	9	feasonable
4	b	Barbara	23	33		21	weather.
5	c	Sabine	24	34	Libra	3
6	d	Nicholas	25	36		15
7	e	Agathon	26	37		27
8	f	Concep. Mary	27	38	Scorp.	9	Cold raw
9		2 Su. in Adv.	28	39		21	misty wea-
10	a	Miltiades	29	41	Sagit.	3	ther.
11	b		0 ♑	42		15
12	c	Valerius	1	43		28
13	d	Lucia Virg.	2	44	Capr.	11
14	e	Nicasius	3	46		24	Frost now
15	f	Abraham	4	47	Aquar.	7	and very
16		3 Su. in Adv.	5	48		22	cold.
17	a	Lazarus	6	50	Pisces	4
18	b	Christopher	7	51		18
19	c		8	52	Aries	2
20	d	Amon Fast	9	54		16	High winds
21	e		10	55	Taur.	0	and cold.
22	f	30 Martyrs	11	56		14
23		4 Su. in Adv.	12	57		23
24	a	Ad. & Eve fast	13	59	Gem.	13
25	b		15	0		27	A thick
26	c		16	1	Canc.	11	gloomy air
27	d		17	3		25	and indiffe-
28	e		18	4	Leo	9	rently cold.
29	f	Jonathan	19	5		2
30		1 after Christ	20	6	Virgo	5
31	a	Sylvester	21	8		17

The Year, Month, and Day, (accounting the Year do begin Jan. 1.) wherein every K. and Q. of Eng. since the Conq. began their Reign.			The number of Years, Months, & Days, that every K. and Q. reigned 28 da. to a month.					The num. of y. expired in this y. since they began to re. as also since they ended.	
K.W. Conq.		1066	Octob. 14	20 y	11 m	22 d	622		
W. Rufus		1087	Sept. 9	12 y	11 m	18 d	501	K.W.Conq.	
Henry	1	1100	August 1	35 y	4 m	11 d	588	W. Rufus	
Stephen		1135	Decem. 2	18 y	11 m	18 d	553	Henry	1
Henry	2	1154	Octob. 25	34 y	9 m	2 d	534	Stephen	
Richard	1	1189	July 6	9 y	9 m	0 d	599	Henry	2
John		1199	April 6	17 y	7 m	0 d	489	Richard	1
Henry	3	1216	Octob. 19	56 y	1 m	0 d	472	John	
Edward	1	1272	Nov. 16	34 y	8 m	6 d	416	Henry	3
Edward	2	1307	July 7	19 y	7 m	5 d	381	Edward	1
Edward	3	1327	Jan. 25	50 y	5 m	7 d	361	Edward	2
Richard	2	1377	June 21	22 y	3 m	14 d	311	Edward	3
Henry	4	1399	Sep. 29	13 y	6 m	3 d	289	Richard	2
Henry	5	1413	March 20	9 y	5 m	24 d	275	Henry	4
Henry	6	1422	Aug. 31	38 y	6 m	16 d	266	Henry	5
Edward	4	1461	March 4	22 y	1 m	8 d	227	Henry	6
Edward	5	1483	April 9	0 y	2 m	18 d	205	Edward	4
Richard	3	1483	June 22	2 y	2 m	5 d	205	Edward	5
Henry	7	1485	Aug. 22	23 y	10 m	24 d	203	Richard	3
Henry	8	1509	April 22	37 y	10 m	2 d	179	Henry	7
Edward	6	1547	Jan. 28	6 y	5 m	19 d	141	Henry	8
Q. Mary		1552	July 6	5 y	4 m	22 d	135	Edward	6
Q. Elizab.		1558	Nov. 17	44 y	4 m	15 d	130	Q. Mary	
James	1	1603	March 24	22 y	0 m	3 d	85	Q. Elizab.	
Charles	1	1625	March 27	22 y	10 m	3 d	63	James	1
Charles	2	1649	Jan. 3	36 y	0 m	7 d	39	Charles	1
James	2	1685	Feb. 6	Long live the King			3	Charles	2

The use of the Table in Example.

King Henry 8 began his Reign in the year of Christ, 1509, April 22. He Reigned 37 years, 10 months, and 2 days. It is since he began his Reign 179 years compleat the 22 of April this year 1688. Now to know the time since the end of his Reign, before his name standing on the right hand, you shall there find 141 years since he died, Jan. 28. And so of the rest.

MARY HOLDEN:

THE

SECOND PART

Of the Woman's

ALMANACK.

FOR

The Year of our Lord God, 1688.

BEING

The *Biſſextile* or Leap-year, and from the Creation of the World 5637 Years :

WHEREIN

Is contained the Deſcription of the Four Quarters of the Year, the Eclipſes, Aſtrological Tables of many uſeful things worth remembrance. Many neceſſary Rules in Gardening, &c.

By Mary Holden *Student in Phyſ. and Aſtrol.*

LONDON,
Printed for the Company of *Stationers.* 1688.

Of *Eclipses happening this Year.*

Our times will the Luminaries be Eclipsed this Year, twice the Sun, and twice the Moon.

The first will be of the Moon, on the 5th day of *April*, about of the Clock in the Evening, in 26 degrees of *Libra*, it will a great Eclipse, but not to be seen of us ; The Moon being der the Earth.

The second Eclipse is of the Sun, on *April* the 20th. at one the clock in the morning, in 11 Degrees of *Taurus*, invisible to us, but will be seen almost in the Meridian of our *Antis*.

The third will be an Eclipse of the Moon on the 29th day of *ember*, about 10 of the clock in the morning ; it happens in degrees of *Aries* the Ascendant of *England* ; invisible is also.

The fourth will be an Eclipse of the Sun on the 14th. day of *her*, about seven of the clock in the morning, in two Degrees of *Scorpio*, the latter part of it may be seen in *England*, the Weather admits.

Description of the Four Quarters of the Year, and first of Winter. *Sol in* ♈ ♎ ♓

"He Winter Quarter begins when the Sun enters the first minute of ♑, that is *December* the 10th. 42 minutes after at night, being Teusday, making with us the shortest day the longest night. The natural inclination of this Quarter old and moist, but the colder and dryer the better for ath. Now the younger fort and chollerick people enjoy Health best, but the aged, and those of phlegmatick constitutions are generally most distempered. In *December* choller phlegm do much increase, which makes people generally heavy, dull and cold ; Therefore you may safely take this month to purge the Head of choller and phlegm, but must be such as are prepared for the same purpose.

A 2

Of the second Quarter called the Spring. Sol in ♈. ♉. ♊.

THe Spring time being the most pleasantest and wholsome season of the four, taketh its beginning on Fryday the 9th of *March* near one of the Clock after Noon ; At this time the Sun riseth at 6, and sets at 6, and maketh the night and day equal. This Spring Quarter continueth till the 11th of *June* The nature of this Quarter is hot and moist ; And of the Sanguine Complextion many are the distempers which proceeds from putrified and corrupted Blood, these being most dangerous : Therefore let them that have any care of themselves take Physick and bleed ; this being the fittest time to ease diseased Bodies ; and to restore Health again to those in whom formerly it has been decayed.

Of the third Quarter of the Year, called Summer. Sol in ♋. ♌. ♍.

THis Quarter takes its beginning at the time of the Suns first entering into *Cancer*, which is this Year on Sunday the 10th of *June*, at 48 minutes past noon, at which time he makes his greatest declination towards the North, and caused the longest day and shortest night in the Year, and this Quarter continueth till the 12th of *September*. This quarter is naturally hot and dry, and the Phlegmatick Constitutions are best in Health, the Chollerick the contrary. This season is more favourable to old Age then to Youth, and therefore care ought to be taken accordingly : The infirmities of this season are many, as bleeding at the Nose, hoarseness, cough, shortness of Breath, Pleurisies, pain in the Head, Eyes, and Stomach, Feavers, and other strange Diseases.

Of the fourth Quarter of the Year, called Autumn, or Harvest. Sol in ♎. ♏. ♐.

THis Quarter beginneth when the Sun toucheth the first minute of the Sign *Libra*, and produceth much the same effects as in *Aries*, *September* the 12th at 8 at night, that is, making the day and night equal, the Sun rising at 6, and setting at 6 ; rising just East, and setteth exactly West ; This is the

second

cond Spring, and a convenient time to take Physick and let
blood, especially labourers, which have taken great pains in
harvest, and have taken great heats and colds, which ingen-
dreth many Distempers if neglected. This quarter is natu-
ally cold and dry, and therefore persons of a sanguine com-
plection are for the most part best in Health, and the Melancholly most subject to Distempers.

Monthly Observations for good Husbandry and good Housewifry.

Januaries Observations.

Plough for Pease, fallow such Land as you intend shall rest
the Year following; Water your barren Meadows, Pasture,
and drain Arable ground, especially if you intend to sow Pease,
Oats or Barly the second time following. Also stub up all
rough Grounds; Trim up your Garden Moulds: Set all kind of
fruit-Trees, for it is best to set such Trees as will endure the
old; they will be forwarder in growth then those set in the
spring: Set Vines, and trim the old ones; nail up your Wall-
fruit, and towards the end graft Pears, Cherries and Plums.
the Weather calm, rear Calves, remove Bees, keep good Diet.

Februaries Observations.

Set Beans, Pease, and other Pulse in stiff ground, begin the
onset, prepare your Garden, prune and trim your Fruit-
trees from Moths, Cankers, and superfluous Branches, plash
hedges, lay your Quickset close, plant Roses, Gooseberry Trees,
and any other Shrub-trees, and graft your tender Stocks; forbear all Phlegmatick Meats.

March's Observations.

Look well to your Ewes, cut up underwood for Fewel,
transplant all sorts of Summer Flowers, comfort them with
good Earth, especially the *Crown Imperial, Narcissus, Tulips,*
and *Hyacinth*; In your barren fruit-trees bore holes, and drive
hard Wedges of Oak, and cover roots of trees close with fat
Earth that are uncovered; Graft fruit trees, and sow Oats,
Rye and Barley, slip Artichoaks, now advise with your Physician;

sician, for in this Month Physick and Bleeding is good to prevent further dangers, for now Blood increaseth, and gross humours abound; let your Dyet be cold and temperate.

Aprils Observations.

Sowe your Hemp and Flax; sowe and set all sorts of Herbs, slip Lavender, Rosemary, Sage, Cyprus, Box, and such like shrubs, open your Hives, and give your Bees their liberty, and let them labour for their living; cut your Oak-Timber, the Bark is now best for the Tanners use; scower your Ditches, gather your Manure together in heaps, gather stones, repair Highways, set Oziers and Willows, and cast up all decayed fences: Physick is very seasonable still, as bleeding and purging to prevent causes of sickness, and for remedy in sickness.

May's Observations.

This Month commands Gentlewomen to set their stills to work, as yet sow sweet Marjoram, painted Beans, Beassel, Time, Carnations, and Herbs that are tender, plant Stock-Gilliflowers in Beds in the full of the Moon, shade your Carnations and Gilliflowers in the heat of the day, fold your sheep, carry forth manure, and bring home fewel; weed Winter Corn, furnish your Dairy, let your Mares go to Horse, fat your dry Kine, and away with them; set your Bees at liberty, look for swarms in this month: In this month it is good to let blood and purge for such as have infirmities in the Head and Eyes, and for Aged People.

June's Observations.

Sow Lettice, Radishes, and such like Herbs at the full of the Moon, then they will not run to seed this month, and the best season for your Herbs to keep dry for the whole year; cut neither Hedges nor Trees these three months, gather Herbs with your fingers, a knife will cause them to dye; distil all sorts of Plants and Herbs whatsoever, cut your rank meadows, fetch home fewel, and carry forth manure, mucus and lime to mend your lands; be sure to make cheese this month, whatever you make the rest of the year.

July's Observations.

Attend your Hay-harvest, shear field sheep, gather your
flowers and seeds at the full of the moon, dry your flowers in
the shade; for the Sun too much exhaleth their vertue; sun
them a little before you lay them up, let the herbs you intend
to preserve run to seed, cut off the stalk of your flowers, and
cover the roots with new fat Earth : Sell your Lambs you intended for the Shambles; beware of violent heats and sudden
colds, which are the chiefest distempers of this month; take
no Physick, unless in extraordinary cases; refrain *Venery.*

August's Observations.

Follow diligently your Corn-Harvest, cut down your Wheat
and Rye, mowe Barley and Oats, put off your fat Sheep and
cattle, gather your Plums, Apples and Pears, make your
summer Perry and Syder; set your slips and Scyons of all
sorts of Gilliflowers, and other Flowers; transplant them that
were set in the Spring, gather your seeds in the full of the
Moon, if dry weather, geld your Lambs, carry manure from
your Dove-coats, put your swine to the early mast; take no
Physick, neither let blood in the Dog days but upon great occasion, if the Air be hot, otherwise, in necessity you may
safely use it; use not to sleep in the Afternoon, for it causeth
headach and Agues, refrain all excess in eating or drinking,
drink that which is cooling.

September's Observations.

Cut your Beans, Pease, and all manner of pulse : On the
land you intend to sowe Wheat and Rye, bestow the best
manure; gather your Winter-fruit, sowe Winter herbs, transplant Physical herbs; towards the end of the month, Earth
up your Winter herbs and plants, remove and set all slips of
flowers, set Roses and Barbaries in the new of the Moon, sell
your Wool, flocks of Bees, and other Commodities you intend to put off; Thatch your Hive of Bees you intend to
keep, and look that no Drones, Mice, or other Vermin be
about them; Thrash your Seed, Wheat and Rye. Use Physick moderately, shun the eating of sweet and rotten Fruit,
avoid surfeiting.

Octobers Observations.

Finish your Wheat-seed, plash and lay your Hedges and Quick-sets, scour your Ditches and Ponds, transplant and remove all manner of Fruit-trees, lay bare the roots of your thriving trees, in Planting, set the same side of your Trees South and West which was so before, otherwise the North wind will kill them, make Winter Perry and Syder, spare your Pastures, and feed upon Corn-fields ; draw Furrows to drain, and keep dry your new sown Corn ; make Malt, rear all new fall'n Calves, all Foals that were foaled in the Spring, wean from the Mares. Sell your Sheep that you do not intend to Winter, and separate Lambs from the Ewes, that you intend to keep. Recreate your spirits by harmless sports, and take Physick by good advice, if need require it.

Novembers Observations.

Cut down your Timber for Ploughs, Carts, Naves, Axle-trees, Harrows, and other offices about Husbandry, or House-wifry ; make the last return of Grass, feed Cattle, take your swine from the mast, and feed them for the slaughter ; rear all Calves that fall now, break all Hemp and Flax that you intend to spend in the Winter season ; remove Fruit-trees, and sowe Wheat and Rye in hot soils, sowe early Beans and Pease, set Crabtree-stocks to graft on in the old of the Moon, sowe Parsnips and Carrots, uncover the roots of Apple-trees, and so let them remain till March. Use Spices and Wine moderately, and if any Distemper afflict the Body, you may make use of Physick still, and Bleeding.

Decembers Observations.

Put your Sheep to the Pease-ricks, kill your small Porks and large Bacons, top Hedges, saw your Timber for building, and lay it to season ; Plough your ground you intend to sowe clean Beans upon : Cover your dainty Fruit-trees, drain your Corn-fields, and water your meadows ; cover your best flowers with rotten Horse-litter. Now all sorts of Fowl are in season ; keep thy self warm with a wholsome Dyet, and avoid all care that may trouble thy spirits, as a thing of dangerous consequence.

FOr as much as some do think that Astrology was invented by the Heathens, I shall endeavour to prove that it was from the beginning of the World, devised by the Sons of *Seth*, and for as much as they feared least their Art should perish before it came to the knowledge of Men, for they had heard their Grandfather *Adam* say, that all things should be destroyed by the universal Flood; they made two Pillars, one of Stone and the other of Brick, to the intent that if the Brick wasted with Water or Storms, yet the Stones should preserve their Letters whole and perfect, and in these Pillars they Graved all that concerned Astrology, or the observances of the Stars; and therefore it is credible that the *Egyptians* and *Chaldes* learned Astrology of the *Hebrews* and so consequently it spread abroad in other Nations; therefore I would not have any to despise the Art of Astrology, the Art and study is both laudable and excellent, and founded upon good principles of Scripture, as you may find from *Gen.* 1. to 14. and from 14. to 18. *Judges* 5. *ver.* 21. *Psalm.* 3. *ver.* 6, 19. *Isaiah* 40. 22, 26. *Job* 38. 31, 32. look in the 7. *chap.* of the *Wisdom of Solomon* from the 17. *ver.* to the 21. and I hope it will satisfie you.

A

A Table of the hour and minute of Sun rising every second day.

days	January ho. mi.	Februa. ho. mi.	March ho. mi.	April ho. mi.	May ho. mi.	June ho. mi.
2	8 4	7 15	6 15	5 14	4 21	3 45
4	8 1	7 11	6 12	5 10	4 17	3 45
6	7 58	7 7	6 8	5 6	4 14	3 44
8	7 55	7 3	6 4	5 2	4 11	3 43
10	7 53	6 5	6 0	4 58	4 7	3 43
12	7 51	6 53	5 56	4 54	4 5	3 43
14	7 48	6 50	5 52	4 50	4 2	3 43
16	7 45	6 46	5 48	4 46	4 0	3 44
18	7 43	6 42	5 44	4 43	3 58	3 45
20	7 40	6 38	5 40	4 39	3 56	3 46
22	7 37	6 34	5 36	4 35	3 54	3 47
24	7 33	6 30	5 32	4 32	3 52	3 48
26	7 29	6 26	5 29	4 29	3 50	3 49
28	7 25	6 22	5 25	4 25	3 48	3 50
30	7 21	6 0	5 21	4 22	3 47	3 52

days	July ho. mi.	Aug. ho. mi.	Septem. ho. mi.	Octob. ho. mi.	Novem. ho. mi.	Decem. ho. mi.
2	3 54	4 39	5 39	6 41	7 27	8 15
4	3 56	4 42	5 42	6 45	7 40	8 15
6	3 58	4 46	5 45	6 49	7 44	8 15
8	4 0	4 50	5 58	6 52	7 47	8 17
10	4 2	4 54	5 51	6 56	7 51	8 17
12	4 5	4 58	5 53	7 0	7 54	8 17
14	4 8	5 2	6 0	7 4	7 57	8 17
16	4 11	5 6	6 6	7 8	7 5	8 16
18	4 15	5 10	6 11	7 12	8 1	8 15
20	4 18	5 14	6 15	7 16	8 3	8 15
22	4 21	5 18	6 20	7 10	8 5	8 14
24	4 24	5 21	6 24	7 22	8 7	8 13
26	4 27	5 25	6 28	7 25	8 9	8 12
28	4 30	5 29	6 32	7 29	8 11	8 10
30	4 34	5 32	6 36	7 32	8 13	8 7

Seek the day of the month ... and right against it in every ... you have
the ho. and minute of Sun rising.
Look ... the ... es the Sun rises after ...
... 8, 7, 6, 5, 4.

A Table

A Table of Annuities and Reversions.

years	What 1 pound to be paid any number of years hence, under 31, is worth in ready money.			What the Annuity to continue any time under 31 years, is worth in ready money at 5 per cent.				What 1 pound will amount to at any time under 31 yea, reckoning Interest upon Interest.			
	sh.	d.	q.	l.	sh.	d.	q.	l.	sh.	d.	q.
1	18	10	2	0	18	10	2	1	1	2	2
2	17	9	2	1	16	8	0	1	2	5	2
3	16	9	2	2	13	5	2	1	3	9	3
4	15	10	0	3	9	3	2	1	5	3	0
5	14	11	1	4	4	5	0	1	6	9	0
6	14	1	1	4	18	4	1	1	8	4	2
7	13	3	2	5	11	7	3	1	10	0	3
8	12	6	2	6	4	4	1	1	11	10	2
9	11	10	0	6	15	0	1	1	13	9	2
10	11	2	0	7	7	2	1	1	15	9	3
11	10	6	2	7	17	8	3	1	17	11	2
12	9	11	1	8	7	8	0	2	0	3	0
13	9	4	2	8	17	0	2	2	2	7	3
14	8	10	0	9	5	10	3	2	5	2	2
15	8	4	0	9	14	3	0	2	7	11	1
16	7	10	2	10	2	1	2	2	10	9	2
17	7	5	0	10	9	6	2	2	13	10	2
18	7	0	0	11	16	6	2	3	17	1	0
19	6	7	1	11	3	2	0	3	0	6	0
20	6	2	3	11	0	4	3	3	4	1	3
21	5	10	2	11	15	3	1	3	7	11	3
22	5	6	2	12	0	10	0				
23	5	2	3	12	6	0	3				
24	4	11	1	12	11	0	0				
25	4	7	2	12	15	8	0				
26	4	4	3	13	0	0	3				
27	4	1	3	13	4	2	2				
28	3	11	0	13	8	1	3				
29	3	9	1	13	11	6	2				
30	3	5	3	13	15	3	2				

By this Table you may readily find the increase of any other sum for such a number of years; for if 1 l. come to so much, then such suppose 5 l. will come to 5 times as much, &c.

T 2

153

The Use of the Tables.

THe first Table shewing the decrease of one Pound yearly at 6 per cent may be used in buying Reversions, &c. As suppose a parcel of Land or House or the like, whose fee simple or real worth is 200 l. and it be Morgaged or Leased out for 20 years, then what is the Reversion thereof after that 20 years worth in ready money? for Answer, I look against 20 years and find that the Reversion of one pound after 20 years is worth but 6 s. 2 d. 3 q. then if 1 l. be worth 6 s. 2 d. 3 d. 200 l. will be worth 200 times as much, which will be 62 l. 5 s. 10 d. for the value of the Reversion required.

The second Table may be used in buying of Leases, &c. as suppose I am to buy a Lease of 10 l. per annum, for 21 years, what ready money may I give at the rate of 6 l. per cent per annum, for Answer, I look against 21 years and find that 1 l. annuity to continue 21 years is worth in ready money 11 l. 15 s. 3 d. 1 q. then I say, if 1 l. annuity for 21 years be worth 11 l. 15 s. 3 d. 1 q. then 10 l. annuity for the same time will be worth 10 times as much, which will be 117 l. 12 s. 8 d. 2 q. for the value of the Lease required.

The third Table may be used in putting out money for a certain time at 6 l. per cent per annum, as suppose 20 l. be let out for 7 years what will it amount to in that time, reckoning Interest upon Interest? For Answer, I look against 7 years, and find that 1 l. will amount to in that time 1 l. 10 s. 0 d. 3 q. then I say 20 l. will amount to 20 times as much, which will be 30 l. 1 s. 3 d.

The use of the following Table is plain and easie, for suppose I am to find Easter this present year 1688 then having found the Golden Number 17 and Dominical Letter G at the bottom of the Table, I look under the Dominical Letter G at the top, and right against the Golden Number 17 at the left hand, and in the Common angle of meeting I find Aprill 15. for Easter Day.

A

A Table shewing how to find Easter *for ever by the help of the Golden Number and Dominical Letter.*

G. N.	A	B	C	D	E	F	G
1	Apr. 9	10	11	12	6	7	8
2	Mar.26	27	28	29	30	31	apr. 1
3	Apr.15	17	18	19	20	14	15
4	Apr. 9	3	4	5	6	7	8
5	Mar.26	27	28	29	23	24	25
6	Apr.15	17	11	12	13	14	15
7	Apr. 2	3	4	5	6	mar.31	apr. 1
8	Apr.23	24	25	19	20	21	22
9	Apr. 9	10	11	12	13	14	8
10	Apr. 2	3	mar.28	29	30	31	apr. 1
11	Apr.16	17	18	19	20	21	22
12	Apr. 9	10	11	5	6	7	8
13	Mar.26	27	28	29	30	31	25
14	Apr.16	17	18	19	13	14	15
15	Apr. 2	3	4	5	6	7	8
16	Mar.26	27	28	22	23	24	25
17	Apr.16	10	11	12	13	14	15
18	Apr. 2	3	4	5	mar.30	31	apr. 1
19	Apr.23	24	18	19	20	21	22

Year of our Lord	1584	1585	1586	1587	1588	1589	1590

G. N.	13	14	15	16	17	18	19
D le	FE	D	C	B	AG	F	E

A

A Catalogue of the Fairs in England *and* Wales ;
Revised, Corrected and Enlarged.

Fairs in January.

THe 3 day at Llanibither, 5 at Hickerford in Lancashire,
6 at Salisbury, Bristol, 7 at Llanginny, 25 at Laighton-buzzard, Bristol, Churchingford, Northallerton in
Yorkshire; Gravesend, 31 at Llandissel.

Fairs in February.

The 1 day at Bromly in Lancashire, 2 at Bath, Bickles-
worth, Bugworth, Farrington, Godlemew, Lyn, Maidstone,
Reading, Beconsfield, the Vizes in Wiltshire, Whirland, 5 at
Boxgrove, Brimley, 6 at Stafford for six days with all kind of
Merchandise without arrest, 8 at Tragirton, 9 at Landall, 14
at Oundle in Northamptonshire, Feversham, 24 at Baldock,
Bourn, Froom, Buckingham, Henly upon Thames, Higham-
Ferries, Tewksbury, Uppingham, Walden, 25 at Stamford,
an horse-fair.

Fairs in March.

The 1 day at Llanradeg, at Llangavellah, at Medrin, 3 at
Bromwel-brakes in Norfolk, 4 at Bedford, Ockham, 6 at
Tragirton, 12 at Spalord, Stamford, Sudbury, Wooburn,
Wrexam, Bodnam, Aston in Norfolk, 13 at Wye, Bodwin
in Cornwal, Mounthowin, 17 at Parrington, 18 at Sturbridge,
20 at Alesbury, Durham, 24 at Llanereberith, 25 at St. Al-
bans, Alhwel in Hertfordshire, Barton, Cardigan, Carwalden,
in Essex, Huntington, St. Jones in Worcestershire, Malden,
Malpas, Newcastle, Northampton, Oney in Buckinghamshire,
Woodstock, Whitland, Great Charr, 31 at Malmesbury.

Fairs

HOLDEN. 1688.

Fairs in April.

The 2 at Hitchin, Northfleet, Rochford, 3 at Leek in Staffordshire, 5 at Wallingford, 7 at Derby, 8 at Fenny-stratford, 9 at Billingsworth and Cobham, 11 at Newport-pagnel, 22 at Stabford, 23 at Amptshil, Bewdley, Bruton, Brigstock, Bolson, Bury in Lancashire; Cattlecombs, Charing, Chichester, Engfield in Suffex, Gisford, Bishops-Hatfield, Henningham, Ipswich, Kilborough, Lonquer, Northampton, Nutley in Suffex, S. Combs, Sawbridgworth, Tamworth, Wilton, Worsham, Rilsborough, Harbin in Norfolk. Sapier in Hartfordshire, 25 at Risborough, Bourn in Lincolnshire, Buckingham, Caln in Wiltshire, Cliff in Suffex, Colebrook, Luton in Bedfordshire, Dunmow in Effex, Darby, Innings in Buckinghamshire, Ockham, Uttoxeter, Winchcomb, 26 at Tenterden in Kent, Clere.

Fairs in May.

The 1 day at Andover, Blackburn in Lancashire, Brickhil, Silfo in Bedfordshire, Chelmsford, Congerton in Chefhire, Fokingham, Grighowel, Kimar, Leighton, Leicefter, Litchfield, Lexfield in Suffolk, Linfield, Hantrident, Louth, Maidftone, Oceftree in Shropshire, Perin, Philips-Norton, Pombridge, Reading, Rippon, Stamsed, Stow the old, Stocknasland, Tuxford in the Clay, Usk, Haveril, Warwick, Wendover, Worsworth if not Sunday; 2 at Powlthesly in Carmarthershire; 3 at Abergavenny, Athborn-peak, Arundel, Bonvard, Bala, Chertfey near Oatlands, Chipnam, Church-Stretton in Shropshire, Cowbridge in Glamorganshire, Darby, Denby, Elftow by Bedford, Hinningham, Methyr, Monmon, Non-Eaten, Huddersfield, Rochdale in Lancashire, Tidnel, Waltham-Abby, Thetford in Norfolk, 5 at Marshenleth in Montgomeryshire, 6 at Almsbury, Hoy, Knighton, 7 at Bath, Beverly, Hanflen, Newton in Lancashire, Hatsbury, Oxford, Stratford upon Avon, Thunderley in Effex, 8 at Maidftore, 10 at Athbornpeak, 11 at Dunftable, 12 at Grays Thorock in Effex, 13 at Bala in Mirion, 15 at Welch-pool in Mountgomeryshire, 16 at Llangarranog in Cardigan, 19 at Mayfield, Odehil, Rochefter.

157

fter, Wellow. 20 at Malmsbury. 25 at Blackburn. 29 at Cranbrook. 30 at Pershore.

Fairs in June.

The 3 day at Alesbury. 6, 7, 8. at Milton-Abby in Dorfetshire. 9 at Maidstone. 11 at Holt, Kinwilgate in Carmarthenshire. Llanibither, Llanwist, Landilzvader, in Carmarthenshh. Maxfield, Newborough, Newcastle in Emlin, Ockingham, Wellington, Newport-Paguel, Shipton upon Stower, Brenel in Norfolk. 13 at Newton in Keddewen in Mountgomeryshire, 14 at Bangor. 15 at Vizes, Perfhore seven miles from Worcester. 16 at Belth in Brecknock, Newport in Keams. 17 at Hadstock, Higham-Ferries, Llanvilling, Scowgreen. 19 at Bridgenorth. 21 at Yftradmerick. 22 at St. Albans, Shrewsbury, Derham in Norfolk. 23 at Barnet, Castle-Ebichin in Monmouth, Dolgelly in Merion. 24 at Afhburn, St. Annes, Awkinborough, Bedford, Bedle, Beverly, Bishops-castle, Broughtongreen-market, Bosworth, Breconock, Broomsgrove, Cambridge, Colchefter, Cranbrook, Croyden, Farnham, Harft, Kingfton in Warwickshire, Kirkham in Aunderness, Lancafter, Leicester, Gloucester, Halifax, Hertford, Hirtkon, Horsham, Lincoln, Fullow, Penway, Prefton, Reading, Rumford, Shaftsbury, Stanftock, Tunbridge, Wakefield, Wenlock, Weftchefter, Windfor, Wormefter, York. 26 at Northop. 27 at Burton upon Trent, Felkfton, Llandogain. 28 at Hefcorn, Merchenleth, St. Pombs. 29 at Afhwei, Bala, Barkhamfted, Bennington, Beballinge, Bolton, Bromly, Buckingham, Buntinsford, Cardiffe, Gorgang, Hodefdon, Holdfworth, Horndon, Highfield, lower Knocksford, Lempfter, Lanergan, Llanbedery, Man field, Marlborough, Mountford, Munfiril, Oney, Peterborough, Peterfield, Pentfiephen, Sarltrange, Sennock, Seatham, Stafford, Stockworth, Sudbury, Therofegrais, Tring, Upton, Wear, Weftminfter, Witny, Wolverhampton, Woodstock, York. 30 at Man field in Chefhire.

Fairs in July.

The 2 at Afhton under line, Congerton, Hunnington, Rickmanfford, Seneath in Bear, Swanfey, Woorwin. 3 at Haverton.

5 at

at Burton upon Trent. 6 at Haverhil, Llanibither, Llanidlas: at Albrighton , Burntwood , Cheppingnorton, Castlemain, happelfrith, Canterbury, Denbigh, Emlin, Haverford, Richmond, Royston, Shelford, Sweaton, Tenbury, Threfhevinrech, fizes, Uppingham. 11 at Lid, Partny. 13 at Fodringbay. 15 Greenfted, Laighton-buzzard, Finchback. 17 at Stevenage, elth, Knelms, Leek , Llanvilling. 20 at Winchcomb , Awfton, Barkway, Betley , Boulton , Bowin , Catesby, Ghimnock, Coolidg, Llanibithener, St. Margarets, Neath, Odiham, Tenby , Uxbridge , Woodftock , Ickleton in Cambridgfhire. at Bernards-caftle , Battlefield , Bicklfworth , Billericay , Bridgnorth , Broughton , Caln , Clithéral , Colchefter. 22 at Chefhham, Ickleton , Kefwich , Kimolton , Kingfton , Mawdchil, Win, Hey, Marlborough ; Newark upon Trent, Norich, Ponterly, Ridwally , Roking, Stonyftratf. Stokesbury, ledbury,Witheral,Withgrig,Yadeland,Yarn, 23 at Carnarvan, thefton. 25 at Cromifh by Wallingford, Abbington,Afhwel,Alkrgam,Baldock, Barkhamfted, Bilfon,Bofton , Briftol,Bromfgove, Bromly, Brodoke,Buntingford,Cambden,Capel-Jago,Chifter, Chilholm, Darby , Doncafter , Dover, Dudly, Erith, Hatfield, St. Jamefes London, St. Jamefes by Northamp. Ipfich, Kingfton, Lifle , Kirkham, Linfield, Liverpool, Louth, Kilpas, Malmsbury, Machenbleth, Ravenglafs , Reading, Richmond in the North, Rofs, Saffron-walden, Schifnal, Skipton, Stamford, Stackpool, Stone, Themblegreen, Thickham, Thrapton, Tilbury, Trobridge , Walden , Warrington, Wetherby, Wigmore. 27 at Afhwel, Canterbury, Chapple-frith, Horfham, 30 at Stafford.

Fairs in Auguft.

The 1 at Bath, Bedford, Chepftow , Dunftable, St. Eeds, Exeter, Feverfham, Flint, Hay, Horfnay, Kaermarthen, Kaergully, Llantriffent, Lawrwin, Ludford, Loughborough, Maling, Newton in Lancafhire, Newcaftle upon Trent, Northam, Church-Rumney, Shrewsbury, Selborn, Selby, Thaxted, Wisbich, Eland , York , at Radnor , Linton , Thunderly, 6 at Bardney, Peterborough. 9 at Aberlew. 10 at Bedford, Alchurch, Banbury , Blackamoor, Bodwin, Brainford, Chidley, Croyley , Frodifham , Fulfea , Harley , Hawkhurft,

D

Horn-

Horn-caftle, Hungerford, Kellow, Kenwilgal, Kilgarron, Lud
low, Marras, Melton-Mowbray, Mearworth, Newborough Owndle
Rugby, Sedule, Snerborn, Tocefter, Waltham-Abby, Wen
don, Wormfler, Winflow. 15 at St. Albans, Bolton, Cam
bridge, Carlifle, Cardigan, Gisborough, Goodhuft, Hinkly
Huntington, Luton, Marlborough, Newin, Northampton. New
port in Monmouthfhire, Stroud, Swinfey, Tutbury, Wake
field, whitland, Ymiuith. 24 at Aberconway, Abrough, Aftor
-de H Zouch Beggers-bufh, Bromly, Brigflock, chordly, Crow
land; Dover, Farmgden, Grimsby, Harwood, Kidderminfter
Loudon, Mountgomery, Monmouth, Nantwich, Northallr-
ton, Norwich, Oxford, Sudbury, Tewksbury, Todinton in
Bedfordfhire, Waderel, 28 at Afhford, Daintry, Sturbridge in
Worcefterfhire, Fahfarn-green, Welch-Pool, 29 at Brecknock,
Colft in Cincolnfhire, Kacrwis, Kearmaithen, Oakham, Wat
ford, Monday after Barthol. at Sanbich.

Fairs in September.

2 At Chapuel-Silby, St. Giles, Neath, 7 at Ware, Wood
bury-hill. 8 Atherfton, Bewmaris, Blackborn, Brewood,
Bury in Lancafhire, Cardigan, Cardifl, Chartom, Chalton in
Chefhire, Drayton, Dryfield, Gisborough, Gliborn, Hartford,
Huntington, Landafel, Waslen, Northampton, Partney, Re
culver, Sneath, Snole, Southwark, Sturbridge, Tenby, Utce
-ter, Wakefield, Waltham on the Woulds, Weft-Nein, White
land. 12 at Wentworth, Woolpit, Tuxford. 13 at Newtown
in Einvin, Powithwily. 14 at Avergavenny, Alesbury, Cheping-
Woccam, Lartley, Church-fretton, Chefterfield, Denbigh,
Eldom, Henbury, Munfton, Newborough, Newport,
Penhad, Rippon, Richmond, Rofs, Rockingham, Snalding,
Stratford-upon-Avon, Walfham-Abby, Wotton under hedge.
16 at Raisdargwy. 17 at Clif. Llanidlas. 20 at Llanvelly, Ru
dian. 21 at Abergwily, Baldock, Bedford, Braintry, Brackly-
malden, Bulwick, Canterbury, Dover, Clapon, Croyden, Daintry, Euftad. St. Edmonsbury, Helmfley, Holden, Katherin-
hill, Knighton, Kingfton in Warwickfhire, Marlborough, Mal
den, Mildnal, Nottingham, Peterborow, Shrewsbury, Strat
ford, Vizes, Wendover, Witheral, Woodftock. 22 at Pan
ridge in Staffordfhire a great horfe-fayr. 24 at Llanvilling,
Malton a week. 26 at Darby. 28 at Dolgeth, Kaermarthen
29 at

the old, Aberton, Aberconway, St. Al-
npeak, Balmstock, Basingstoeke, Bishop-stratford,
Bruningh_am, Buckland, Barwel, Canturbury,
ester, Cockermouth, Market-deeping, Michael-dean,
ally, Hay, Higham fieries, St. Jves, Kingston, Killingworth,
ingland, Lavenham, Lancaster, Leicester, Landils, Llan-
h-angel, L'ocher, Ludlow, Malden, Marchenleth, Biethvr,
ewbury, Selby, Shefiord in Beckhire, Sittingbourn,
Snow in Lincolnshire, Tuddington, Uxbridge, Weshil, Wey-
ner seven days, Westchester, Witham, Woodham-ferry in
Esex, Bookham.

Fairs in October.

1 at Banbury, Caster. 2 at Salisbury. 3 at Bolton in the
Moors. 4 at St. Michaels. 6 at Havent in Hampshire, Maidstone
in Kent. 8 at Bishop-stratford, Chichester, Hertford, Llanibi-
ter, Pontstephen, Swanfey. 9 at Ashburn-peak, blith, De-
vises, Gainsborough, Harborough, Sawbridgeworth, Throck-
God-s. 11 at Newport-Pagnel. 12 at Bolton in Furnace, Llan-
pveth. 13 at Aberrow, Charing, Creton, Colchester, Drai-
on, Edmunsrow, Gravesend, Hitchen, Newport in Mon-
mouthshire, Hodnet, Laiton buzzard, Marshfield, Royston,
Stopforth, Stainton, Tamworth, Windfor, Graychester in
Essex. 18 at Henden in Wiltshire, Ashwel, Banbury, Barnet,
Whittle, Brickhil, Bridgnorth, Bishops-Hatfield, Burton upon
Trent, Charlton, Clift-Regis, Ely, Faringdon, Henly in Arden,
Holt, Kidwelly, Isk, Lowhaddon, Marlo upon Thames, Mid-
dlewich, Newcastle, Radnor, Thirst, Tisdale, Tunbridge,
Uphaven, Wellingborough, Wigham, Wrickley, York. 19
at Fridefwid by Oxford. 21 at Saffron-walden, Oeester, Co-
ventry, Hereford, Llanibither, Lentham, Stokesley. 22 at
Bicklesworth, Knotsford-lower, Ratsdale, Preston, Whit-
church. 25 at Beverly. 27 at Darnton. 28 at Biddenton in
Bedfordshire, Aberconway, Ashby de la Zouch, Bidderden, Hal-
derden, Hulston, Hartford, Lempster, Llanedy, Newmarker,
Preston in Aunderness, Stamford, Talliern-green, Warwick,
Wilton, Wormcester. Friday before Simon and Jude at Oxford. 31 at Abermales, Chelmsford, Ruthin, Powlethelly,
Stokesly, Wakefield.

B 2   Fairs

Fairs in November.

1 At Bicklefworth, Caftlemain, Kellom, Mountgomery, Ludlow. 2 at Blechingly, Bifhops-caftle, Elfmere, Kingfton upon Thames, Leek, Loughborough, Mayfield, Maxfield, York. 3 at Kaermarthen. 5 at Welch-Pool, 6 at Andover, Bedford, Brecknock, Hertfort, Lesford ; Mailing in Kent, Marron in Holdern, Newport-pond, Pembridge, Salford, Stanley, Trigney, Wellington, Wetfhod. 10 at Aberwingreen, Lenton in Nottinghamfhire, Llanibither 7 days. Rughby, Schifnal, Wem. 11 at Aberkennen, Bettingham, Dover, Folkingham, Marlborough, Monmouth, Newcaftle in Emlin, Shaftsbury, Skipton on Craven, Tream, Withgrig, York. 13 at St. Edmondsbury. 15 at Llanithinery, Marchenleth, Willington. 17 at Harlow, Hide, Lincoln, Northampton, Spalding. 19 at Horfham in Kent. 20 at St. Edmondsbury, Health, Ingerftone. 20 at Penivont, Sawthy, 23 at Bangor, Bwelth, Caerlin, Froom, Ludlow, Katefcrofs, Sandwich in Kent, Tuddington in Bedfordfhire. 25 at Higham-Ferries. 28 at Afhbornpeak. 29 at Lawreft. 30 at Ampthil, Baldock, Bedford in Yorkfhire, Bewdley, Bofton-mart, Bradford, Collingborough, Cobham, Cubley, Engfield, Gargreen, Greenfted in Suffex, Harleigh, Kimolton, Maidenhead, Maiden-brackley, Narbert, Oceftry, Peterfield, Pecores, Prefton, Rochefter, Wakefield, Warrington.

Fairs in December.

1 At Turbury. 5 at Dolgeth, Newton, Pluckley. 6 at Arundel, Cafed, St. Geds, Exeter, Grantham, Heddingham, Hethin, Hornfey, Nortwich, Sennok, Spalding, Woodftock. 7 at Sandhurft. 8 at Bedford, Bewmaris, Clitheral, Helxome, Kaerdigan, Kimar, Leicefter, Malpas, Northampton, Whitland. 11 at Newport-pagnel. 21 at Hornby. 22 at Llandilavawr. 29 at Canterbury, Royfton, Salisbury.

The

The moveable Fairs.

From Chriſtmaſs till June, every Wedneſday at Northaller-
to. 3 Mondays after twelfth-day, at Hinkley in Leiceſterſhire.
Jueſday after Twelfth-day, at Meltonmowbray, and an Horſe-
air at Salisbury. Thurſday after Twelfth-day at Banbury, Lit-
ctworth; and every Thurſday 3 Weeks after. Friday after
twelfth-day at Lichfield. Shrove-monday at Newcaſtle under
me, Barkhamſted. Aſh-wedneſday at Abington, Candain in
Gloceſterſhire, Ciceter, Dunſtable, Eaton by Windſor, Exeter,
Folkingh. Lichfield, Royſton, Tamworth, Tunbridge, 1 Thurſday in Lent at Banbury. 1 Monday in Lent at Cherſey, Chicheſter, Wincheſter. 1 Tueſday in Lent at Bedford. 4 Monday in Lent at Odiham, Saffron-walden, Stimford. Friday
and Saturday before the 5 Sunday in Lent at Hartford. Monday before Annunciation at Denby, Kendal, Wisbich. 5 Monday in Lent at Grantham, Helxom in Suſſex, Salisbury, Sudbury. Wedneſday before Palm-ſunday at Draitor. Thurſday
before Palm-ſunday at Llandiſſel. Palm-ſunday Eve at Alisbury,
Leiceſter, Newport, Pomfract, Skipton, Wisbich. Palm-mon-
day at Billingſworth, Kendal, Llandauren, Worceſter. Wedneſday before Eaſter at Kaerlin, Llanvilling. Maund-thurſday
at Kettering, Sudminſter. Good-friday at Acton-burnel, Amp-
hil, Biſhops-caſtle, Bruton, Bury, Charing, Engfield, Gilford,
Hinningham, Ipſwich, Lonquer, Mellain, Nutly, St. Pombs,
Risborough, Rotheram. Tueſday in Eaſter-week at Brails, Daintry, Hitchin, North-fleet, Rochford, Sanbich, Aſhby de la
Zouch. Wedneſday at Wellingborough, Beverly, Redburn.
Friday at Darby. Saturday at Skipton in Craven. Monday after Low-ſunday at Bickleſworth, Eveſham, Newcaſtle under
line. 3 Monday after Eaſter at Lowth. Rogation-week at Beverly, Engfield, Rech. Aſcention-Eve at Abergelly, Darking.
Aſcention-day at Bewmaris, Biſhopſtratford, Braſled, Brun-
ningham, Bridgnorth, Burton, Chappel-frith, Chappelknion,
Eccleſhal, Egleſrew, Hallaton, Kidderminſter, Lutterworth,
Middlewich, Newcaſtle, Rippon, Roſs, Stapport, Sudminſter,
llizes, Wigan, Yarn. Monday after Aſcention at Thaxſtead,
Burſington. Wedneſday after Aſcention at Shrewsbury. Friday after Aſcention at Ruthin. Whiſſon-Eve at New-Inn,

B 3   Skipton

Skipton upon Craven, VVisbich. VVhitſun-monday at Crib
Kerbyſteven, Lenham, Rochdale. Rvhſ, Saliſbury, Ogmond
ſham, Amerſſim, Appleby, Bickleſworth, Bradford, Bromi-
ard, Burton, Chicheſter, Cockermouth, Darrington, Eveſham,
Exeter, Harſgreen, St. Jves, Linton, Owndle, Rigate, Sſelford,
Sittingborn, Sleeford, Midlome, VVhit-church. Darrington in
the North, Driſſeld, Stokecheer. VVhit-reuſday at Aſhby dela
Zouch, Canterbury, Daintry, Elſemere, Epping. Faringdony
Knotsford, Laiton-buzzard, Lewes, Lonquer, Ione Milford,
Llanimthevery, Melton-mowbray, Midhurſt, Monmouth, Pe-
rith, Bochford, Oringſtoke. VVedneſday at Llanbedder, Llan-
ydeby, Leek, Newark upon Trent, Peutſtephent. Royſton,
Sandñar. Thurſday at Cakeſield, Kington. Friday at Cockñal,
Darby, Stow in Guillin. Trinity-Eve at Peinſret. Rowel, Skip-
ron in Craven. Monday at St. Marv-Awke, Kendal, Hounſlow,
Southcove, Stokeſly, Criſwel, Raiſy, Spiſby. Uſk, VVatſord,
Tunbridge, Vizes. Tueſday at Abergiveony, Radner. VVed-
neſday at Aberſcow. Corpus Chriſti at St. Agnes, Banbury,
Biſhop-ſtratford, Bremingham, Carewid, Egleſrev, Ballron,
Haligh, Kidderminſter, Llanwiſt, Llanimerhen ſt, Neath,
Newport in Monmouthſhire, Preſcot, St. Eedes, Stamford,
Stopport, Newbury, Hemſted, Roſs. Friday after at Coventry,
Chepſtow in Monmouthſhire. Monday after at Belton, Stam-
ford. Monday after July 3 at Haveril. Monday fortnight after
Midſummer at Foddringhay. Monday after Bartholomew at
Sanbich in Cheſh. Monday after St. michael at Ea ly, St.
Faiths by Norwich. St. michels. Tueſday at Saliſbury. Thurſ-
day at Banbury. monday fortnight after VVhitſunday, at Darn-
ton, and every monday fortnight after until Chriſtmas. The
Friday before Simon and Jude at Litchfield.

ADVERTISEMENTS.

THat I may do all the good I can, I Publish this to the World, that I have Excellent Remedies for all Women troubled with Vapours, Rising of the Mother, Convulsion fits; to the Canker in the Mouth, with so much ease, that the Patient will hardly feel it; and all other Diseases incident to my own Sex. *Mary Holden.*

1. SAlmon's Select Physical and Chyrurgical Observations, containing divers Remarkable Histories of Cures done by several famous Physitians, above 700 Eminent Cures.

2. Also *Salmon's* Systema Medicinale, a Compl. System of Physick, containing the Method of Curing all the principal Diseases happening to the Bodies of *Men*, Women, and Children, Translated out of Latin into English, out of the most learned *J. Dolæus.*

3. *Salmon's* Polygraphice, or the Art of Drawing, Engraving, Etching, Limning, Painting, Washing, Varnishing, Guilding, Colouring, Dying, Beautifying, and Perfuming; in Seven Books, exemplified in the Drawing Women, Landskips, Countries and Figures of various forms: To which also is added many Chymical Secrets fit for publick or private uses. All Three Printed for *Tho. Passinger* at the three Bibles in *London-bridge.*

Mary Holden's *The Womans Almanack: Or, An Ephemerides for the Year of Our Lord, 1689* (Wing 1827A) is reprinted from the copy at the Folger Library (Shelfmark 1827A). The text block of the Folger copy is 75×135 mm.

For passages that are blotched, please consult Appendix B, 'A Key to Difficult-to-Read Passages'.

THE
Womans ALMANACK:
OR
An EPHEMERIDES

For the Year of Our LORD, 1689.
Being the First after Biſſextile, or Leap-Year,
And from the Creation of the World, 5638.
Wherein is Contained (beſides the State of the YEAR)
the Solar Ingreſſes, Various Configurations, Aſpeds,
Conjunctions, and Diurnal Motions of the Planets.
With the Riſing and Setting of the Sun; With other
Neceſſaries that may conduce to the compleating ſuch a
Work; Alſo the time of High-Water at *London-Bridge*.
With the Moons Age: Calculated for the Meridian of
LONDON, whoſe Latitude is 51 Degrees, 32 Minutes,
and may ſerve for any other part of *ENGLAND*

By MARY HOLDEN, *Midwife in Sudbury*, *and Student
in Phyſick and Aſtrology.*

London, Printed by *J. Millet*, for the Company of
STATIONERS, 1689.

Julian			the Roman Account
	18	The Golden Number	18.
	F	The Dominical letter	B
	8	The Epact.	8
		The Cycle of the *Sun*	18
Feb.	10	Shrove Sunday.	Feb.	20
March	31	Easter-Day.	April	10
May	9	Ascension-Day,	May	19
May	9	Whit-Sunday.	May	27
May	26	Trinity-Sunday.	June	5
December	1	Advent-Sunday.	Decemb.	11

The Anatomy of Mans Body.

♉	♊
Neck & Throat	Arms & Shoul.
♋	♌
Breast & Stom.	Heart and Back
♍	♎
Bowels & Belly	Reins & Loyns
♏	♐
Secret members	The Thighs.
♑	♒
the Knees	The Legs
♓ The Feet	

The Most Material Aspects, with Characters of the Planets.

☌ Conjuction.	when	1	0	♄ Cold and moist.
⚹ Sextile.	Planet	2	60	♃ Hot and moist.
☐ Quartile.	is di-	3	90	♂ Hot and dry.
△ Trine.	stant	4 signs	120 de-	☉ Hot temperate.
☍ Opposition.	from	6 or	180 grees	♀ Cold temperate.
☊ Dragons head	ano-			♀ Cold and dry.
☋ Dragonstail.	ther.			☽ Cold and moist.

A Table of the 4 Terms, and their Returns, for this present Year, 1689.

Hillary Term begins January 23, ends February 13.

Return or essoyn Days.	Exception.	Return. brev.		Appearance.
Octab. Hill. Jan. 20	Iana 21 Jan.	22 Jan.		23
Quind. Hill. Jan. 27	Ian. 28 Jan.	29 Jan.		30
Craft. Purif. Feb.	Febr. 4 Feb.	5 Feb.		6
Octab. Purif. Feb. 9	Febr. 10 Feb.	11 Feb.		12

Easter Term begins April 17, ends May 13.

Quind. Pasch. Apr. 15	Apr. 15	Apr. 16	Apr.	15
Tres. Pasch. Apr. 22	Apr. 22	Apr. 23	Apr.	24
Mens. Pasch. Apr. 29	Apr. 29	Apr. 30	May	1
Quinq. Pasch. May 6	May 6	May 7	May	8
Craft. Ascen. May 10	May 11	May 13	May	13

Trinity Term begins May 31, ends June 19.

Craft. Trin. May 20	May 28	May 29	May	31
Octab. Trin. June 3	June 3	June 4	June	5
Quind. Trin. June 11	June 11	June 12	June	13
Tres. Trin. June 18	June 18	June 19	June	20

Michaelmas Term begins October 23, ends November 28.

Tres. Mich. October 20	Octob. 21	Octob. 22	Octob.	23
Mens. Mich. October 27	Octob. 28	Octob. 29	Octob.	30
Craft. Anim. November 3	Nov. 4	Nov. 5	Nov.	6
Craft. Mart. November 12	Nov. 13	Nov. 15	Nov.	
Octab. Mart. November 19	Nov. 20	Nov. 20	Nov.	21
Quind. Mart. November 26	Nov. 27	Nov. 28	Nov.	30

Note, that the Exchequer openeth 8 days before any Term begins, except the Term of Trinity, in which it openeth but 4 days before.

Note also, that the bright Planet *Venus*, will be our Glorious Evening Star till the 13th. of *June*; And then making her Conjunction with the Sun, She is our bright Morning Star to the end of the year.

A Table whereby may be known the Moons age
every day this year, 1689, by help whereof may
be found the time of full Sea at London bridge

Day	January	February	March	April	May	June	July	August	September	October	November	December
1	23	21	20	21	24	25	24	25	27	2d	29	
2	21	22	21	22	23	24	25	27	23	29	30	
3	22	23	22	23	2	25	26	28	29	30		
4	23	24	23	24	25	26	27	29	1		2	3
5	24	25	24	25	25	27	28	1	2	2	7	3
6	25	26	25	26	27	28	29	1	2	3	3	4
7	26	27	26	27	28	29	1	2	3	4	4	5
8	27	28	27	28	29	1	2	3	5	5	6	
9	28	29	28	29	30	2	3	4	6	7	18	
10	29	1	29	1	1	3	4	5	7	7	8	9
11	30	2	30	2	2	4	5	6	8	8	9	10
12	1	3	1	3	3	5	6	7	9	9	10	11
13	2	4	2	4	4	6	7	8	10	10	11	12
14	3	5	3	5	5	7	8	9	11	11	12	13
15	4	6	4	6	6	8	9	13	12	12	13	14
16	5	7	5	7	7	9	10	11	13	13	14	
17	6	8	6	8	9	10	11	12	14	14	15	
18	7	9	7	9	9	11	12	13	15	15	16	
19	8	10	8	10	10	12	13	14	16	16	17	18
20	9	11	9	11	11	13	14	15	17	17	18	19
21	10	12	10	12	12	14	15	16	18	18	19	20
22	11	13	11	13	13	15	16	17	19	19	20	21
23	12	14	12	14	14	16	17	18	20	20	21	22
24	13	15	13	15	15	17	18	19	1	21	22	
25	14	16	14	15	16	13	19	20	22	22	23	24
26	15	17	15	17	17	19	20	21	23	23	24	
27	16	18	16	18	18	20	21	22	24	24	25	26
28	17	19	17	19	19	21	22	23	25	25	26	
29	18		18	20	20	22	23	24	26	26	27	28
30	19		19	21	21	23	24	25	27	27	28	
31	20		20		22		25	26		28		

January hath XXXI Days.

account English

Last Quarter the 3 Day, at 1 in the Afternoon.
New Moon the 11 Day, at 10 in the morning.
First Quarter the 18 Day, at 8 in the morning.
Full Moon the 2[illegible] Day, at 10 in the morning.

[illegible]		Saints Days	☉	♑	☽	♍	Lunar Aspects & W.		
1	a	Circumcision	22	5		25	☌♃☾. ☌♀☾.		1
2	b	Adler. Ab	23	10	♎	11	The Year	15	[illegible] 1
3	c	Melior. M.	24	11		2	□☉☾. △♀☾		[illegible] 1
4	d	Chrom. Mo.	25	12	♏	5	⚹♄☾. □♃☾. ⚹♄☾		1
5	e	Ed. K. Conf.	26	14		17	⚹☉☾. begins with		1
6	f	Epip.	27	15		29	⚹♃☾. □♀☾ as		[illegible]
7	g	Ced. B. Lon.	28	16	♐	11	⚹♂☾. strange un-		1
8	A	Will. B. Yor.	29	17		2[illegible]	⚹[illegible]☾. ⚹♀☾		1
9	b	Adrin	0 ♒	18	♑	[illegible]	⚹ ☾. settled wea-		1
10	c	Sechred V.	1	19		1	☌☉☾. □♄☾.		2
11	d	Hyginus	2	20	♒	[illegible]	⚹♃☾. ⚹♂☾.		2
12	e	Benedict.	3	21		1	Now Snow,		2
13	f	1 past Epip.	4	22	♓	[illegible]	△♄☾. ☍♀☾. or		2
14	g	Hillary	5	23		1[illegible]	□♂☾. ⚹[illegible]☾. Sleet.		2
15	A	S. P. Maurus	6	24		28	[illegible]☉☾. ⚹♃☾.		2
16	b	Mar. P. M.	7	25	♈	1[illegible]	△♂☾. [illegible]☾.		2
17	c	Anthony	8	2[illegible]		2[illegible]	⚹♀☾. Right winter		2
18	d	Chair S. Pet.	9	27	♉	11	△♄☾. weather		2
19	e	VVolstan	10	28		25	△☉☾. △♃☾. ☌♂		2
20	f	2 past Epip.	11	29	♊	1[illegible]	△♄☾. with □♀☾		3
21	g	S. Agnes	12	30		2[illegible]			[illegible]
22	A	Vincent	13	31	♋	7	△♀☾. wind		[illegible]
23	b	Term begins	14	31		2	☍☉☾. □♄☾. ☌♃		[illegible]
24	c	Timothy	15	32	♌	[illegible]	△♂☾. and ☍♀☾		4
25	d	Conv. S. Paul	16	32		1[illegible]	⚹♄☾. trouble		[illegible] 5
26	e	Pollicarp.	17	33	♍	[illegible]	Air.		[illegible] 6
27	f	Septuagesima	18	34		1	□♂☾. ☍[illegible]☾.		[illegible]
28	g	Agnes App.	19	35		25	△♃☾. △[illegible]☾.		[illegible]
29	A	Gildus Ab.	20	36	♎	7	△☉☾. ⚹♂☾.	8	[illegible]
30	b	Martina	21	37		1[illegible]	☌♄☾. □♃☾.	9	[illegible]
31	c	Adamnan.	22	38	♏	1			[illegible]

February hath XXVIII Days.

English account.

Last Quarter the 2 Day, at 11 in the morning
New Moon the 9 Day, at 11 at Night
First Quarter the 16 Day, at 5 at night
Full Moon the 24 Day, at 2 in the morning.

Roman account.

		Saints Days	☉	♒	☾	m	Lunar Aspects & Wea.	
1	d	St. Bridget	23	39		13	☌⊙☾. ☌♄☾. □☿☾.	11
2	e	Purif. V. M.	24	40		25	△♀☾. mix'd	12
3	f	Sexagesima	25	40	♐	7	✱♃☾. weather,	13
4	g	Gilbert Conf.	26	41		19	✱⊙☾. ✱☿☾. cold.	14
5	a	Agatha V.	27	42	♑	1	✱♄☾. ☌[illegible]☾. □♀☾.	15
6	b	Dorothy V.M	28	4[illegible]		1[illegible]	dark, with high winds,	16
7	c	Richard K.	29	42		27	□♄☾. ✱☿☾.	17
8	d	Edelf Abbeſs	0 ♓	43	♒	11	⚺♃☾. inclining to	18
9	e	Apollo V. M.	1	43		25	⚺⊙☾. △♄☾. ⚺☿☾.	19
10	f	Shrove Sund.	2	44	♓	9	✱♂☾. Froſt;	20
11	g	Schollaſti V.	3	44		24	□♂☾.	21
12	a	Ethelrald B.	4	44	♈	8	✱♃☾. ⚺♀☾.	22
13	b	Aſh W. Tet. c.	5	45		23	✱⊙☾. ☍♄☾. very	23
14	c	Valentine	6	45	♉	7	□♃☾. △♂☾. ✱☿☾.	24
15	d	Fauſtin M.	7	45		22	changeable weather,	25
16	e	Lancon B.	8	45	♊	6	□⊙☾. △♃☾. □☿☾.	26
17	f	Quadrageſima	9	46		19		27
18	g	Simeon B.	10	46	♋	3	△⊙☾. △♃☾. ☍♂☾.	28
19	a	Acca B.	11	46		17	□♀☾. △♀☾. to'ard	Mar.
20	b	Ember Week	12	46	♌	0	□♄☾. the end	2
21	c	Lubret V.	13	46		13	☍♃☾. of the month.	3
22	d	hair of s.p.a.	14	45		26	✱ ☾. △♀☾.	4
23	e	Malburg V.	15	46	♍	9	☍⊙☾. △♂☾.	5
24	f	St. Matthias	16	46		21	☍☿☾.	6
25	g	Fulkus Abb.	17	46	♎	3		7
26	a	John B.	18	45		15	△♃☾. □♂☾.	8
27	b	Sexolph F.	19	45		27	⚺♄☾. ⚺♀☾.	9
28	c	Oswald B. Y.	20	45	♏	9	∠⊙☾. □♃☾. ✱♂☾.	10

March hath XXXI Days.

Last Quarter the 4 Day, 7 at Night.
New Moon the 16 Day, at 9 morning.
First Quarter the 18 Day, 1 in the morning
Full Moon the 25 Day, at 6 at night

Day		Saints Days	☉		☽		Lunar Aspects & W.	Roman Account
1	d	S. David	21	45		21	☌☉☾. ☌☾.	11
2	e	Chad, B.	22	45	♐	14	△☉☾ Very dark	12
3	f	*3 Sund. Lent*	23	45		14	□☉☾. ✶♃☾. Clouds	13
4	g	Cassimirus	24	44		24	✶♄☾. △♀☾. and	14
5	A	Piran B.	25	44	♑	5	□☾. likely	15
6	b	Fridolin	26	43		40	✶♀☾. □♄☾. ☌♂☾.	16
7	c	S. *Tho.* of *Aq.*	27	43	♒	53	□☿☾. ✶☿☾. to	17
8	d	Perpetua	28	42		34	☌♃☾. Snow;	18
9	e	Francisca	29	42	♓	41	△♄☾ ✶♀☾.	19
10	f	*4 Sund. Lent*	30	♈ 41		9	☌☉☾. ✶♂☾.	20
11	g	Oswin K.	1	41	♈	2	☌☿☾. toward the	21
12	A	St. Gregory	2	40		56	✶♃☾. □♂☾	22
13	b	Vigan Monk	3	39	♉	52	☍♄☾. middle	23
14	c	Geonulph K.	4	38		36	□♃☾. ☌♀☾. good	24
15	d	Aristobul.	5	37	♊	17	✶☉☾ △♂☾. Wea-	25
16	e	Alrede Ab.	6	36		33	△♃☾ ✶☿☾. ther	26
17	f	*5 Sund. Lent*	7	35	♋	29	□☿☾ △♄☾. with	27
18	g	Edw. K. & M.	8	35		4	✶♀☾. □☿☾. gentle	28
19	A	S. Joseph.	9	34		25	□♄☾. ☍♂☾. showrs	29
20	b	Joachim	10	33	♌	9	△☉☾. ☍♃☾. △☿☾.	30
21	c	Benedick	11	32		5	☾. □♀☾.	31
22	d	Ord. of S. Ben.	12	31	♍	42	Storms and	Apr.
23	e	Egbert K.	13	30		2	△♀☾. Wind,	2
24	f	*Palm Sunday*	14	29	♎	14	△♂☾. ☍☿☾.	3
25	g	Annun. B. V.	15	27		18	☍☉☾. △♃☾.	4
26	A	S. William	16	26		16	☌♄☾.	5
27	b	Archibald	17	25	♏	0	□♂☾. wind and	6
28	c	Fremund K.	18	24		0	□♃☾. Rain.	7
29	d	Baldred	19	23		52	✶♂☾. ☍♀☾. △☿☾.	8
30	e	Patron	20	22	♐	47	△☉☾.	9
31	f	Easter-Day	21	21		49	✶♄☾. ✶♃☾.	10

April hath XXX Days.

Last quarter the 2 Day, at 10 at Night
New Moon the 9 Day, at 7 at Night
First quarter the 16 Day, at Noon
Full Moon the 24 Day, at Noon.

		Saints Days	☉ ♈		☽		Lunar aspects and W.	Roman account
1	g	[illegible] M. Mag	22	2		0	[illegible] ♄ ☾ . □ ☿ ☾ . The	11
2	a	Francis Conf.	23	16		18	□ ☉ ☾ . Moon [illegible]	12
3	b	Richard B.	24	1	♒	1	□ ♄ ☾ . ☌ ♂ ☾ . △ ♀	13
4	c	Guir Priest	25	15		14	[illegible] ☉ ☾ . [illegible] ♃ ☾ begins	14
5	d	Vincent Conf.	26	1		28	△ ♄ ☾ . with mod'rate	15
6	e	Eisseld K.	27	12	♓	11	□ ♀ ☾ . weather	16
7	f	Low Sunday	28	4		26	[illegible] ♀ ☾ . and gentle	17
8	g	Dusianus	29	5	♈	11	✱ ♂ ☾ . ✱ ☿ ☾ [illegible]	18
9	a	Tristan B.	0 ♉	8		26	[illegible] ☉ ☾ . ☍ ♄ ☾ . ✱ ♃ ☾	19
10	b	Eschilus B.	1	6	♉	11	□ ♂ ☾ . Showers	20
11	c	Leo Pope	2	4		25	□ ♃ ☾ . ✱ ♀ ☾ [illegible]	21
12	d	Hugh B.	3	3	♊	11	△ ♂ ☾ . ☌ ☿ ☾ . □ ♀ ☾	22
13	e	Hermenegi	4	1		25	✱ ☾ [illegible] ☾ . △ ♄ ☾ . △ ♃ ☾	23
14	f	2 past Easter	5	59	♋	1	Storms those	24
15	g	Tra. S. Osw. B	6	57		24	□ ♄ ☾ . Days, perhaps	25
16	a	Anicetus, P.	7	55	♌	7	□ ☉ ☾ . △ ☿ ☾ . some	26
17	b	Term begins	8	54		2[illegible]	☍ ♃ ☾ . ☍ ♂ ☾ . ✱ ♀ ☾	27
18	c	Oswin Monk	9	52	♍	2	△ ☉ . ✱ ♄ ☾ [illegible]	28
19	d	Elphege, B.	10	50		15	□ ♀ ☾ . Frosts, but	29
20	e	Gealwald K	11	48		27	not to hurt	30
21	f	3 past Easter	12	45	♎	[illegible]	☍ ♀ ☾ . the Spring	May.
22	g	Soter & Cajus	13	44		21	[illegible] ☾ . △ ♃ ☾ . △ ♂ ☾	[illegible]
23	a	St. George	14 ☉	42	♏	3	△ ☿ ☾	[illegible]
24	b	Melitus	15	40		1[illegible]	☍ ☉ ☾ . [illegible]	[illegible]
25	c	S. Mark Evan.	16	37		26	□ ♃ ☾ . □ ♂ ☾ [illegible]	[illegible]
26	d	Cletus P.	17	35	♐	8	Clouds ☌ ♀ ☾ . △ ☿ ☾ .	[illegible]
27	e	Vital. [illegible] V.	18	33		2[illegible]	✱ ♄ ☾ . ✱ ♃ ☾ . ✱ ♂ ☾	[illegible]
28	f	4 past Easter	19	31	♑	2	and Rain.	[illegible]
29	g	Peter Mart.	20	29		15	△ ☉ ☾ . □ ♀ ☾ .	[illegible]
30	a	Katherine Siena	21 ♀	26	♒	27		[illegible]

May hath XXXI Days.

Laſt quarter the 2 Day, at 10 in the morning.
New Moon the 9 Day, at 2 in the morning.
Firſt quarter the 15 Day, at 12 at Night.
Full Moon the 24 Day, at 2 in the morning.
Laſt quarter the 31 Day, at Noon.

		Saints Days	☉	♉	☽		Lunar Aſpects & W.	
1	b	S. Phil. & Jac.	21	24		10	□☉☾. Winds,	11
2	c	Athanaſius	22	21		23	△♄☾. [illegible]♃☾.☌♂♀	12
3	d	Invent. ✠	23	19	♓	6	with Clouds	13
4	e	Monica.	24	17		20	⚹☉☾. and ſhowers	14
5	f	4 paſt Eaſter	25	15	♈	4	□♀☾. of Rain,	15
6	g	Rogat. Mond.	25	12		19	☌♄☾. ⚹♃☾. and	16
7	A	Staniſlaus	27	10	♉	4	⚹♂☾. ⚹♀☾. ☌♀☾	17
8	b	Micha. Ap.	28	7		19	☌☉☾. □♃☾. thunder	18
9	c	Aſcenſion	29	5	♊	5	□♂☾. in many	19
10	d	Gordian	0 ♊	2		20	△♄☾. △♃☾. places.	20
11	e	Freemund K.	0	59	♋	5	△♂☾. ☍♀☾. ⚹☿☾	21
12	f	5 paſt Eaſter	1	57		19	⚹☉☾. □♄☾.	22
13	g	Term ends	2	55	♌	3	Now temperate	23
14	A	Boniface	3	52		16	and ſeaſonable	24
15	b	Olympn. V.	4	50		29	□☉☾. ⚹♄☾. ☌♃☾	25
16	c	Ubaldus B.	5	47	♍	11	☍♂☾. weather.	26
17	d	Reſtitut. M.	6	44		24	△☿☾.	27
18	e	[illegible]cival B.	7	42	♎	6	△☉☾. □♀☾.	28
19	f	VVhit-Sund.	8	39		18	Something	29
20	g	Ethalbert B.	9	36		29	☌♄☾. △♃☾. △♀	30
21	A	Godrick Erm.	10	33	♏	11	△♂☾. windy,	31
22	b	Ember VVeek	11	31		23	□♃☾.	June
23	c	Will. Roche.	12	28	♐	5	☍☉☾. ☍☿☾.	2
24	d	Joan VVidow	13	25		17	□♂☾. likely	3
25	e	Urban	14	22		29	⚹♄☾. ⚹♃☾. ☍♀☾.	4
26	f	Trinity Sund.	15	20	♑	12	⚹♂☾. to Thunder	5
27	g	Bede Prieſt	16	17		24	□♄☾. In many	6
28	A	Jonas Ab.	17	14	♒	7	△☉☾. places.	7
29	b	Burin V.	18			20	△♄☾. ☌♃☾. △☿☾	8
30	c	Felix	19	8	♓	3	△♀☾.	9
31	d	Term begins	20	6		15	□☉☾. ☌♂☾. □☿☾	10

June hath XXX Days.

English account. | New Moon the 7 Day, at 8 in the morning. First Quarter the 13 Day, at 1 in the afternoon. Full Moon the 22 Day, at 4 in the afternoon. Last Quarter the 3d Day, at 1 in the morning. | Roman account.

		Saints Days	☉	II	☽ ♈		Lunar aspects, and W.	
1	C	Pamph. M.	21	3		(	□ ☾	11
2	F	1 past Trinity	22	0		14	⚹☉☾ (⚹♄☾.	12
3	G	Eluthe Erm.	22	57		28	☍♄☾.⚹♃☾.⚹♀☾	13
4	A	Petroch B.	23	54	♉	13	⚹♂☾ Clouds and	14
5	b	Boniface B.	24	51		28	□♃☾. Rain,	15
6	C	Norbet B.	25	48	♊	13	⚹☉☾.□♂☾.	16
7	D	Rob. Abbot	26	45		28	△♄☾.△♃☾.☌♀☾	17
8	E	William B.	27	43	♋	13	(☌☿☾.	18
9	F	2 past Trinity	28	40		27	□♄☾.△♂☾.	19
10	G	Margaret Q.	29	37	♌	11	Thunder and	20
11	A	Barnaby	0♋	34		25	⚹☉☾.⚹♄☾.☍♃.	21
12	b	Basilides	1	31	♍	8	Lightning, (⚹♀☾	22
13	C	Anthony	2	28		21	□☉☾.⚹☿☾.	23
14	D	Corpus Chri.	3	25	♎	2	☍♂☾.□♀☾.	24
15	E	Vitus	4	22		14	□☿☾. Variable	25
16	F	3 past Trinit.	5	21		26	△☉☾.☌♄☾.△♃☾.	26
17	G	Botolph Ab.	6	16	♏	8	weather to (△♀☾.	27
18	A	Mace, and M.	7	13		20	□♃☾.△☿☾.	28
19	b	Term Ends	8	10	♐	2	△♂☾. the Months	29
20	C	Edw. K.	9	7		14	End.	30
21	D	Alban M.	10	4		26	⚹♄☾.⚹♃☾.□♂☾	July 1
22	E	Alchatius	11	1	♑	8	☍☉☾ (□♀☾	2
23	F	4 past Trinity	11	58		21	□♄☾	3
24	G	S. John Bap.	12	56	♓	4	⚹♂☾.☍☿☾.	4
25	A	Amphibalus	13	53		16	△♄☾.△♀☾.	5
26	b	John and Paul	14	50	♓	0	☍♃☾.	6
27	C	Levine B.	15	47		12	△☉☾.□♀☾,	7
28	D	Leo Pope	16	44		26		8
29	E	S. Pet. & Paul	17	41	♈	10	□☉☾.☌♂☾.△☿☾	9
30	F	5 past Trinit.	18	38		24	☍♄☾.⚹♃☾.⚹♀☾.	10

July hath XXXI Days.

English account | Roman account

New Moon the 6 Day, at 6 at Night
First quarter the 14 Day, at 1 in the morning
Full Moon the 22 Day, at 4 in the morning
Last quarter the 29 Day, at 6 in the morning.

		Saints Days	☉	[illegible]	☾ ♉	Lunar aspects and W.	
1	g	Roind. B.	19	35	8	✱☉☾.□♀☾.	11
2	a	Visit. V. M.	20	32	27	□♃☾. Fair and	12
3	b	Cornelius	21	29	♊ 7	✱♂☾.✱☿☾.plesant	13
4	c	Eliz. Widdow	22	27	22	△♄☾.△♃☾.☍♀☾	14
5	d	Mudween	23	24	♋ 7	□♂☾. weather,	15
6	e	Sexburg Q.	24	21	21	☌☉☾.□♄☾. but	16
7	F	5 past Trinity	25	18	♌ 5	△♂☾.Clouds ☌☿☾.	17
8	g	Grimbald	26	15	19	✱♄☾.☍♃☾.✱☿☾.	18
9	a	Edleb Q.	27	12	♍ 3	fair, sometimes	19
10	b	7 Brethren	28	10	16	□♀☾. likely to	20
11	c	Pius Pope	29	7	28	✱☉☾. thunder, with	21
12	d	Nabor	0 ♌	4	♎ 10	☍♂☾. Showers.	22
13	e	Anac. P. M.	1	1	22	□☉☾.☌♄☾.△♃☾.	23
14	F	7 past Trin.	1	58	♏ 4	heat prevails, △♀☾.	24
15	g	Swithen B.	2	56	16	□☿☾.	25
16	a	Osm B.	3	53	28	△☉☾.□♃☾.	26
17	b	Kenelm B.	4	50	♐ 10	Glorious Weather,	27
18	c	Ared. B. M.	5	47	22	✱♄☾.✱♃☾.△♂☾.	28
19	d	Dog days beg	6	45	♑ 4	Now Clouds	29
20	e	S. Marg. V.	7	42	17	□♃☾.□♂☾: and	39
21	F	8 past Trin.	8	40	♒ 0	☍☉☾.□♄☾.	31
22	g	Mary Mag.	9	37	13	☍♀☾. Showers	Aug.
23	a	Apolinares	10	36	26	△♄☾.☌♃☾.✱♂☾	2
24	b	Fast.	11	34	♓ 9	of Rain. △♀☾.	3
25	c	S. James	12	32	32	□♀☾.	4
26	d	Anne M. V. M	13	29	♈ 7	△☉☾ △☿☾. ✱♀☾	5
27	e	Joseph Arem.	14	27	21	☍♄☾.✱♃☾.☌♂☾.	6
28	F	9 past Trin.	15	24	♉ 5	□☉☾.□♀☾.	7
29	g	Martha V.	16	21	19	□♃☾.	8
30	a	Abdon & C.	17	19	♊ 3	✱♀☾. ✱♂☾	9
31	b	Ignatius	18	17	17	✱☉☾.△♄☾.△♃☾	10

August hath XXXI Days.

New Moon the 3 Day, at 3 in the morning.
First Quarter the 12 Day, at 11 at Night.
Full Moon the 20 Day, at 4 in the afternoon.
Last Quarter the 27 Day, at Noon.

English Account		Saints Days	☉ ♌		☽ ♋		Lunar Aspects & W.	Roman Account
1	c	Peter ad Vinc	19	12		1	△ ♄ ☾. ☌ ♀ ☾. Showr	11
2	d	Stephen P. & M.	20	9		16	□ ♂ ☾. Fair	12
3	e	Invent. S. Step.	21	7	♌	0	□ ♄ ☾. ☌ ☿ ☾ [illegible] Ver	13
4	f	10 past Trini.	22	5		14	☌ ☉ ☾. ☍ ♃ ☾. hot	14
5	g	B. Lady ad In.	23	2		27	✶ ♄ ☾. [illegible]	15
6	a	Transf. our L.	23	51	♍	10	Thunder and	16
7	b	Donatus B. M.	24	57		23	Lightning;	17
8	c	Cyrius Largus	25	55	♎	6	□ ♀ ☾. ✶ ☿ ☾.	18
9	d	Hugh B. Ely	26	53		18	✶ ☉ ☾. △ ♃ ☾	19
10	e	Laurence, M.	27	51	♏	0	☌ ♄ ☾. ☍ ♂ ☾. □ ☿ ☾	20
11	f	11 past Trin.	28	49		12	△ ♀ ☾. Clouds, and	21
12	g	Clare Virgin	29	47		24	□ ☉ ☾. □ ♃ ☾ some	22
13	a	Hypol. & Cassi.	0 ♍	45	♐	6	△ ☿ ☾. Showers.	23
14	b	Usibius Conf.	1	43		18	✶ ♃ ☾.	24
15	c	Assum. B. V.	2	41	♑	0	△ ☉ ☾. ✶ ♄ ☾ △ ♂ ☾	25
16	d	Thomas Mon.	3	39		12	☍ ♀ ☾. Heat and	26
17	e	Tho. of Hartf.	4	37		25	☌ ♃ ☾ □ ♂ ☾. Lightn-	27
18	f	12 past Trin.	5	35	♒	8	☍ ☿ ☾. (ing	28
19	g	Clintank K. M.	6	33		21	△ ♄ ☾. ☍ ♃ ☾	29
20	a	Barnard Abb	7	31	♓	5	☍ ☉ ☾. ✶ ♂ ☾	30
21	b	Rich. of St. An.	8	29		19	△ ♀ ☾. brisk winds	31
22	c	Tim & his Fe.	9	27	♈	3	and Clouds to the	Sept.
23	d	Justinia. Mon.	10	25		17	✶ ♃ ☾. □ ♀ ☾. △ ☿ ☾	2
24	e	St. Bartholme.	11	24	♉	1	△ ☉ ☾. ☍ ♄ ☾. ☌ ♂ ☾	3
25	f	13 past Trin.	12	22		15	□ ♃ ☾. ✶ ♀ ☾. □ ☿ ☾	4
26	g	Zepherine Po.	13	21	♊	0	[illegible] nchs end.	5
27	a	Dog days ende	14	19		14	□ ☉ ☾. △ ♃ ☾	6
28	b	Austine B.	15	17		28	△ ♄ ☾. ✶ ♂ ☾. ✶ ☿ ☾	7
29	c	Decol. of Joh. B.	16	15	♋	12	✶ ☉ ☾.	8
30	d	Felix	17	14		26	□ ♄ ☾. ☌ ♀ ☾.	9
31	e	Adrin B. Conf.	18	12	♌	5	□ ♂ ☾.	[illegible]

September hath XXX Days.

English account | Roman account

New Moon the 2 Day, at 4 in the afternoon.
First quarter the 11 Day, at 5 in the afternoon.
Full Moon the 19 Day, at 2 in the morning.
Last quarter the 25 Day at 7 at Night.

		Saints Days	☉	♍	☽	♌	Lunar Aspects & W		
1	f	14 past Trin.	19	11		3	♄ ☾. ☍ ♃ ☾.	[illegible]	11
2	g	Adam Ab.	20	5	♍	[illegible]	△ ♂ ☾. ☌ ☿ ☾. Cold	[illegible]	12
3	A	Foillan B.	21	6		19	☌ ☉ ☾. [illegible]	[illegible]	13
4	b	Transl. S. Cut.	22	6	♎	2	⚹ ♀ ☾. some hasty	[illegible]	14
5	c	Altho. Abbot	23	5		14	[illegible] ☾. △ ♃ ☾.	[illegible]	15
6	d	Bega V.	24	4		26	☍ ♂ ☾. showers	[illegible]	16
7	e	Transl. S. Dun.	25	2	♏	8	□ ☿ ☾. of hail	[illegible]	17
8	f	15 past Trin.	26	1		20	⚹ ☉ ☾. □ ♃ ☾. ⚹ ☿ ☾.	[illegible]	18
9	g	Gorgonus M.	27	59	♐	2	△ [illegible] ☾. or Rain.	[illegible]	19
10	A	Nicholas Con	28	58		14	⚹ ♃ ☾.	[illegible]	20
11	b	Protus	29	57		26	□ ☉ ☾. ⚹ ♄ ☾. △ ♂ ☾.	[illegible]	21
12	c	Eansured. Abb.	30 ♎	56	♑	8	High winds or	[illegible]	22
13	d	Werenfri.	1	54		20	△ ☉ ☾. storms,	[illegible]	23
14	e	Exalt. ✠	2	53	♒	3	□ [illegible] ☾. □ ♂ ☾. △ ☿ ☾.	[illegible]	24
15	f	16 past Trin.	3	52		16	♃ ☾. ☍ ♀ ☾.	[illegible]	25
16	g	Corne. & Cyp.	4	54		29	△ ♄ ☾. ⚹ ♂ ☾.	[illegible]	26
17	A	Steph. & Socr	5	51	♓	13	fair weather.	[illegible]	27
18	b	Ember Week	6	50		27	☍ ☉ ☾.	[illegible]	28
19	c	Januar. B. M	7	49	♈	12	⚹ ♃ ☾. △ ♀ ☾. ☍ ☿ ☾.	[illegible]	29
20	d	Eustra. Mart.	8	48		27	☍ ♄ ☾. ☍ ♂ ☾.	[illegible]	30
21	e	S. Matthew	9	47	♉	11	□ ♄ ☾. □ ☿ ☾.	[illegible]	Octo.
22	f	17 past Trin.	10	47		16	Now Turbulent.	[illegible]	2
23	g	Tecla, V. M.	11	45	♊	10	△ ☉ ☾. △ ♃ ☾. △ ♄ ☾.	[illegible]	3
24	A	Winbald. A.	12	45		25	△ ♃ ☾. ⚹ ♂ ☾. ⚹ ☿ ☾.	[illegible]	4
25	b	Geofrig. Ab	13	45	♋	9	□ ☉ ☾. dark with rain.	[illegible]	5
26	c	Cyprian	14	44		22	□ ♄ ☾. □ ♂ ☾. □ ☿ ☾.	[illegible]	6
27	d	Cosmas	15	44	♌	6	⚹ ☉ ☾. fair weather,	[illegible]	7
28	e	Lioba Abbes	16	43		19	☍ ♃ ☾. ⚹ ☿ ☾. windy.	[illegible]	8
29	f	S. Michael	17	43	♍	2	⚹ ♄ ☾. △ ♂ ☾. ☍ ♀ ☾.	[illegible]	9
30	g	Jerom Abbes	17	43		15	[illegible]	[illegible]	10

October hath XXXI Days.

English account.	New Moon the 3 Day, at 8 in the morning First quarter the 11 Day, at Noon Full Moon the 18 Day, at 1 in the afternoon Last quarter the 25 Day, at 4 in the morning.	Roman account.

		Saints Days	☉ ♎		☾ ♍		Lunar aspects, and W.	
1	A	Remigius	18	42		28	Hight Winds and	11
2	b	Thomas Bi	19	42	♎	10	△♃☾. Clouds,	12
3	c	Gerard	21	42		22	☌☉☾.☌♂☾.	13
4	d	Francis Conf.	21	41	♏	5	⚺♄☾.✶♀☾.☌☿☾	14
5	e	Placid	22	41		17	□♃☾.	15
6	f	19 past Trin.	23	41		28	Snow, or Rain,	16
7	g	Mark P.	24	40	♐	10	✶♃☾.□♀☾.	17
8	A	Bridget Wid.	25	40		22	✶☉☾.△♂☾.	18
9	b	Dennis	26	40		4	✶♄☾ △♀☾.✶☿☾	19
10	c	Paulin B. Yo.	27	40	♑	16	Warm,	20
11	d	Edelburg Ab.	28	40		28	□☉☾.□♄☾.□♂☾.	21
12	e	Willford *b. yo*	29	40	♒	11	☌♃☾.□☿☾.	22
13	f	20 past Trin.	o♏	40		24	△☉☾.✶♂☾.	23
14	g	Calistus pope	1	40	♓	7	△♄☾. consid'ring the	24
15	A	Terisia V.	2	40		21	☍♀☾.△☿☾.	25
16	b	Lullus *b. mentz*	3	40	♈	4	Season;	26
17	c	Transl. S. Audr.	4	40		26	✶♃☾.☌♂☾.	27
18	d	S. Luke	5	40	♉	5	☍☉☾.☍♄☾.	28
19	e	Fridiswide V.	6	41		20	□♃☾.△♀☾.☍☿☾.	29
20	f	21 past Trin.	7	41	♊	5	Very Cloudy and	30
21	g	Ursula V.	8	41		20	△♃☾.✶♂☾.□♀☾	31
22	A	Cordula V.	9	42	♋	5	△☉☾.△♄☾. Cold	Nov.
23	b	Term Begins	10	42		19	□♂☾. inclining *to frost*	2
24	c	Moglore B.	11	42	♌	3	□☉☾.□♄☾.✶♀☾	3
25	d	Crysant & D	12	43		16	☍♃☾.△♂☾. (△☿☾	4
26	e	Evaristus P.	13	47		29	✶♄☾.□♀☾.	5
27	f	22 past Trin	14	43	♍	12	✶☉☾. Cloud, winds	6
28	g	Sim. and Jude	15	44		25	and Rain;	7
29	A	Eadfin B. Can.	16	44	♎	7	⚺♀☾.✶☿☾.	8
30	b	Aglenoth B.	17	45		19	△♃☾.☍♂☾.	9
31	c	Eoilan B. M.	18	45	♏	1	⚺♄☾.	10

November hath XXX Days.

English account

New Moon the 2 Day, at 1 in the morning
First quarter the 16 Day, at 6 in the morning
Full Moon the 16 Day, at 10 at Night
Last quarter the 23 Day, at 6 at Night

Roman account

		Saints Days	☉	m	☽		Lunar aspects, and W	
1	d	All Saints	19	45		31	☌ ☉ ☽ . ☌ ♀ ☽ . □ ♃ ☽.	11
2	e	All Souls	20	47		25	Good weather, the	12
3	f	23 past Trin.	21	47	♐	7	⚹ ♀ ☽ . ☌ ☿ ☽ . season	13
4	g	Vitalis	22	48		19	⚹ ♃ ☽ . △ ♂ ☽ . consi-	14
5	a	Malachy B.	23	49	♑	1	⚹ ♄ ☽ . dered.	15
6	b	Winoch Ab.	24	50		13	□ ♂ ☽ . □ ♀ ☽ .	16
7	c	VVhildford B	25	50		25	⚹ ☉ ☽ . Cold Rains,	10
8	d	4 Crow'd Mar	26	51	♒	7	□ ♄ ☽ . ⚹ ☿ ☽ . with	18
9	e	Dedic. Christ	27	52		20	□ ☉ ☽ . ☌ ♃ ☽ . ⚹ ♂ ☽	19
10	f	24 past Trin.	28	53	♓	2	△ ♄ ☽ . □ ☿ ☽ . (△ ♀ ☽	20
11	g	Martin B.	29	54		16	winds.	21
12	a	Martin P.	0 ♐	54		29	△ ☉ ☽ . ⚹ ♃ ☽ , △ ☿ ☽	22
13	b	Kilian B.	1	55	♈	13	☌ ♂ ☽ . Now good	23
14	c	Laurence B.	2	56		28	☍ ♄ ☽ . ☌ ♀ ☽ . wether	24
15	d	Maclove B.	3	57	♉	7	□ ♃ ☽ . for the	25
16	e	Edm. B. Cant	4	58		28	☍ ☉ ☽ . ☍ ♀ ☽ . time	26
17	f	25 past Trin.	5	59	♊	13	△ ♃ ☽ . ⚹ ♂ ☽ . of the	27
18	g	Dedic. p. chair	6	0		29	△ ♄ ☽ . △ ♀ ☽ . Year.	28
19	a	Pontion Pope	7	1	♋	14	□ ♂ ☽ .	29
20	b	Edm. K.	8	2		28	△ ☉ ☽ . □ ♀ ☽ . △ ☿ ☽	30
21	c	present B. V.	9	3	♌	12	□ ♄ ☽ . ☍ ♃ ☽ . △ ♂ ☽	Dec.
22	d	Cicily V.	10	4		26	□ ♀ ☽ .	2
23	e	Clement P.	11	5	♍	9	□ ☉ ☽ . ⚹ ♄ ☽ . ⚹ ♀ ☽	3
24	f	26 past Trin.	12	6		22	⚹ ☿ ☽ . Clouds,	4
25	g	Katherine V.	13	8	♎	4	⚹ ☉ ☽ . Rain, or	4
26	a	Peter B. Alex	14	9		16	△ ♃ ☽ . ☌ ♂ ☽ .	5
27	b	Oda. V. Scot.	15	10		28	Snow.	6
28	c	Term Ends	16	11	♏	10	☌ ♄ ☽ . ☌ ♀ ☽ .	7
29	d	Setermine M.	17	12		22	□ ♃ ☽ . ☌ ☿ ☽ .	8
30	e		19	13	♐	4		9

December hath XXXI Day.

The Engl. Account.		Roman Account.
	New Moon the 1 Day, at 8 at Night.	
	First Quarter the 9 Day, at 6 at Night.	
	Full Moon the 16 Day, at 10 in the morning.	
	Last Quarter the 23 Day, at 11 before Noon.	
	New Moon the 31 Day, at Noon.	

		Saints Days	☉		☽		Lunar Aspects & W	
1	f	Advent Sund.	20	14		10	☌ ☉ ☾. ⚹ ♃ ☾. ∠ ☿ ☾	11
2	g	Daniel	21	16		28	Cold Ayr, likely	12
3	A	Francis Xav.	22	17	♑	10	⚹ ♄ ☾. to be Frosty	13
4	b	Lucius K.	23	18		22	□ ♂ ☾. ⚹ ♀ ☾. ⚹ ☿ ☾.	14
5	c	Barbara V.	24	19	♒	4	□ ♄ ☾.	15
6	d	Sabbas Abb.	25	21		17	⚹ ☉ ☾. ☌ ♃ ☾. ⚹ ♂ ☾.	16
7	e	Ambros B.	26	22		29	□ ♀ ☾. (□ ♀ ☾.	17
8	f	2 Advent	27	23	♓	12	△ ♄ ☾.	18
9	g	Ethalgin.	28	24		24	□ ☉ ☾. △ ♀ ☾. △ ☿ ☾	19
10	A	Melch. P.	29	25	♈	9	Good Weather,	20
11	b	Damas. P.	0 ♑	26		22	△ ☉ ☾. ⚹ ☿ ☾. ∠ ♂ ☾	21
12	c	Elfred V.	1	27	♉	7	☍ ♄ ☾. and seasonable	22
13	d	Lucy V.	2	28		21	□ ♃ ☾. ☍ ♀ ☾.	23
14	e	Membornie	3	30	♊	6	☍ ☿ ☾.	24
15	f	3 Advent	4	31		22	☍ ☉ ☾. △ ♃ ☾. ⚹ ♂ ☾	25
16	g	Bean P.	5	32	♋	7	△ ♄ ☾, toward the	26
17	A	Lazarus	6	34		22	□ ♂ ☾. End, Cold	27
18	b	Ember Week	7	35	♌	7	□ ♄ ☾. △ ♀ ☾. △ ☿ ☾	28
19	c	Macharius	8	36		21	☍ ♃ ☾. △ ♂ ☾. Rain	29
20	d	Con.eg. Abb	9	37	♍	5	△ ☉ ☾. ⚹ ♄ ☾. □ ♀ ☾	30
21	e	S. Thomas	10	39		18	☿ ☾ □. or Snow,	31
22	f	4. Advent	11	40	♎	0	□ ☉ ☾.	Janu.
23	g	Inthw. V.	12	42		13	⚹ ♀ ☾.	2
24	A	Ruth. Monk	13	44		25	△ ♃ ☾. ☍ ♂ ☾. ⚹ ☿ ☾	3
25	b	Christmas	14	45	♏	7	⚹ ☉ ☾. ∠ ♄ ☾.	4
26	c	S. Stephen	15	46		19	High winds	5
27	d	S. John	16	47	♐	1	□ ♃ ☾. ends	6
28	e	S. Innocents	17	48		13	the Year.	7
29	f	Tho. B. Cant.	18	50		24	⚹ ♃ ☾. △ ♂ ☾. ☌ ♀ ☾	8
30	g	Eastrach Abb.	19	52	♑	7	⚹ ♄ ☾. ☌ ☿ ☾.	9
31	A	Sylvester	20	54		19	☌ ☉ ☾.	10

MARY HOLDEN

THE
SECOND PART
Of the Woman's
ALMANACK.
FOR
The Year of our Lord God, 1689.

BEING

The First after *Bissextile* or Leap-year, and from the Creation of the World 5638 Years:

WHEREIN

Is contained a Description of the Suns entrance into the four Cardinal Signs : Also an account of such Eclipses as will happen this present Year ; with useful Tables. Likewise an Astronomical Description of the seven Planets ; with an account of the Eighth, or Starry Heaven : The Ninth, or Crystalline Heaven : The Tenth, or first Mover : And the Eleventh or Imperial Heaven,

By Mary Holden *Midwife, and Student in Physick and Astrology.*

LONDON,
Printed for the Company of *Stationers.* 1689.

A Table of the Latitude of the Planets, ♄ ♃ ♂ ♀ ☿, for the
first, eleventh, and one and twentieth days of each Month
this Year 1689. In this Table N. *signifies* North
and S. *signifies* South.

Month	Day	♄		♃		♂		♀		☿	
January	1	2	24	0	37	0	10	1	39	0	19
	11	2	22	0	40	0	7	1	29	0	19
	21	2	20	0	42	0	3	1	11	1	57
February	1	2	18	0	44	0	2	0	42	1	51
	11	2	16	0	47	0	6	0	9	1 S.	8
	21	2	15	0	50	0	11	0	28	0	47
March	1	2	15	0	37	0	18	0	59	2	23
	11	2	14	0	40	0	27	1	39	3	22
	21	2	14	0	42	0	37	2	18	1	48
April	1	2	14	0	44	0	48	2	55	0	57
	11	2	15	0	47	0	49	3	20	2	31
	21	2	15	0	50	1	13	3	34	2	56
May	1	2	16	0	52	1	26	3	33	2	23
	11	2 N.	18	0	55	1	45	3	13	0	59
	21	2	19	0	58	2 N.	2	2	23	0	44
June	1	2	21	1	0	2	20	0	48	1	55
	11	2	23	1 S.	2	2	36	1	17	1	43
	21	2	25	1	4	2	52	3	35	0	31
July	1	2	28	1	5	3	12	5	21	1	35
	11	2	31	1	4	3	23	6 S.	3	3	40
	21	2	33	1	3	3	45	5	55	4	52
August	1	2	35	1	2	3	59	5	15	3	20
	11	2	37	1	1	4	14	4	20	0	26
	21	2	38	1	0	4	22	3	21	1	24
September	1	2	40	0	59	4	20	2	15	1	47
	11	2	40	0	58	4	22	1	17	0	59
	21	2	40	0	57	4	8	0	25	1	7
October	1	2	39	0	57	3	31	0	21	1	17
	11	2	37	0	57	2	33	0	59	2	14
	21	2	36	0	57	1	52	1	27	2	41
November	1	2	34	0	57	1	13	1	48	2	1
	11	2	33	0	57	0	30	1	50	0	51
	21	2	29	0	58	0	13	1	55	3	38
December	1	2	27	0	59	0	7	1	46	1	55
	11	2	25	1	0	0	23	1	29	0	44
	21	2	21	1	1	0	31	1	7	0	2

A 2   A Table

A Table of the Mutual Aspects.

January.

□ ♄ 3 ♃	4	♏ ♒
□ ♄ ☿	5	♏ ♑
△ ♄ 3 ♀	11	♏ ♓
□ ☉ ♄	14	♒ ♏
☌ ☉ 3 ♃	17	♒
□ ♄ ☿	24	♏ ♒
☌ ♃ 3 ☿	27	♒
□ ♂ ♀	28	♐ ♒

February.

☌ ☉ ☿	7	♒
✱ ♄ 3 ♂	10	♏ ♑
✱ ♂ ☿	11	♑ ♓
△ ♄ 3 ☿	12	♏ ♓
✱ ♃ ♀	13	♒ ♈
△ ☉ 3 ♄	14	♓ ♏
✱ ☉ ♂	20	♓ ♑

March.

☍ ♄ ♀	2	♏ ♒
□ ♃ 3 ♀	17	♒ ♉
□ ♄ ♂	22	♏ ♒
☌ ☉ 3 ☿	23	♈
☽ Ecli. vi.	25	♎
✱ ♂ 3 ☿	27	♒ ♈
✱ ♀ ☿	31	♊ ♈

April.

✱ ☉ ♃	4	♈ ♒
☍ ☉ 3 ♄	12	♉ ♏
✱ ♂ ♀	19	♒ ♊
△ ♃ 3 ☿	24	♒ ♊
☌ ♃ ♂	25	♒
△ ♄ 3 ♀	29	♏ ♋
△ ♂ ♀	30	♓ ♋

May.

✱ ♃ ☿	2	♒ ♈
☍ ♄ 3 ☿	3	♏ ♉
△ ♂ ☿	5	♓ ♋
✱ ♀ 3 ☿	6	♋ ♉
✱ ♂ ☿	7	♓ ♉
□ ☉ 3 ♃	10	♊ ♒
△ ♄ ♃	18	♏ ♓
□ ♃ 3 ☿	20	♓ ♊
☌ ☉ ☿	26	♊
□ ♂ ☿	29	♓ ♋

June.

△ ♄ ☿	2	♎ ♊
△ ♃ 3 ☿	3	♓ ♋
☌ ♀ ☿	5	♋
△ ☉ 3 ♄	10	♊ ♎
□ ☉ ♄	11	♋ ♎
△ ♂ ♀	12	♈ ♋
☌ ☉ 3 ♀	13	♋
△ ♃ ♀	16	♓ ♋
□ ♂ 3 ♀	17	♈ ♋
□ ♄ ☿	11	♎ ♋
△ ♄ 3 ♀	19	♎ ♊
△ ♂ ☿	25	♈ ♌

July.

△ ♄ ♃	6	♎ ♒
□ ☉ 3 ♄	12	♌ ♎
△ ♂ ☿	19	♈ ♌
△ ♃ 3 ♀	21	♒ ♊
△ ♄ ♀	25	♏ ♋
✱ ♃ 3 ♂	28	♒ ♈
☌ ☉ ☿	30	♌

August.

☌ ♄ ♂	6	♏ ♉
☍ ☉ 3 ♃	8	♌ ♒
✱ ☉ ♄	14	♍ ♏
△ ☉ 3 ♂	17	♍ ♉
☍ ♃ ☿	23	♒ ♌
✱ ♄ 3 ☿	28	♏ ♍
△ ♂ ☿	30	♉ ♍

September.

□ ♄ ♀	1	♏ ♌
□ ♂ 3 ♀	5	♉ ♌
☌ ☉ ☿	12	♎
☍ ♃ 3 ♀	18	♒ ♌
☽ Eclip.	19	♈
☍ ♄ 3 ♂	22	♏ ♉
△ ♃ ☿	24	♒ ♎
△ ♂ 3 ♀	29	♉ ♍

October.

☍ ♂ ☿	1	♉ ♏
✱ ♄ 3 ♀	2	♏ ♍
☌ ♄ ☿	3	♏
△ ☉ 3 ♃	4	♎ ♒
✱ ♀ ☿	10	♍ ♏
☍ ☉ 3 ♂	12	♎ ♈
□ ♃ ☿	14	♒ ♏
☌ ☉ 3 ♄	21	♏
✱ ♀ ☿	31	♎ ♐

November.

□ ☉ ♃	4	♏ ♒
✱ ♃ 3 ♂	6	♒ ♈
☍ ♂ ♀	9	♈ ♎
△ ♃ 3 ♀	10	♒ ♎
☌ ☉ ☿	17	♐
☌ ♄ 3 ♀	26	♏

December.

△ ☉ ♂	7	♐ ♈
□ ♃ 3 ♀	8	♒ ♏
✱ ☉ ♃	9	♐ ♒
✱ ♃ 3 ♂	15	♒ ♈
✱ ♃ ☿	25	♓ ♐
✱ ☉ 3 ♄	26	♑ ♏
△ ♂ ☿	27	♉ ♑

A Table of high Water at London-Bridge.

☽ Increaſe	1	2	3	4	5	6	7	8	9	10	11	12	13	14	15
☽ Decrea.	16	17	18	19	20	21	22	23	24	25	26	27	28	29	30
Full ⎰ Hou	3	4	5	6	7	7	8	9	10	11	11	12	1	2	3
Sea. ⎱ Min	48	36	24	12	0	48	35	24	12	0	48	36	24	12	0

The Uſe of this Table.

Look for the day of the Moneth in the foregoing Table, and againſt that day is the Age of the Moon in any moneth this year ; which find in this Table in the two upper lines, and right under it is the hour and minute of high Water at *London-Bridge*. For Example : The firſt day of *January*, I find the Moon to be 20 days old : Then I ſeek this Table, and find the Moon 20 days old Decreaſing ; and under it 7 hours, 0 minutes, which is the time of High Water at *London-Bridge*.

A 3

A Table

A Table of the Moons Latitude for every other day, at Noon for the Year 1689.

Days	Janua. d. m.	Febru: d. m.	March. d. m.	April. d. m.	May. d. m.	June. d. m.
1	1 S. 48	2 M 19	3 M 1	5 M 14	4 M 42	1 M 0
3	0 M.27	4 2	4 32	5 3	3 6	1 S 32
5	2 39	5 15	5 15	3 45	0 44	3 51
7	4 19	5 A 12	4 58	1 38	1 S 58	5 9
9	5 10	4 19	3 A 31	1 S 6	4 13	5 D 3
11	5 A. 9	2 4	1 8	3 32	5 15	3 46
13	3 55	0 S 33	1 S 32	5 1	4 D 56	1 48
15	1 48	3 2	3 56	5 D 12	3 35	0 M 22
17	0 S. 50	4 42	5 6	4 12	1 33	2 29
19	3 11	5 D 17	5 D 10	2 30	0 M 33	4 9
21	4 D.45	4 41	4 9	0 27	2 38	5 8
23	5 16	3 11	2 24	1 M 48	4 16	5 A 10
25	4 36	1 10	0 15	3 40	5 10	4 13
27	3 2	0 M 38	1 M 54	4 52	5 A 9	2 22
29	0 55	0 0	3 44	5 A 16	4 6	0 S 3
31	1 M.17	0 0	4 54	5 8	2 14	1 13

Days	July. d. m.	August d. m.	Septem. d. m.	Octob. d. m.	Novem. d. m.	Decem. d. m.
1	2 S 34	6 S 13	3 S 35	0 S 35	3 M 21	5 M 5
3	4 29	4 54	0 33	1 M 38	4 46	5 A 13
5	5 15	3 24	0 M 41	3 32	5 15	4 25
7	4 D 40	1 17	2 48	4 48	4 A 54	2 52
9	3 6	0 M 58	4 23	5 A 17	3 33	0 S 33
11	1 0	3 2	5 A 12	4 49	1 33	1 58
13	1 M 12	4 32	5 4	3 24	1 S 6	4 4
15	3 12	5 15	4 2	1 10	3 28	5 13
17	4 36	5 A 1	1 59	1 S 27	5 D 0	4 56
19	5 A 16	3 48	0 S 36	3 58	5 10	3 D 24
21	4 56	1 33	2 6	5 8	4 1	1 6
23	3 33	0 S 54	5 D 5	5 D 5	2 5	1 M 10
25	1 22	3 19	5 D 16	3 52	0 M 13	3 12
27	1 S 9	4 53	4 32	1 53	2 24	4 36
29	3 28	5 D 15	2 48	0 M 22	4 6	5 15
31	4 56	4 26	1 46	2 29	4 M 42	5 A 0

Here Note, The Letters M. and S. tell you whether it be Meridional or Septentrional, South or North, and how long it will continue so, and the Letters A. and D. shew you when the Moon is ascending or descending in her Latitude.

Of the Winter Quarter, or the Sun in ♑ ♒ ♓.

Which begins the Sun first entring the Tropical sign Capricorn, which will be this Year, *December* the 11th. 31 minutes after 1 in the morning; making the shortest day and the longest night to all that inhabit on this side the Equator; at which time 21 degrees 31 min. of ♋ upon the Meridian; and 16 degrees of ♎ ascends.

The Distempers that are most likely to afflict us this Quarter, are Coughs, Rhumes, Pleurisies, and inflammation of the Lungs, distillations, hoarsness, pains in the Breasts : The Winter maladies are for the most part durable.

―――――――― ―――――――― ――――――――

An Astrological Description of the other Three Seasons; and first of the Spring.

THE Spring or Vernal Equinox beginneth at that time the *Sun* (the Fountain of Life) entereth the first scruple of the Celestial sign *Aries* ; which this year happeneth *March* the 9th. 7 hours 31 min. past morning, and the figure of Heaven is as followeth.

A 4   In

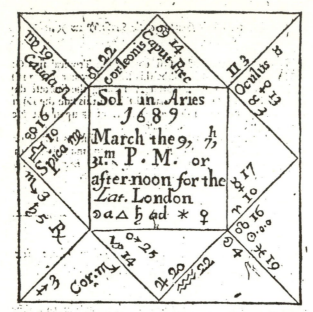

In this figure we have the first degrees of the Equinoctial sign Libra ascending, and ♀ and ♂ chief Rulers of this Spring Quarter. By the Sun entering into ♈, we are to judge of the event and success of the accidents of the Spring Quarter; and not without good reason, since the Sun, (the Soul and Life of the World) that gives life unto all the Creatures by a singular Blessing and Providence of the Creator; which is clearly manifested by the increasing quality of humidity; the Earth, and all things thereon, do abound plentifully with at that time.

The days do increase, and the nights diminish; and all things do flourish, and appear in their greatest lustre and splendour.

In the Scheme, the Angles are all moveable, and of the Fiery

Fiery, Earthy, Airy, and Watry Triplicities ; and it Is further obferved, that two Planets are pofited in a Fiery fign,
and two in VVatry figns, and two in Earthy figns, and one in
an Airy fign ; fo that the four Elements are herein concerned.
As to the actions of this Spring Quarter, the Moon is pofited
in a double fign near the cufp of the 6, between the △ of ♄,
and the ✳ of ♀. As to the actions of this Quarter, they
may be very fignificant, fince the Moon fuffers an Eclipfe before the month is out ; and likewife a quadrat Afpect of ♄
and ♂ near the Eclipfe, and ♄ ℞ in ♏ is moft malicious and
unfortunate : But I dare not adventure to fay any more, being unwilling to give the leaft offence ——— As to Difeafes, ♂
portends corruptions of Blood, Tertian Feavers, acute Difeafes, heats the Blood of fuch as are in their prime. In the
Air he ftirs up great heat, hot peftilent Winds, very peftife-
rous and infectious : Alfo Thunder, Lightnings, Whirlwinds,
exceffive Dearth —— In the Seas, he ftirs up ftorms, fudden
Shipwrack ; but in regard ♂ is applying to a △ Afpect with
♀, much of the evil fignification is mitigated, Jupiter and
Venus are Planets of its benevolent Nature, and ♀ in the
Scheme is very potent.

This is likely to be a very fickly year ; many perfons will
be moft intolerably afflicted from old Surfeits, now breaking
out to purpofe into Dropfies, Agues, Coughs, Confumptions,
Tympanies ; and it is to be feared fome Peftilential Diftem-
pers. —— Now is the time to confult with your Phyfitian before it be too late. I fhall forbear to inlarge any farther at
this time, humbly befeeching Almighty God in his infinite
Mercy to divert all further Judgments whatfoever, and continue perfect Peace and Unity.

Of Summer, or the progrefs of the Sun through ♋ ♌ ♍.

THis Quarter begins, the Sun entering into the firft fcruple
of ♋, which is this year *June* the 11th, 2 hours 40
minutes paft mid-night ; caufing to us, and all who inhabit
on this fide of the Equator, longeft day and fhorteft night.
The natural conftitution of this Quarter is hot and dry, fym-
pathizing

pathizing with choler and melancholly. The phlegmatick this Quarter are best in health, the cholerick most afflicted; it revives decrepid old Age, and debilitates Youth, because they are full of blood and choler, and thereby much exposed to Feavers, especially tertian; for the Distempers that arise from the excess of blood and choler, are more dangerous than those that take their original from blood and phlegm. The phlegmatick persons enjoy the greatest freedom from sickness; because the powerful heat of the Sun in this season dryes up the superfluous moisture that accustometh to discompose them, but to the cholerick persons the Sun too potently exhales the radical moisture : Extremity of heat we see cleavs the Earth it self, and must needs therefore afflict those bodies, that are aptly disposed to its fury.

The Diseases this Quarter signified by the sixth House, are Cancers in the Breasts, ill digestion in the Stomach, Surfeits, Giddiness of the Head, Apoplexy, yellow Choller, and saltish humours in the Face and Stomach, pains in the Feet, and Faintness in the Limbs.

Of Autumn, or the Suns motion through ♎ ♏ ♐ .

WHich takes its beginning this year *September* the 12th. 1 hour 16 min. after noon, the Sun then crossing the Worlds Axis with a right Angle, makes equal day and night all the World over betwixt the Polar circles.

This season is by nature cold and dry, and agrees to melan-cholly, resembling Age. The sanguine constitution is best in health, the melancholly much afflicted ; the best time for Youth, the worst time for Age. Those Diseases (for the most part) that are taken this Quarter, are hardly to be cured ; cholerick persons, and those of a phlegmatick constitution must expect the invasion of unwelcome Diseases ; and there-fore ought to take good advice, and antidote themselves a-gainst the assaults of the enemies of nature before it be too date; This is a fit time being the second Spring;

Of

HOLDEN. 1689.

Of Eclipses happening this Year, 1689.

There is no Eclipse of the Sun this year, only two of the Moon, and both total : The first happeneth on *March* the 25th near seven at night, and is celebrated in the 15 degrees of ♎ ; it begins in the 12th Angle, the Angle of Sorrow, Labour and Imprisonment ; and ends in the 10th Angle, the Angle of Honour and Dignity. ♀ Rules the place Eclipsed, and ♄ in the ascendent ℞ in ♏ doth partake in the signification ; and ♂ also is shearer being received by ♄.

Seeing this Eclipse happens in the Spring, in which time the Earth is preparing to receive the Seed, the signification of this Eclipse hath much to do in such things or seeds that are to be sown about this time ; or on such Plants or Trees, which do put forth themselves either in sprouting or budding.—— We must expect Winds or Blasts, in regard it falls in the Spring —— The Moon governs the 9th House, which signifies dammage at Sea ; ♀ opposes the ☽, he is the forerunner of inordinate mutations of Weather, and Wind quickly changing from one Quarter to another, causing Shipwracks, as also Thunder and Lightening. ♂ Lord of the sixth House, signifies Mortality amongst the lesser sort of Cattle, proceeding from some strange and violent distempers which may reign among them.

The second Eclipse happeneth on *September* the 19th about two of the clock in the morning, and is celebrated in seven degrees of Aries. In the Figure hereof ♀ opposes the Moon, as in the former ; and Saturn and Mars are in opposition.

The Eclipse happens in the house of death, and ends in the Angle of quarrels, strifes and contentions—— ♂ is chief Ruler of this Eclipse, the first decanad of Aries being governed by ♂ ——— An Eclipse, or conjunction of the Luminaries, in a sign belonging to ♂, produceth, or is the signifier of diseases, tending unto death ; the more in regard it happeneth in the 8th House being in ♈ ; it afflicteth the sick with Frenzies,

zies, Lethargies, Apoplexies, the falling Evil, and fluxes of
Rheums diftilling from the Head, and confequently Peftilential Feavers. Inflammations and fmall Pox in abundant——
♈ being a Beaftial fign, and ♂ Lord of the Eclipfe in ♉,
both Beaftial figns, therefore we may fear a rot of Sheep, and
fome Peftilential ficknefs amongft great Beafts, as Horfes,
Cows, and Oxen.

A Defcription of the feven Planets; and firft of the Moon.

THE Moon is the leaft of all the Planets; (except Mercury) fhe feemeth to us to be great, becaufe fhe is next
to us. Her form is round; fhe is of nature cold and moift.
Her Light is borrowed from the Sun; as it is eafily demon-
ftrable in the Moon when fhe oppofeth the Sun; and is then
commonly called the full Moon, which is her true figure:
For as a Looking-glafs well pollifhed, tranfports or cafts the
light of the Fire, or of the Sun againft a Wall; fo doth the
Moon receive, or retain the Light of the Sun; and in a clear
and fair night, caufeth that Light to reflect againft the Earth.
But farther, to make it appear that the Moon hath its light
by reflection from the Sun, take thefe two Arguments: The
firft is from the feveral Afpects of the Moon in her variations;
the fecond from her Eclipfes. Firft, from the Afpects of the
Moon it appears that her Light is fo borrowed, becaufe fhe is
inlightened only on that fide the Globe which has its Afpect
towards the Sun, or upon which the Sun hath its Afpect.——
So in the firft Quarter, the Sun being new fet in the Weft,
that part of the Moon is enlightned which is towards the
Weft: And though it be full half of her Globe, yet is there
to us, but a fmall part vifible, *viz.* that illuminated femi-cir-
cle, which increafes more and more, as they both grow into
a direct oppofition; and when they are diametrically oppo-
fite,

fite, then doth that half of her that is enlightned, fully appear to us ; which we call full Moon, or her being in the full, from which time the Moon paffing her circuit more flowly than the Sun, his reflection upon her is from the Eaft ; the Eaftern fide of her Globe is then enlightned : Thus we fee that the light of the Moon is more or lefs to usward, according as her pofiture is towards the Sun.

The fecond Argument from the Eclipfe does fomewhat more clearly prove, becaufe it fhews the Moon to be but a dark Body, when fhe is in fuch a line of oppofition to the Sun, as that the Earth (being a grofs body) interpofing, cannot receive her reflection from the Sun. It is yet further manifefted by the beginning and ending of the Eclipfe, as fhe gradually lofes and gains her Light, until they both removing into a line of oppofition, where there is no fuch interpofure, fhe becomes again wholly enlightned.—— Therefore we may fafely conclude, that though they are both great Lights, and that the Sun is fo effentially; yet the Moon is fo only by mutation or reflection from the Sun.

There are five things to be confidered of the Moon : Flrft, her fweet temper, which does quallifie the extream heat of the Sun, that the Elemental World is thereby preferved, and fubfifteth ; to which purpofe this Lunary Body runs through the Zodiack thirteen times in a year, and does commodioufly move or meet in figns, or places of Heaven fit and proper in imitation of the Sun : So that in Winter fhe (as it were) choofeth the figns of Summer, and in Summer the figns of Winter ; whereby the extremities of thofe qualities are moderated ; and cafts back the Sun beams here below on the Earth with admirable temperature.

Secondly, In regard fhe changeth every month, fhe is called the true Kalender (in her changes, increafe, full, and decreafe) of Feftival days.

Thirdly, She is ordained to be the Miftrefs and Governefs of the Night. *Gen. 1. 16. Pfal. 136. 9.*

Fourthly, She is Sirnamed the Princefs of the Sea ; upon the ebbing and flowing fhe hath a marvellous power ; for if fhe decline, or be in the firft Quarter then the Tide is weak ; but when fhe change, or is at the full, then is the Tide violent and ftrong : Upon which occafion, it is this Planet that

rules

miles over the humidity and moisture, causeth the mass or heap of waters in the Sea so to swell and increase, and carry them to and fro according as she her self is in the East, or as she bends downward toward the West.

Fifthly, She hath a marvellous power over all kind of Animals and living Creatures. She is less than the Earth 40 times. She retains the Earth for her Center ; about which she performs her revolution in 27 days, 7 hours, 40 minutes. She is distant from the Earth 160426 miles ; her diameter is 1828 miles ; the circumference of her Circle is 962556 miles. She hath ♋ to her House, a Constellation consisting of 15 Stars.

Secondly, Of the Planet *Mercury* : He is but a little seen with us, by reason of his stay and abode near the Sun, whose lustre and brightness defaceth and putteth out (as it were) all other Lights that approach near unto it : It declines or falls from beyond the Ecliptick line, against the Meridional part, toward which it does ordinarily bend, leaving the Planet Venus alwayes on the North side.—— This Planet continually waiteth on the Sun, and followeth him continually as a Servant follows his Master, and is near 18 degrees from him,—— This Planet is 356102 miles above the Moon, he is 3140 times less than the Earth, yet of it self it is a great Light. The Diameter thereof is 430 miles, the Circumference of his Heaven is 3 millions 9168 miles. He governs the Twins, a Constellation consisting of 29 Stars ; and the Virgin, consisting of 39 Stars.

Thirdly, Of *Venus* : This Planet with Mercury does faithfully accompany the Sun ; for they are nothing near so far distant from the Sun as those Planets above him are ; but in comparison of the other Planets they seem to be near him ; especially this Planet Venus, which is one Cœlestial Sign and a half, and somewhat more ; and Mercury a little less than a sign ; both which Planets turn continually about the Sun ; and does accompany him in an orderly course : But this Planet being left by Mercury on the North-side, is a great and glorious Light ; for by her declining she is removed so far from the Sun, that she cannot be obscured by the Light thereof :

And

And yet notwithstanding she doth so truly and faithfully accompany him, that oftentimes she rises in the morning before him, and at other times she follows him very close towards the evening, and the rest of the time she is hid from our sight by being so near the Sun.—— This Planet is 315298 miles above Mercury.—— She is distant from the Earth 831826 miles; she is 32 times less than the earth : Her Diameter is 1986 miles : The Circumference of her Heaven is 4 millions, 990956 miles.—— She ruleth Taurus, a Constellation consisting of 43 Stars, and Libra consisting of 18 Stars.

Fourthly, Of the Sun : This Planet is placed in the middle between the other six Planets, having ♂ ♃ ♄ above him, and Venus, Mercury, and the Moon under him ; for if it were higher or lower than it is, then the seasons of the Year would be quite out of order ; wherefore observe that the Sun in his proper and in his regular courses, (occasioned by the motion of the first moveable) doth (in the Heaven where God placed him) temper and allay by his heat the extream coldness of the Sky, Saturn and the Moon.—— Now if the Sun were in the place or circle of the Moon ; and the Moon above in the circle of the Sun, the earth would be burned with the heat thereof ; so on the contrary, if the Sun were in the Heaven of Saturn, it would be too far distant from the earth ; which would wax cold by reason of the Moon, and too little heated by the Planets, Mercury, Venus, Mars and Jupiter; so that it would bring forth nothing.

Here is the Wisdom of the Creator seen, in placing the Sun where it is, for the good of all superiour and inferiour Bodies. This glorious Planet is the continual fountain of heat, the head of bright shining light, the life of the Universe, the eye and torch of the World, the ornament, grace and beauty of the Firmament, the King of the fixed Stars and Planets, the Prince of the Cœlestial Fires, and the hottest of all the Cœlestial Bodies, as you may find, Psalm 19. 56. Matth. 13. 6.

We find evidently the several parts of the Earthly Globe to be differently hot or cold, accordingly to the remoteness of the Suns Body.—— The giving life, growth, augmentation to all Animals, Vegetables and Minerals, is from the real imparting

ing of actual heat from the *Sun* ; therefore in the absence or distance of the *Sun* in the Winter, the defects is supplied by the application of that which is actually hot ; the *Sun* like-wife does cause the nights and days to appear ; he turns conti-nually the one half of our Hemisphere the one half of the day, and in like manner the other half he turns about the other Hemisphere which is opposite to ours ; but in his ab-sence from us, while he remains there, the night comes upon us, by reason of the shadow of the earth, the extent of which shadow is 74602 miles ; his dayly course is 25 millions 19732 miles, although we perceive him not to move, nor know any thing of his course, yet in one minute of an hour he runs 17381 miles, as have been observed by Astronomers ; the *Sun* being carried about the Heaven and the Earth in 24 hours, brings a sweet benefit ; gives rest, ease, and content-ment, and delight to us, and all other living creatures. Be-sides, it is the will of God that the Sun should carry the Light round the World every day, that thereby the excellent Riches and Beauty of his Work might the better appear ; so that Life and Light are the effects of the *Sun*, which rules the day as the Moon does the night.——— He governs Leo, a Con-stellation consisting of 40 stars. This glorious Planet is 3 mil-lions 339796 miles above Venus ; the *Sun* is distant from the Earth 4 millions 169955 miles. It is 166 times bigger than the Earth : His Diameter is 45450 miles ; the Circumference of his Circle is 25 millions of miles : The Sun is 6640 times greater than the Moon.——— When we seriously consider what good all inferiour Bodies receive by the greatness, swiftness, and distance of this Planet from us ; his dayly oblique course, his substance, form, eclipses, motion, and conjunction of con-trary motions. We shall have just cause to adore and reve-rence the admirable Wisdom and Power of the Creator in such an excellent and wonderful Body, as that of the Sun ; and not to pass it over as the most do, but stand amazed thereat.

Fifthly, Of *Mars* : The word Mars signifies War, also it signifies red or inflamed, because it is next to the Sun, and by its influence makes the sublunary bodies fierce and violent.— This Planet is one million 936786 miles above the Sun. He

is

is 6 millions 108408 miles from the earth : He is half as big again as the earth : His Diameter is 9456 miles : His Circumference is 36 millions 650448 miles. He governs Aries, a Constellation consisting of 21 stars : And Scorpio consisting of 10 stars.

Sixthly, Of *Jupiter* : It is observed the influence of this Planet is very temperate ; and that one while it warms the coldness of the Planet Saturn, and another while it moderates the heat of the Planet next under it, which is Mars. It does graciously help and relieve the inferiour Bodies. It is hot and moist, temperate. He is Lord of Sagittary, containing 16 stars, and Pisces, consisting of 36 stars. This Planet is 37 millions 891592 miles above Mars. He is distant from the earth 44 millions of miles. He is 91 times greater than the earth : The Diameter thereof is 31200 miles, and the circumference of his Heaven 264 millions of miles.

Seventhly, Of *Saturn* : This Cœlestial body is nearest unto the eighth Heaven of the fixed stars, and is exceeding cold (partaking thereof) because he is the nearest (of all other Planets) unto the Cœlestial waters, (which are above the Firmament) where the heat of the fixed stars are quallified by that exceeding great store of waters. All Ages, and modern Experience knoweth that when *Saturn* is in conjunction or radiation with the Sun or Moon, the two great Lights ; he diminisheth heat in the hot seasons of the year, and augmenteth cold in the cold times : Besides his propinquity to the starry Heaven, great distance from the earth, his intrinsecal hidden qualities of cold operations ; he prohibiteth the heat to descend ; likewise the cold influence of this Planet makes the Body chill, melancholly and dry.——— This great Planet is twenty eight millions of miles above Jupiter. He is distant from the Earth seventy two millions of miles. He is ninety six times greater than the Earth, and although ♄ and ☉ appear to us almost equal in bigness, yet ♄ is 301723 times bigger than ☉ ; and the reason is because of the exceeding distance that is between them, one above the other ; which is seventy one millions 483800 : The Circumference of

B
its

Its Heaven is four hundred thirty two millions of miles. He ruleth Capricorn, consisting of twenty eight Stars, and Aquarius consisting of forty one Stars.

Of the Eighth, or Starry Heaven.

IT is that Heaven commonly called the Firmament, *Gen.* 1. 6. which Heaven compasseth, and comprehends all the aforesaid Heavens or Circles of the seven Planets : It is not of a thin substance, as the Water, Air, or Fire is ; nor of a gross obscure substance as the Earth, *Exodus* 24. 10. but being of a substance, without comparison, finer and thinner than any under it ; gives place to those bodies that are more solid. Those six principal Circles (by Astronomers) first, the Æquator, or Æquinoctial, which is a great Circle placed in the middle of the Sphere, between either or both Poles, by equal spaces the Heavens, and crosses the Zodiack in two parts, *viz.* Aries and Libra, which when the Sun comes to it, causes equal day and night throughout the World, under the Poles excepted. Secondly, The Zodiack which is so called because it is the path of the Sun, who is called the Author of Life. It is a bowing Circle, and crossing thwartly the Æquinoctial and first mover ; and appears bending in respect of the Poles of the World, and from them is unequally distant : It is one of the six and greatest circles in the Firmament, in which the Twelve Signs are placed, having a circle line in the midst thereof, called an Ecliptick line. Thirdly, The two Colours which are generally called the great circles, drawn by the Poles of the World, they are never seen wholly in the turning about as the other circles are. Fourthly, Meridian, which is a circle that goeth by the Poles of the World, and the height of, and place. Fifthly, The Horizon, which is a circle that divideth the upper half Sphere, which we see not. Sixthly, The two Tropicks, which turn again when the Sun is digressed from the Æquator, and comes in those points when he

turns

turns back again. Thefe two touch the Zodiack at the beginning, ♋ and ♑ : ♋ being Northerly, and the Summer circle to thofe on this fide the Æquator, and ♑ Southerly, and the Winter circle to us, but contrary to thofe that are on the other fide of the Æquinoctial ; likewife the circle of the Zodiack is oblique, or overthwart, for the better diftribution of the heat of the Planets to feveral places or parts of the Earth ; for if they (efpecially the Sun) fhould move in a ftrait courfe, and not oblique, but a fmall part of the Earth would have injoyed the comfort of their heat and influences; and that alfo in fo high a degree, and that it would have rendered even the part uncomfortable for Habitation as is under the Æquinoctial ; whereas now by their oblique courfe they communicate themfelves in fome proportion to the whole Earth; begetting thereby the deftination of times, and the various feafons of the year; and the different temperature of feveral Regions and Countreys. —— There are alfo 12 Signs in the Zodiack, reprefenting 12 feveral forms or figures ; fome of Humane fhape, and fome of other Creatures, fo called for diftinction fake ; as *Aries* is called the *Ram*, and *Taurus* a *Bull*, and fo for the reft ; not that there is any creature in the Zodiack, or that they have any real refemblance, but that they are fo called for diftinctions fake, as aforefaid. There are alfo certain Stars mentioned in Scripture, as *Arcturus*, *Orion*, and *Pleiades*, Job 9. 9. *Mazzaroth Arcturus* with his Sons, chap. 38. 32. *Arcturus* is the North ftar with thofe about him, the crooked ferpent, *Amos* 5. 8. which is a figure of a ftar fafhioned like a ferpent becaufe of the crookednefs ; fome of thofe Stars are of a conftringent or freezing nature, as *Orion* which confifts of 39 Stars; others of a moift nature, producing pleafant fhowers, as the *Pleiades*, or the feven Stars : The North and South Poles are the two ends or points of the Aftronomers Axle-Tree, upon which the Heaven is imagined to turn

Of the Ninth, or Cristal Heaven.

AND it may be called so, for the Creator having made of nothing within nothing the principles and grounds of things, made this Firmament of Waters so perfectly clear and purified as it is; which waters were the waters that were divided from the waters that were under the Firmament, *Gen.* 1. 6, 7. and mentioned, *Psal.* 148. ver. 4. which Firmament, or Heaven of fixed Stars, divideth those waters from the waters below.——— Now those waters above all the Heavens hitherto described are clear and transparent as Cristal, through which one may see any thing beyond, *Rev.* 22. 1. So that you see there is a store of Waters beside that which is in the Clouds, and the Sea, as hath been proved, and may farther appear, if we consider the universal Flood, for *Moses* says, the sluces and the flood-gates of Heaven were let go, *Gen.* 7. 11. which could not be understood of the waters of the Clouds, but of some other store surpassing all Humane understanding. This Heaven is carried about by the Tenth Heaven, and hath its special motion, by vertue whereof it carries the Eighth Heaven, but very slowly and leasurely from the East to the West.

Of the Tenth Heaven, or first Mover.

THE Tenth Heaven is named by Astronomers the great and first moveable : This Heaven continually moving with an equal gate from East to West, doth by reason of its violent swiftness, carry and turn about all the other Heavens in twenty four hours from East to West between the two Poles, drawing with it all the other Heavens, Globes, and Cælestial Bodies, (yea the Elements which are more light and nimble) so that they make their own proper revolutions, which are

contrary.

contrary from Weſt to Eaſt, every one in longer or ſhorter time, according as they be far or near diſtant from the ſame, and are carried about in their circle, as a man is in a Chariot upon the Land, or as a Ship is in the Waters ; for though a man be in a Chariot or Ship, he is not ſo faſtned thereunto, but that he may remove himſelf from one ſide, or from one end to another. And thus you have had a brief deſcription of the Cœleſtial Heavens.

Of the Eleventh, or Imperial Heaven.

THE Eleventh Heaven, which is called the Imperial or higheſt Heaven, it excells in purity and clearneſs all the other Heavens. In the Holy Scriptures we read of three Heavens, by thoſe three Heavens are meant the three unmeaſurable Heavens above the Starry Heaven; the higheſt of which is the aforeſaid Imperial Heaven, which St. *Paul* calls the third Heaven, 2 *Cor.* 12. 2.

Adver

I Make a rare Electuary, that cureth any Fits, caused by Wind, Vapours, the rising of the Mother, Convulsion: It seldom fails of curing any Fits whatsoever.

I With the Blessing of God cure the Canker in the Mouth, with so little disturbance to the Patients, that they shall scarce feel it, or any other Distemper incident to the mouth or Throat.——— The reason I publish this last, is because I see such great cruelty in them that cure by plucking out of Teeth, and breaking of Jaw-bones in young Children, that they never have any Teeth in their places.

THere be three Fairs in a year at *Sudbury*, the first is kept on the 27th and 28th of *April*. The second is on the Feast of St. *Peter* and St. *Paul*, the day before and the day after. The third is on the 24, 25, 26 of *September*.
Last year I writ neither of Fairs, Horses nor Mares, but it was Mr. Printers Pleasure.

IF any Gentleman, or other Person would have his Land Surveyed, or any Building or Edifice measured, either for Brick-layers, Carpenters, Masons, Plaisterers, &c. Mr. *Saunders* will perform the same either for Master, or Work-men, and if any Persons would have about his House or Garden, any Sun-Dyals, either Direct, Declining, Inclining, Reclining, Concave, Convex, or Reflective, he will make or prepare for them such as they shall desire.

WEather Glasses also are prepared and carefully adjusted by Mr. *Saunders*, for any that have a desire to have them.

From *Ouston* in *Com. Leicester*,
Jun. the 25th. 1688.

That

THat most Noble and Incomparable Medicine known by the name of *Clarks* Compound Spirits of *Scurvy-grass*, both *Golden* and *Plain*, and are of themselves so excellent and infallible a Remedy against the Scurvey, Dropsie, and all cold Distempers of the Stomach; are rightly prepared by the said *Henry Clark*, and sold at his House at the sign of the Lamb near *Somerset-House* in the *Strand*, and at all the Chief Towns in the Three Kingdoms, and most parts of the Habitable World. Price One Shilling each bottle.

F I N I S.

Dorothy Partridge's *The Woman's Almanack, For the Year 1694* (Wing 2016A) is reprinted from the copy at the Bodleian Library (Shelfmark Wood Alm. F [8]). The text block of the Bodleian copy is 75 × 135 mm.

For passages that are blotched, please consult Appendix B, 'A Key to Difficult-to-Read Passages'.

The Woman's Almanack,

For the YEAR 1694:

Calculated for the Meridian of City and Country.

Containing many choice, useful, pleasant, and most necessary Observations, adapted to the Capacity of the Female Sex, and not to be found in other Almanacks. As,

The Good House-wife's Calendar. A Table of Expences. The Critical Days of the Year. Observations on New-Year's Day. Of Dog-Days, and Unfortunate to the Female Sex. How to know the Hour by the Moon. Observations on Moles: How to know whither a young Woman be a Maid or not, by a new Way of Astrology. To know tell which shall die first a Man or his Wife. How to make Love-pinder. Choice Rarities, discovering to both Wives, and young Succisom Widows, their Fortune by the Stars; as, whether Rich or Poor, long Life, Marry or not; how many Husbands, whether marry the Person they desire, and whether rich or poor in their married State: What Voyages are Fortunate. Also excellent Cosmeticks to beautifie the Complexion of old Ladies, making one of sixty six serve as well as a young Girl of sixteen. How to procure a new Set of Teeth to grow in an old Woman's Mouth. To Cure a Red-face. Likewise what time of the Moon 'tis best to get Children.

By Dorothy Partridge, Midwife, Student in Astrology.

London Printed for J. S. in the Great Old-baily, 1694.

The Woman's Almanack, &c.

Monthly Observations in Goodhousewifrey, for the Year 1694.

JANUARY.

Pen Bee-hives, uncover Roots of Trees, cut Vines in one of the twelve days; take away superfluous Branches from Fruit-trees. Fruits in prime, Winter-musk (bakes well) Winter-norwich (excellently baked) Kentish-pepin, Russet-pepin, Holland-pepin. Set up your Traps for Vermin, especially in your Nurseries and Flower-gardens. A lusty squab fat Bedfellow very good Physick at this Season.

FEBRUARY.

Kitchen garden-herbs may be planted. Half-open your passages for the Bees. Now also plant out your Colly-flowers to have early; and begin to make your Hot-bed for the first Melons and Cucumbers. Continue Vemine-traps, &c. A good Season to get Children in.

MARCH.

Slip and set Sage, Rosemary, Lavender, Thyme, &c. By this time your Bees sit; keep them close Night and Morning. If Weather prove ill, plant and graft Fruit-trees, carry out Mannure; sow all seeds, whose roots are round, as Onyons, &c.

A-

208

APRIL

PRune Fruit-trees, plant and sow strange Flowers, plant Artichock-slips, set French-beans. This Month *Venus* is very rampant; get a lusty Husband, least worse befal ye.

MAY.

SEt Gilly-flowers close in Bed, repair Hedges. Now set your Bees at full liberty, look out often, and expect Swarms, &c. Ply the Laboratory, and distil Plants for Waters, Spirits, &c.

JUNE.

PLant, graft, or set tender Herbs or Flowers. Also fold in Sheep, and make them beat off the Dew with their feet in the morning before they feed. Sow Parsneps, Pumbions, Cucumbers, Melons, and Gourds, in a hot fair Day.

JULY.

GAther Flowers and Preserve. Replant such Herbs as you would not have Seed off. Sow Cabbage or Lettice in the old Moon.

AUGUST.

ABstane from the Feats of *Venus*, the Learned hold it very bad to use it this Month. Now cut down Wood for Winter-fire. Geld Lambs, &c.

SEPTEMBER.

SLip Garden-flowers, and re-plant them; and cast up Drains to keep the Land dry in Winter.

A 2. OCTO.

OCTOBER.

SEt Pears, Plums, and Apples, remove Trees that bear Kernels.

NOVEMBER.

ROugh, hew, and fashion Plough-timber, and lay it up to Season; the Ash is good, the Elm better.

DECEMBER.

KIll Swine; open Dreins to prevent Inundations; now use *Venus*.

Critical Observations on New-year's Day.

SOme observe that *New-year's Day* being red, portends great Tempest, and War. If it falls upon Sunday, then a pleasant Winter followeth, and a tempestious Spring, a dry Summer, a plentiful Vintage, Cattle grow, Honey aboundeth, and Women dye, Plenty and Peace. If upon Monday, a various Winter, a good Spring, Summer dry, hard Vintage, and Mens Health changeable, Bees dye, and Wonders shall be seen. If upon Tuesday, a Winter cloudy, a wet and tempestuous Spring, a dry Summer, a small Vintage, though at first hopeful, Women shall dye. If upon Wednesday, the Winter will be sharp and cold, the Spring hard and boysterous. If upon Thursday, a pleasant quiet Winter, a troublesome Spring. If upon Friday, a changeable Winter, a good Spring, Summer dry, a great Plenty of Corn, Sheep shall dye. If upon Saturday, a fearful Winter, for violent Gusts of Wind, a turbulent Spring, and Corn nought, with a rot of Sheep, old Women shall dye, and much burning abound.

of

210

THe Dog-days are so called, because of the influ-
ance of those Stars called the Dog, and they
continue in force so long as the Sun by his nearness
co-operateth with them, beginning about the 20th
day of *July*, and ending the 17th of *August*. *Diophantes*
would have us observe the rising of the Dog-Star,
in what Sign the Moon is in that time : for if she be
found in *Aries*, there useth to be small store of Grain,
but in *Gemini* great abundance, and so likewise in
Taurus ; in *Virgo*, corruption of Grain ; in *Sagitary*,
abundance, and so in *Capricorn* ; in *Aquarius*, scarcity ;
in *Piscibus*, Plenty ; in *Libra* abundance of Fruits,
with shells of Nuts, &c. Moreover, some do reckon
33 Unfortunate Days (as they call them) in a Year,
In *January*, the 1, 2, 4, 5, 10, 15, 17, and 19. In
February, the 8, 10, and 17. In *March*, the 15, 16,
19, and 28. In *April*, the 16, and 21. In *May*,
the 7, 17, and 20. In *June*, the 4, and 7. In *July*,
the 15, and 20. In *September*, the 6, and 7. In *October*, the 6. In *November*, the 15, and 28. In *December*, the 6, 7, and 9. Others also say that there
are in the Year six most Unfortunate Days to be let
Blood, or, to be Born : *January* the 3. *July* the 1.
October the 2. *April* the 3. *August* the 1, and 2. And
amongst many the 28 Day of *December*, called *childer-
miß-day, Cross-day*, and *Innocents-day*, Is taken for a very
evil Day. But it becometh Christian People not to
subject themselves unto Hours and Days, as did Pa-
gans of old.

Observations on the Weather.

THe Judgment of the Weather is very various and
uncertain, especially in an Island, such as is *England.*

land, *Scotland*, and *Ireland*, wherein one day the Season changes so often, as that the Morning may be cold like Winter, and the middle of the Day hot like Summer, and again the Night cold as Winter; and sometimes contrariwise it is hot in Winter, *&c.* But the mixture or confusion as it were of Sea and Land, with the often and sudden change of the Wind, are no little causes hereof. Wherefore frequent Observations and Experience in each particular Place, is very Necessary: Without which a learned Person may Err more grossely than he that hath no more Knowledge then Observation alone, as we see ordinarily in Shepherds and plain Husband-men that are much abroad by Day, and by Night. Whereas an Artist must observe the rising, culminating, and setting of the greatest Stars, the Ingress of the Sun into the four Cardinal Points, Eclipses, the Aspect of the Planets, but especially the Moon, and her Mansions and Lunations, *&c.* Which are here too Obscure, and too Tedious to Treat of, as they ought. Wherefore we will speak most of such ordinary Signs as Husband-men and Good Housewives do observe.

Signs of fair Weather.

IF it doth Lighten the day being clear, or if it Rain presently after a great Wind; when the Crow or Raven gapeth against the Sun in Summer; also the gaping of Dawes in the morning, the swarming of Bees, the flying of Humble-Bees, Droanes, or Bettles about the Doors in the Evening, the howling of the Owl in rainy Weather, and Ants removing of their Eggs; all these are signs of fair Weather.

Signs of foul Weather.

RObin Red-breast singeth under Hedges before Rain, but upon the tops of Trees before fair Weather. Hens lay abroad if it rain long, but under a Roof if it rain not long. The Herb *Tidsolly* looketh rough against a Tempest, and the Leaves stand staring; Hens resort to the Pearch or Roof covered with dust: Also the alteration of the Cock's crowing, the pruning and washing of Birds in Winter, the wallowing of Dogs, the ample working of the Spinner ver in the Air, the Ant busied with her Eggs, the Bees in fair Weather not going far, Rain suddenly dried up, the heaviness of Head and Eyes, the falling of Soot from Chimnies, the biting of Fleas, Flies and Gnats, the pissing often of Dogs, when Cattel eat greedily, and lick their Hoofs, if they suddenly run here and there, making a noise, and breathing into the Air with open Nostrils, also the croking of Frogs, Moles tairs up the Ground, the unaccustomed noise of Poultry or Swine, the crying of Crows twice or thrice quick calling, are signs of tempestuous Weather to follow. . Little Rain in Winter, is sign of a wet Spring to follow; and a hot dry Summer, is sign of a wet Winter: When it beginneth to freeze with an East-wind, cold Weather is like to continue.

How to judge of Weather by the Clouds.

BLack Clouds flying from the East, is Rain at Night, from the West, is Rain the next Day; if they fly low and appear to settle on the tops of Hills, it is cold Weather; if they be full charged, and appear whole like Towers, it Hails at hand: If white Clouds appear in Winter two or three days together at Sun-rising, it is Cold and Snow, but black Clouds are Rain. A red Sky in the Evening and a gray Morning, is a fair Day. Mists falling in the Morning in Spring or Harvest, also Mists over Ponds or Waters in the Morning, shew Rain. If Smoke ride swiftly in the Air, it is Wind from thence, especially from North to South. If Mists descend from Hills, and settle in the Valleys, it is fair hot Weather next day. If the Summer be moist, wet and cloudy, it is bad for Corn and Fruit, &c.

Of the Critical Days in the Year.

IN feaverish Diseases, and such like, the Physicians do observe Critical Days, that is to say, Days upon which there is a great alteration of Sickness, either towards Health or Death in the Patient: Such are reckoned to be the first day of the Sickness, the 14 day, the 20, and the 27. Indeed the Moon altereth those times somewhat by the swiftness or slowness of her motion. They have also days whereupon they do pass judgment of the Critical Time that cometh after, such are the 4 day of the Sickness, the 11, the 17, and

and the 2 . So likewise in Astrology, according to the Weather, (for the other is according to the temperament of the Body) there are some days, or rather seasons, seeing we look not altogether upon only one day, which are critical in regard of the Weather, and so consequently of Dearth and Epidemical or Raging Diseases, all which are to be understood to fall out so often, or for the most part, but not always. Nay, some are of opinion, that it is changed many days back in our times, but Experience and Observation can best satisfie in all these: Thus if the 22d day of *January* be clear without Clouds, it is a sign of a good Year for Wines

If on *Candlemas-day* the Sun shine, it is a sign of more Winter to be remaining than is already past. So if upon the 22d of *February*, it freeze or be cold, it will continue a Fortnight.

Also the 24th day of *February*, altereth the Weather from Frost to Thaw, or from Thaw to Frost.

So many Mists in *March*, so many hoary Frosts after *Easter*. If the Frogs be heard before the 24th day of *April*, so many days after are they silent.

A dry *March*, a moist *April*, and a cold *May* is thought to be a good Spring.

If the Sun shine the 25th day of *May*, Wines prosper. And if it rain the 24th of *June*, Nuts do not prosper. If the 24th of *June* be wet, it is a sign of a bad Harvest.

If it rain the 2d of *July*, there will much Rain follow.

If the Wind do not change the 24th day of *June*, the Night following it is held good.

If it rain the 4th day of *July*, it lasteth so four Weeks.

The 8th day of *July*, if fair, the Vintage shall be good, but if dark, bad.

If the 25th day of *July* be fair, it is a sign of a good Harvest.

So if the Leaves do not fall betimes in Harvest, it is a sign of a sharp Winter.

If the 24th day of *August* be fair, it is a sign of a good Harvest.

If it rain on the 1st day of *September*, it is a sign of a dry Harvest to come.

The

If the Deer on Rood-day lye down, and rise up dry,
Then forty days fair follow usually.

So many days old the Moon is the 29th day, so many floods that Winter. If the 17th day of *November* be cloudy, it sheweth a wet Winter; if dry, a sharp Winter. And as is the 11th so is the Winter.

From the 6th day of *September*, to the 21st, are called *Halcion-days*, because no Winds use to blow near to the shortest day of the Year. If the 25th day of *December* come is the new Moon, it is a token of a good Year: And the nearer to the new Moon the better: The contrary in the decrease. If the Sun shine the 12th day, or 6th of *January*, shall be much Wind: Such is Solstice or 11th day of *December*, such is the Winter. How many days the first Snow is, before new Moon, so many Snows are to come. Thunder on *Shrove-Tuesday*, foretelleth Wind, store of Fruit, and Plenty, the Sun-beams being early abroad: Others affirm, So much it shineth that day, the like it shineth every day of *Lent*. If it rain on *Ascension-day*, it betokeneth scarcity of Food for Cattel; but if it be fair, plenty.

How to know what of the Clock by the Moon.

LOok upon any Sun-dial, and see what of the Clock it is by the shadow of the Moon, as you do by the Sun, observing how much it wanteth, or is past 12, for so much it wanteth, or is past the hour of her coming to the South; and knowing the Age of the Moon at that time, you shall find the time of her coming to the South, by the Table of the length of Moon shining, which is aforesaid. As for example, Let the shadow of the Moon point at 11 of the Dial, and if it be the 10th day of the Moon, she cometh to the South, or shineth by the Table 8 Hours; then subtract 1 from 8, and there remaineth 7 of the Clock, for the Hour of the said time.

B   The

Expences for one Day	One Week			One Month			One Year			
	Shillings	Pence	Farthings	Shillings	Pence	Farthings	Pounds	Shillings	Pence	Farthings
A Farthing		1	3		7				7	7	1
A half-peny	1	3	2		1	2			1	2	2
A Penny		7	0					1	1	5	
Two Pence		2	2		2	4		3	0	10	0
Three pence is for	1	9	is f.	4	8	is for	4	11	3	0
A Groat	2	4		9	4		5	14	0	0
Five pence	2	11		1	0	0	7	12	1	0
Six pence	1	3	6	14	0	0	9	2	6	0
A Shilling	7		1 l.	8			18	5	0	0

Here are four several Tables, one for a Day, the second for a Week, the third for a Month, the fourth for a Year. As to know what the expence of one Farthing a Day is for one Week together, to wit, one Penny three Farthings a Day is for one Week together, to wit, one Penny three Farthings; for a Month, seven Pence; and for a Year, seven Shillings, seven Pence, and one Farthing. And this is to be observed That so many Pence by the Day, make by the Year just so many Pounds, half Pounds and Groats, as seven Pence a day is by the Year, seven Pounds, seven half Pounds, and seven Groats.

Of Riches and Poverty.

The Letter A in the Root of the Fore-finger, promises great Riches and Gain; likewise many Lines from the Root of the Thumb, between the Thumb and Line of Life, pointing toward the Ring-finger, promises great Riches. A Mark like a Ladder on the Mount of the Fore-finger, signifies a poor Woman, subject to great losses.

of

Lines reaching from the Mount of the Thumb, over the Mount, (towards the Line of Life) shew the Number of Husbands; therefore observe how many there be; and she shall have so many Husbands, or at least a *Bolus* to keep her from the *Green-Sickness*; I mean, a Friend in the corner.

Of short Life.

The Line of Life, if it be short, it shews a short Life, and by how much the more it inclines to brevity, so much the more it is feared.

Of Buxsomness and Lust.

The Sister of the Line of Life, on the Mount of the Thumb, long and redish in the Hand of a Woman; also the Mount or ring of the Thumb big, and elevated with many cross disordered Lines, with Lines chequerwise near the Wrist of the Hand; all these denotes and intimates the Woman will kiss in a Corner, or beat her Puss-past with her Neighbour's Rowling-pin; one that cannot fix her Humours to a constant Diet.

How to make Hair as red as a Fox, a lovely Brown.

Take of Lead calcined with Sulphur one part, and another part of quick Lime, mix them with Water, then let it dry, then wash it very clean with Soap and Water, and it will be a very natural Brown: the longer it lieth the better it groweth.

To Cure a Lady's Red Face.

Take Lilly-roots four Ounces, boil them in two Pints of Water until half be consumed; then take it off, strain it out, and keep it for your use.

To make an old Woman's Teeth white, recover a new Set, beautifie the Face, and take out the furrow'd Rinkles as smooth as a Girl of Sixteen.

Take Loaf-sugar 1 Pound, Allom 3 Ounces, the flower of Beans, Fumitory, and Water-lillies, a handful of each, 4 Limons sliced, the Crumb of 2 white Loaves, Goats-milk and White-wine, of each 2 Pints; bruise what is to be bruised; then mix them together in a Glass Alembick, distil them in *Balneo Mariæ*: keep the Water as most excellent for the abovementioned uses.

of

Of Moles; how to know whether any Person hath them.

A Mole on the Nose of a Man, or Lip of a Woman, denotes another on the Privy Parts: A Mose on the Nape of the Neck, another on the Buttocks; and if it be on the Cheek, another on the Belly; a Mole on the Forehead, another on the Breast; a Mole under the Eye-brow, another on the Navel: And this very seldom fails.

How to know whether a Woman be a Maid or no.

Take a spoonful of the Spirit of Seagreen, House-leek, the Powder of Crabs-teeth, one dram; half an Ounce of *Jamaica* Pepper beaten very small, and mixt together, and presented in a Glass of Wine, Beer, or roasted Apple; if the party do not sneeze in half an Hour after, you may suspect her Virginity; if she do, be confident she is virtuous.

How to know which shall die first, the Husband or Wife.

Note, That there are seven Letters in the Cross-row that stand for Numbers, as, C for 100, D for 500, L for 50, M for 1000, V for 5, X for 10. Therefore to know which Party shall die first, write down the Man's Christian and Sirname, and then the Woman's Maiden name also, and count which of their Names by those Letters can make the greatest Number, and that Party shall over-live the other.

How to make a Philtre, or Love-powder.

Take a Swallow's Nest, young ones and all, and digging a hole in the Earth, put them in, and cover it up; let them lie there 48 hours, then opening the place, take the young swallows out, and dry them to Powder very small; and this, some say, hath strange effects: Otherwise, the breathing the Basilick Veins, and distilling it after, is the best Love-powder.

Licensed according to Order.

Mother Shipton's *The Prophesie of Mother Shipton In the Raigne of King Henry the Eighth* (Wing 3445) is reprinted from the copy at The British Library, Thomason Tracts Collection (Shelfmark E.181 [15]). The text block of the British Library copy is 100 × 135 mm.

For passages that are blotched, please consult Appendix B, 'A Key to Difficult-to-Read Passages'.

THE
PROPHESIE
OF
MOTHER SHIPTON

In the Raigne of King
Henry the Eighth.

Fortelling the death of Cardinall *Wolsey*, the Lord *Percy*
and others, as also what should happen in
insuing times.

LONDON,
Printed for Richard Lownds, at his Shop
adjoyning to Ludgate. 1641.

1

The Prophecie of Mother *Shipton*,
in the Raigne of King *Henry*
the eighth.

Hen shee heard King *Henry* the eighth should be King, and Cardinall *Wolsey* should be at *Yorke*, shee said that Cardinall *Wolsey* should never come to *Yorke* with the King, and the Cardinall hearing, being angry, sent the Duke of *Suffolke*, the Lord *Piercy*, and the Lord *Darcy* to her, who came with their men disguised to the King's house neere *Yorke*, where leaving their men, they went to Master *Besley* to *Yorke*, and desired him to goe with them to Mother *Shiptons* house, where when they came they knocked at the doore, shee said Come in Master *Besley*, and those honourable Lords with you, and Master *Besley* would have put in the Lords before him, but she said, come in Master *Besley*, you know the way, but they doe not. This they thought strange that she should know them, and never saw them, then they went into the house, where there was a great fire, and she bade them welcome, calling them all by their names, and sent for some Cakes and Ale, and they drunke and were very merry. Mother *Shipton*, said the Duke, if you knew what wee come about, you would not

A 2

not make us so welcome, and shee said the messenger
should not be hang'd ; Mother *Shipton*, said the Duke you
said the Cardinall should never see *Yorke* ; Yea, said shee,
I said hee might see *Yorke*, but never come at it ; But said
the Duke, when he comes to *Yorke* thou shalt be burned ;
Wee shall see that, said shee, and pluckling her Hand-
kerchieffe off her head shee threw it into the fire, and it
would not burne ; then shee tooke her staffe and turned it
into the fire, and it would not burne, then she tooke it and
put it on againe ; Now (said the Duke) what meane you
by this ? If this had burn'd (said she) I might have burned. Mother *Shipton* (quoth the Duke) what thinke you
of me ? my love said she, the time will come you will
be as low as I am, and that's a low one indeed. My
Lord *Percy* said, what say you of me ? My Lord (said she)
shooe your Horse in the quicke, and you shall dye well,
but your body will bee buried in *Yorke* pavement, and
your head shall be stolne from the barre and carried into
France. Then said the Lord *Darcy*, and what thinke you
of me ? Shee said, you have made a great Gun, shoot it
off, for it will doe you no good, you are going to warre,
you will paine many a man, but you will kill none, so
they went away.

Not long after the Cardinall came to *Cawood*, and
going to the top of the Tower, hee asked where *Yorke*
was, and how farre it was thither, and said that one
had said hee should never see *Yorke* ; Nay, said one,
shee said you might see *Yorke*, but never come at it.
He vowed to burne her when hee came to *Yorke*. Then
they shewed him *Yorke*, and told him it was but eight
miles thence ; he said that he will be soone there : but being sent for by the King, hee dyed in the way to *Lon-*
don

don at *Lecester* of a lacke ; And — wife said to Mister *Besley*, yonder is a fine Hall built for the Cardinall in the Minster, of Gold, Pearle, and precious stone, goe and present one of the pillers to King Henry, and her did so.

Mister *Besley* seeing these things fall out as shee had foretold, desired her to tell him some more of her Prophesies : Mester, said she, before that Ouse Bridge and Trinitie Church meet, they shall build on the day, and it shall fall in the night, untill they get the highest stone of Trinitie Church, to be the lowest stone of Ouse bridge, then the day will come when the North shall rue it wondrous sore, but the South shall rue it for evermore ; When Hares kindle on cold harth stones, and Lads shall marry Ladyes, and bring them home, then shall you have a yeare of pyning hungar, and then a dearth without Corne ; A wofull day shall be seen in England, a King and Queene, the first comming of the King of *Scots* shall be at *Holgate* Towne, but he shall not come through the barre, and when the King of the North shall bee at *London* Bridge, his Tayle shall be at *Edesborough* : After this shall water come over *Ouse* bridge, and a Windmill shall be set on a Tower, and an Elme-tree shall lye at every mans doore, at that time women shall weare great hats and great bands, and when there is a Lord Major at *Yorke* let him beware of a stab ; When two Knights shall fall out in the Castle yard, they shall never bee kindly all their lives after : When all Colton Hagge hath borne seven yeares Crops of corne, seven yeares after your heare newes, there shall two Iudges goe in and out at *Mongate* barre.

Then Warres shall begin in the spring,
Much woe to England it shall bring :
Then shall the Ladyes cry well-away,
That ever we liv'd to see this day.

Then best for them that have the least, and worst for
them that have the most; you shall not know of the War
over night, yet you shall have it in the morning, and
when it comes it shall last three yeares, betweene *Cadron*
and *Aire* shall be great warfare, when all the world is as a
lost, it shall be called Christs crost, when the battell begins, it shall be where Crookbackt *Richard* made his fray,
they shall say, To warfare for your King for halfe a crown
a day, but stirre not (she will say) to warfare for your
King, on paine on hanging, but stirre not, for he that goes
to complaine, shall not come backe againe : The time will
come when *England* shall tremble and quake for feare of
a dead man that shall bee heard to speake, then will the
Dragon give the Bull a great snap, and when the one is
downe they will goe to *London* Towne : Then there will
be a great battell betweene *England* and *Scotland*, and they
will be pacified for a time, and when they come to *Bram-
mammore*, they fight and are again pacified for a time, then
there will be a great Battell at *Knavesmore*, and they will
be pacified for a while : Then there will be a great battell
betweene *England* and *Scotland* at *Sandesyde :* Then will
Ravens sit on the Crosse and drinke as much blood of
the Nobles, as of the Commons, then woe is mee, for
London shall be destroyed for ever after : Then there will
come a woman with on : eye, and she shall tread in many
mens bloud to the knee, and a man leaning on a staffe by
her, and she shall say to him, What art thou ? and he shall
say.

say, I am King of the Seas, and she shall say, Goe with
me to my house, for there are three Knights, and he will
goe with her, and stay there three dayes and three nights,
then will *England* be lost; and they will cry twice of a
day *England* is lost. Then there will be three Knights in
Petergate in *Yorke*, and the one shall not know of the other.
There shall be a Childe borne in *Pontfret* with three
thumbes, and those three Knights will give him three
Horses to hold, while they win *England*, and all Noble
bloud shall be gone but one, and they shall carry him to
Sheriffe *Nuttons* Castle six miles from *Yorke*, and he shall
dye there, and they shall choose there an Earle in the
field, and hanging their Horses on a thorne, And rue the
time that ever they were borne, to see so much bloud-
shed; Then they will come to *Yorke* to besiege it, and
they shall keepe them out three dayes and three nights,
and a penny loafe shall bee within the barre at halfe a
crowne, and without the barre at a penny; And they will
sweare if they will not yeeld, to blow up the Towne
walls. Then they will let them in, and they will hang up
the Major, Sheriffs and Aldermen, and they will goe into Crouch Church, there will three Knights goe in, and
but one come out againe, and he will cause Proclamati-
on to be made, that any man may take House, Tower, or
Bower for twentie one yeares, and whilest the world en-
dureth, there shall never be warfare againe, nor any more
Kings or Queenes, but the Kingdome shall be governed
by three Lords, and then Yorke shall be London. And after
this shall be a white Harvest of corne gotten in by women. Then shall be in the North, that one woman shall
say unto another, Mother I have seene a man to day,
and for one man there shall be a thousand women, there
shall

shall be a man sitting upon St. *James* Church hall and play his fill, And after that a Ship come sayling up the Thames till it come against *London*, and the Master of the Ship shall weepe, and the Marriners shall aske him why hee weepeth, being he hath made so good a voyage, and he shall say, Ah what a goodly Citie this was, none in the world comparrable to it, and now there is scarce left any house that can let us have drinke for our money.

Vnhappy he that lives to see these dayes,
But happy are the dead Shiptons wife sayes.

FINIS

Shinkin ap Shone's *The honest Welch-Cobler* (Wing 3436A) is reprinted from The British Library, Thomason Tracts Collection (Shelfmark E.379 [4]). The text block of the British Library copy is 100 × 165 mm.

For passages that are blotched, please consult Appendix B, 'A Key to Difficult-to-Read Passages'.

The honeſt

4.

VVELCH-COBLER,

for her do ſcorne to call her
ſelſe the ſimple *Welch-Cobler;*

Although her thinkes in all her

Conſciences, if her had as many as would ſtand
betweene *Paules* and *Sharing-Croſſe* that her have
not ſo much wit as her Brother Cobler of *A-*
merica, yet her thinke her may have as much
knaverys and though her have not ſo much *Greek,*
which her holds to be *Heathenish;* nor *Hebrew,*
which her holds to be *Shewish* Language; nor
Latine, which is the Language of *Rome,* yet her
ſhall endever her ſelſe to deliver her ſelſe in as
cood Tialect as her can for her hait plood, for the
petter underſtanding of all her friends and kindred, whether *Comro* or *Siſ,* wherein her ſhall
find variety of counſells, profitable inſtructions,
ſeaſonable cautions, to prevent tangers that may come
upon ill her countrymen here; Her also ſhall find ſome
truth, little honeſty, ſome wit, and a creat teale of kna-
verie.

BY

Shinkin ap Sheni, ap Griſfith, ap Searard, ap Sitles, ap
Shoſeph, ap Lewis, ap Lawrince, ap Richard, ap Tho-
mas ap Sheffre, ap Shewmes, ap Taſſel ap Hrris,
All Shentlemen in WALES.

Printed by M. *Shinkin,* Printer to S. *Taſſie,* and
are to be ſold at the Signe of the Owen the
march 11th Welch Mountaine. 1647. 1646

The honest Welch Cobler.

Hen her take into teep and serious consitteration the many abuses and reproaches cast upon her teer friends and countrymen, it many times makes her scratch where it toth not itch, & finding no redresse tat way, put rather more trouble and perplexitie poth in her head and mind, her resolved with herselfe of another course for her owne and her countrey mens sadication, tat is as much as to say, to publish to the world some little Tract or Treatise, for her is sery eloquent, wherein her is minded to show to the world the candour of her ententions, and the excellencie of her inventions, the sharpnesse of her wit, & the rashnesse of her Judgment, which her had rather call the ripenesse of Shudgment, her skill in Philosophy, her dexteritie in Divinitie, her magnanimous Chavaldrie in Martial Discipline, & her knowledge in State-Maximes, as her may so call it, put to tell her the truth, and no more put the truth, her cane wes not the meaning of the word, put onely her makes pold to use the word, to shew her elegancie of speech, though her pee no more able to understand it then her is able to understand one of the creat mountaines in VVales. Put now her think ont, her can understand more of her Welch mountaine then her can of her hard srates, for her can coop up to the top of her Welch mountaine, and tigg stones and tirt enough to preake her pack, and lay it on her head or shoulder, and then her unterstands it, mark her tat now. Put to avoid prolixitie, her wil preak est presacing any longer, put sall close to her pusinest. put now her talke of pusines, fill her had pett doe her pusines that none can doe put her selfe, for seare her make a peastly piece of worke ont, put sirst her will sing a song pesore her coe any further.

> Taffie was prave, and her puilt her a Cave,
> under the foot of a Mountaine,

Taffie

Taffie was fine, and her tranke of the whit,
the water out of the Fountaine: &c.
Taffia ate Apple-Crabb, put her love was a Trubb,
for strokeing the whey out of her firking.
Put all the long day of her Harpe her will play,
and make the lowse sance in her Sherking.

There was a time when her Welch wit would worke like her Welch wind, otherwise called *Matheglim*, and lick up roddy is her countreymen use to lick up Welch *Flummery*, yet further wit now our honestie will pay any thing its hee Welch Mistees, her must set her selfe flat and close to her Trade of Cobling, and first I shall beekin with the greatest piece of worke I have, though it may be worst payd for it, and this is *Prince Rupert* Boots to sale, and he useth to pay folkes with his Pole-ax. You may remember, as I was informed by some of her owne Countreymen, and those none of the pest qualitie, tat made a shift to save her selves by the nimble agilitie of her heeles at *Marston* fight, that *Prince Rupert* save her selfe, ran over the Beane field, and there her lost either one or both her soles, her ftack so fast in the Clay is that to her oldator pet commend her for her wit, for hoe is sure her will never pe hang'd for her honestie, tat her would parfel her selfe with her Cossens of *Wales*, tat when her see her could not overcome by fighting, to save her selfe by flying: and for tat trick and one more that her canowes her will let her on a piyse of the pest soler tat her wore in her life gratis, because her canow tat her lost all tere & at *Naseby*, and never cot any toud fortune since, except a purge and a broken shyn at *Abbington*, and a little strong beere at *Bristo*, and tere her was forced to leave the greatest part behind him, because he could not stay to drink it but upon those conditions, first that her come no more a plundring into her Welch territories, to tarry away her toud Welch sheep, tat her should cott for her nows selfe, her wife and shildren, which though her says her selfe, is made as cleanly as any Shees in all *Wales*, for her wife strained it through the skirt of her foule smock, for feare there should be any hayres of her Cow or Goat in her Shees to shoake her.

Secondly, tat if her ever shance to come againe into *England* or *Wales*, and to have any of her countrymen under her command,

tat her pring tem no further on, ten her can cnow how to pring
tem off with credit, and not run away from tem in te midst of te
pattle, and leave tem to shift for temselves, while her selfe fall to
plundring of waggons and so her selfe cet all te money, while her
countreymen get knocks : and upon the performances of these
conditions, her will give her some advice which will doe her no
hurt, if her will take it: and first, tat her come no more into *England*
or *Wales*, if her can help it, to fight, for though her be a man of valour, and loves to fight when her cannot shule, yet her knowes by
experience that her may meet with her match in *England*, tat will
past her sides, and preake her pate, and send her home to her owne
countrey for a plaster, and what will her get by tat ?

Secondly, tat her use her utmost endever to make her peace with
cood Parliament & people of *England*: for if her wel consider with
her selfe what cood tey have done for her, and what mischiese her
hath done for them, her will find cause enough to looke about her,
I warrant her. But her seele her selfe not well, call in some of her
kindred, for her is resolved to make her Will, and set her house in
order, pefore her goe away and pe seene no more, and if her shance
to mend, her will follow her owne Trade againe: put in the meane
time her will make an Inventorie of all her cood and bad moveables and immoveables, and make her Cozen *Maurice* Executor.

*Imprimis, in her ped-shamber one foule wife and five small shil-
dren, those being part of her moveable pads, I wish from her heart
they were removeable.*

*Item, in another shamber two payre of surst Queanes tongues,
or tongs should I call them, no, its no matter, they will pinsh worse
then tongs, they are moveables Ile warrant you.*

*Item, in her Pride-shamber one payre of Hornes upon her peds
head, tat her may thank her wife for, and these are unmoveable coods.
*Felix quem faciunt aliena pericula cautem ; *Happie is her whom
other mens Hornes doe make to beware.*

*Item, one proken pate owing to her by one of her neighbours for a
cood turne her tid tem seven years agoe, that is desperate debt.*

*Item, five hundred shrewd turnes owing to me from her Cosens of
*England, *for and in consideration of divers Horse, Cowes and Sheepe
her stole from them, put these are desperate debts also.*

Pu.

5

Put now her spirits pegins to come to her regine, and therefore one word to Prince *Maurice*, for her hath peen a great Taper in her time, and her is doubtfull that her soles of her poops begin to weare out, and therefore her will pestow a payre of soles upon him, if her thought her would take it in good part, and her would give her good counsell with all her heart plood: first, that her would not tance any more after such ungodly measures, tat her hath done in former times, in firing houses, killing good Ministers, and rivers of her owne teare countreymen, which cave her her cause at all. I would have her consider, tat it were too bale a culling for one of her plood and qualitie to turne *Lyme*-burner, if her remember when and how well her was payd for her paines, when her were apout to purne *Lyme*, her should consider, that it was unfit for her Highnesse to purne whole Townes in *England* when her had never a House nor Cottage of her owne, little or pig, to make satisfaction for the wrongs which her had done; and though her prother was made Duke of *Cumberland*, yet it were put firmly; what is her Title worth now? in her judgment it is not worth the smoake of one of her Welch Ladies, when her wife makes Leeke-pottage: and therefore her say, Prince, if her pee wise, keepe her away while her is well, for as her is a Prince of the plout Royall, if her never be catch, her can never be questioned; and thinke her have given her good counsell, and her hope her will not pee crusty, though her pee somewhat hard-bake, if her should heare, that her and her prother peeing growne men, have helpt to rob five hundred tat helpt to feed tem when tey were shildren.

And pesore her forget her, forget her did her say, her warrant her her shall never forget her while her live, nor twentie yeare after, the Marquis of *Newcastle*, a pox on her picture, her thinks her was no witch, pur her made her selfe as plack as a Divell with her Coale-dust, no matter if her had peen choakt with it, for her made many of her friends and countreymen in and about *London* to fret themselves hot, and at last many were glad to sell or pawne all tat her selfes, and her wifes and shildren had worke for all hers life time, to get her some bite. Pur, if ever her catch her in her Welch Territories, her will make her run as fast as her did when her run away beyond Sea after.

after *Marston-moore*, and therefore if her canow when her is well, let her keepe her selfe where her is, and if her have worne out her poots in her running march its pest for her to go to her Couzen Cobler in *America*, and her will patch her poot for her *cratis*, for her do tell her in plaine tennes it is not safe for her to come upon our *Welch* or *English* coasts, for fear her shou'd catch a blocish Ague, as her Couzen *Strafford* did or the Beshits Crick of *Canterbury*, and many others which her could name, for if the Parliament chance to feele her pulses and find her not well quallified for to take some Parliament physick to purge away all her Malignant humours, yet her will go neere to let her plood in the neck, and then her mind will be quite shanged her will never be cood after it, and so her takes her leave of her Marquis of *Newcastle*, better take her leave here then at the------.

Next her would intreat the new Lord *Capell*, a Lord of te last Edition, her do scorne to call her Cow-stealer, her father was an honest Shentleman, and kept a cood house, her little thought of leaving a Son so famous for Coward ze and Cow-stealing, but *Tawsone*, her will say no more, onely her would entreat her never to come more into *VVales*, for her do tell her, tat her is like to loose her labour if her come, for her have almost no Cowes left in *VVales*: Therefore her tad as cood keepe her where her is as come to trouble her and her Countrymen and her selfe, too I could tell her her none, but her spares her because her was lately created Baron of *Haddam*, but now her thinkes her may now be called Baron of *Hadland*, for her could tell her how many creat Pig-houses her had in *Hartfordshire*, where her Baronie of *Hadland*, *Haddum* I should say lies, where her knowes her urship had Parks where were as many horned Beasts as there are apps in her *VVelch* Sheneologes, and so her have done with her urship for this time, onely her would entreat her urship if her have any Cow-Hides left, tat her would put them to tanning for feare her should want leather to sole her poots, and so *Du Cat en ough*.

Put roome for *Cottington* that *Spanish* Fox, her had more familiaritie with *Romish* keese then were fit for her urship to have, for they have hatcht many Cockatrice eges against the Clue and Parliament, and they proved gallant Godsling in his eye for the time,

time, but now they are all dashte, her heard that her urship was
made Lord High Treasurer, but now her tall Cedar like Honour
is laid in the dust, but her will tell her one infallible truth which
her urship will not deny : Since her left her Urships great House
in *ProadStreet*, there hath pin more money told then all her Honour is worth, if her Honour were to be sold by weight, but her
urship hath found by her none experience, that there pee shurch
in *England* that will unkennell the subtilest old Fox in *Spaine*: If
her come heere to give evill counsell, her would wish her urship
to carch her selfe in some other soyle , if her love her selfe and
her eares, come not into her Welch territories, for her have but
few sheep or Lambs, nor Goats, nor Kids, nor Tucks, nor Hens,
nor Keese, nor Kocksins, lest in her principallity of *VVales*, and
beside her have Foxes *Diggon* in *VVales*, and therefore her desires none of her company in *Wales*, to devoure her Welch
Poultry, so farewell and be —— *Foxes never fare better then when*
they are curst.

Put now her can forbeare no longer, her was ready to preake
packwards, and then her should long her good flanell shirt which
cost two croats put halfe a year agoe, when bee tall to mind one
of her owne countrymen flesh, plood and pone, her cannot chuse
but admire at her, her meane the Pishop of *Torke*, the Weather-
Cock, the wonder of her age, her should have said, but her hope
her Preterne of *England* will pardon her expressions, I hope her
will not deny her wonted priviledge, that is, to tell her tale twice
her being a Welchman put to her matter in hand, her countryman
is mettall to the hard ars, for her can use her *Paules* Sword, as
well as her *Peters* Keyes, her may see that while there is life there
is hopes, her had as many thought to see the Tevill turn Presby-
ter as her countryman and k nisman *Williams*, put now her thinke
a Wind-mill would better become her head then a Miter, and so
her will take her leave of her countryman.

And then there is her Cozzen *Wren*, that little Bird, but her
was serry full of mischief as her sheese use to be full of Maggots,
this is her that kept the Taylors wife at *Cambridge* and made her
Husband looke throngh a payre of horning Spectacles, all the
Soape and Sophistrie in *Cambridge* will not wash out that spot in
her Lawne Sleeves, her was put to silence above threescore Ministers

kers at one Fiſh, her was creat jnſtrument in placing ſcanda ous
Prieſts up and towne her Country, where her had to do, ſuch as
was in her owne Country, that would read ſervice in the fore
noone and pe trunke jn the after-noone, nay, perhaps be trunk
all the weeke after, and yet they were ſo covetous, tat her had put
thirteene eggs in an Neſt and her went to lay with her, and
made her ſpend ten pounds, pecauſe her gave her but one for Tythe
but now her little Wren is met withall, now her cannot do miſ
chief as her did before, her is in the Tower, and her do pray her
Lieutenant and her Warders to looke well to her, for her is poor
little Pird, and can get out at a little hole, and her would pray
her to keepe her wings clipt, for ſeare her ſhould fly away, her
thinkes in Conſcience her cood Parliament might doe well to
ſend her to New-England to work for her living, for her have bin
ſo cood in Old England that no pody cares for her companie and
beſide ſhange of Aire may ſhange his chind, for her have heard
men ſay tat ſhange of paſture makes ſat Calves, and why not
ſhange of climates make ſat Knaves, her canow that her preterme
of England would be glad to be rid of him, & ſo much for Wren.

Her had almoſt forgot her Lordſhip Littleton, that ran away
with the Creat Seale, her was never the wiſer man for that, nor
never the honeſter man, to play the knave with them that dealt
ſo well with him: but her have not much ro ſay to her, becauſe
her have but little acquaintance with her, onely take heed to her
ſelfe, for her knowes what is the reward of a pick-pocket better
then her ſelfe.

And then there is the Lord Hopton, a man of mettall, and a
wiſe man, or elſe he ſhould be, for there is not one hair betweene
her and the sky, it is pitty her was ever engaged in ſuch a quarel,
her was fayne to ſell her honeſty to buy her a petiwig of honour,
a Titular Baronie, and now her is glad to hop away, and leave
her Houſe and Land behind her, and carry nothing with her but
her Periwig, which is but light of carriage, her may carry it whi
ther her will with her, except her come to London, and then her
muſt lay it downe, but her thinke hardly her will come there,
farewell ſcolt, if her never come againe there is nothing loſt.

F I N I S.

Shinkin ap Shone's *Shinkin ap Shone Her Prognostication for The ensuing Year, 1654* (Wing 2385) is reprinted from the copy in The British Library, Thomason Tracts Collection (Shelfmark E.731 [5]). The text block of the British Library copy is 100×165 mm.

For passages that are blotched, please consult Appendix B, 'A Key to Difficult-to-Read Passages'.

Shinkin ap Shone   5.

HER

PROGNOSTICATION

FOR

The ensuing Yeer, 1654.

FORE-TELLING

What Admirable Events are like to

fall out in the Horizon of *Little Britain* beyond *Mawburn*
Hills, and in all other places in *Europe, Asia, Africa,*
and *AMERICA.*

As also a true Storie of the beginning of the *Welsh-men,* their Rise
and Progress, and how they came first to inhabit the *Welsh Moun-*
tains, never heretofore discovered either in Print or Writing, and now published for the comfort and con-
solation of aul her countreymen now living,
and for the benefit of Posterity.

Likewise an Astrological Prediction, concerning the Gazing Star,
seen by thousands of people in and about *London,* the
22. and 23 of *February* 1653.

Calculated for the Meridian of Mawburn-hils, *where the Pole Artick*
is elevated eight foot and twelve inches above the Welsh Alps,
and may serve indifferently for all Kingdoms, Coun-
treys and Continents.
March, &6: 1654

Printed for the Author, and are to be sold at his shop at the Sign
of the Cows Bobby behind the Welsh Mountain.

242

1

Shinkin ap Shone her Prognostication.

IT was spoken long since by her cosen, a wise and learned Welsh Shentleman, that art had no enemy but ignorance; and therefore her shall not speak much by way of Preface, Preludium or Exordium, for her do not doubt in the least but to give her understanding Countreymen good content, and for carping zoiluses and mumbling Mommuses, her takes no care to please, but for her ingenuous sons of art, her hopes her will take her pains and industry in good part, and so her begins her Prognostication, and because divers of her learned Astrologers, especially her own cosens and her Country men, differ about which moneth should be the first in the yeer, som taking it to begin in *Ianuary*, others in *March*, therefore her will deliver her sence concerning that point, and says that in her judgment the yeere begins in *March*, and that for these her welsh reasons: First, because according to her rules of her welch art, the first day of *March* is St. *Taffies* day, at which time the Leeks be ripe and fit for her pot, and if her mistake not, there will be a new Moon about the eighth day of *March*, five quarters of an hour past 5 at night; and therefore her doz conclude, by these her welsh reasons, that the yeer begins in *March*. Another of her reasons is, because her own cosen and countreyman *Lewis ap Shone*, being a fery learned shentleman, in the Mathematical Science, doz confirm her in her judgment; and now to her prognostication. In this Moneth her shall have fair weather if it be not foul, in this moneth also is a very good time for her to eat Leeks and Onions, especially in her welsh porrage, it will moke her good plood, and will cleanse her veins from excrementuous humours: in this Moneth her is fearful divers of her cosens and countreymen will be in great danger, by reason of some malevolent Planets influence upon her deer countrymen; for if her be not mistaken in her *Annals*, her Cosen *Lewis Keeg Gwiden* was hang'd at *Presteign* much about this time of the yeer, and if her countreymen be not ferry careful of their own safeties, there will be many of her Countreymen go the same way: for her know, that when the sign is in the neck, as it is on the 11 day of this moneth, her Countreymen are in much danger, of which her is

A 2   ready

ready to give them warning, which her prayes all her Countreymen to take in time; for if her do not take her counsell in time, it will be worse for her, and therefore if her love her neck peware apout this time, great plots and conspiracies are like to be found out, but hope, though her bee not fery sure, that her honest countreymen wil have nothing to do with such deeds of darkness, for her own part, her do declare her shudgement freely, her thinks it best and safest to sleep in a whole skin, and her say again, and again, tat for her own part, let whose neck wil come into a halter, her is resolved to keep her neck out, if her can; for her do wel remember, tat if her head be once cotten in, its hardly cotten out again quickly; for her own father was a Shentleman of good quality, for a Welshman, and was shoakt with a halter, and yet her was no plotter nor conspirator, but a fery honest shentleman of good repute among her neighbors, only her borrowed five yoke of Oxen of her neer kinsman *Rice ap Hugh*, witkout her consent; which misfortune, her cannot attribute to any thing but her destinie and malevolent stars; and terefore her shal conclude tiss moneths Observations with te words of a wise man, *viz. He tat pewares not pefore, shal pee sorry afterwards.*

Aprills Observations.

Tiss moneth peginste fift day, according to te shudgement of the ancient, and for her own part, her is of the same shudgement, and tat for tiss reason, pecause as her humbly conceives, tere is a new Moon te seven day, apout three quarters of an hour past three of te clock in te morning; and dux her think a new Moon can pee made in less time than seven days, and some few odd hours and minuts? Truly her thinks not for her owne part, neither duz her pelieve tat te best or most skilfullest in aule her country can make one new moon in twice te time, let her prate what her wil, if her knows not te Law her duz but lose her labor, and make her self pee laught at; for her tat wanteth knowledg art and science is but the outside of a man, without an inside: For now her call to her memory, her have read a Story of *Alexander* and his great horse, for they were both wise: it is reported of his horse, tat when he had his trappings and rich furniture

niture on, he would suffer none but his Master *Alexander* himself to come neer him, but when his rich turniture was off, hee
was so gentle that any one of his Masters servants might get upon his back and ride him at pleasure : for which her wisdom, as
her humbly conceives, it was that her Master *Alexander* loved
her so wel, for *Alexander* was a man, that loved learning and
learned men intirely, her made so creat account of knowledg and
learning, tat her would oft times say, tat her thought her selfe
more peholding to *Aristotle* for her learning, than to *Philip* her
father for her life, pecaus as her conceived, the one *viz.* Learning, is immortal, and te other, *viz.* Life, but shoit and momenta-
ry. But her must not dwel here, her hope her countrymen will
pardon her long and needful digression, peing in commendation
of learning and learned men, and now to hor business. Tiss month
as her have read in sery cood Authors, was te Mountains of
Wales first inhabited by ker Ancestors and Predecessors, and pecaus many prophane and ignorant *Englishmen* have presumed to
traduce her teer friends and countrymen with sundry opprobri-
ous languages, as first, tat her countreymen spring first of all
from a horseturd left upon te top of *Maburn-hills* by *Buce-
phalus, Alexanders* creat horse, others of them say, tat when
Brutus first entred *Wales* her horse left a *Surrevesence* uponte
top of *Mawburn-hills*, and from thence came her countrymen,
and terefore tey call her Countrymen *Brutes*, as if they were
Beasts, others of tem say, tat te first peginning of her countreymen sprang from a *Baw Gnithie*, or a *Goose*——— breathed upon *Pigmalions* Image, te Poets feigning tat te gods made her a
live; and te first time she blew her nose she threw te snot from
her, which falling upon a *Goose*——— from that *precious compound*
came te Welshman : But in all tese tings tey are deceived, not
having read, te *writings* of te *Ancients* : For first, her cannot
finde in all her *Welsh Histories*, tat ever *Alexander* te
creat ever was in her *Countrey*, and if ever her was at
Mawburn-hills, which her cannot peleeve, *Mawburne-
hills* is not in her *Countrey*, and terefore tat can pee
no disparagement to her, or her *Countrey-men*, and for cillling
her *countreymen brutes*, or *beasts*, her understands not in te
least, nor her thinkes no body els tat ever her knew,
or

or could ever hear of; and therefore her will wave that, and the
rest, and give her Countreymen a clear demonstration of her
pedigree from the first inhabiting of *Wales*, her Ancestors antient Inheritance, and to the everlasting praise of her Countreymen be it spoken: It is thus. It was in antient time, but her
thinks it was since *Noahs* Flood, *England* was governed by seve-
rall Kings, and at that time *Carnwall* was a Kingdome of it self,
distinct from the rest, and the King of *Cornwal* having occasion
to use a great number of Oars at Sea, more then her own Dominions was able to furnish her withall, whereupon the King of
Cornwal called a Council together to advise with her about
her business, being of great weight to her small Common-
wealth; whereupon it was unanimously agreed, that her Majesty of *Cornwal* should write a Letter in Cornish to her Majesty
of *France* for a supply of French Oars for her Cornish Galleys,
but when her Majesty of *France* had received her Majesty of
Cornwals Letters, and her Majesty of *France* not well understanding the Cornish tongue, understood these Oars to bee
Whores, of which kind of good creatures *France* did abound,
insomuch that they might be well spared, her Majesty of *France*
willingly consented, and accordingly sent over to *Cornwall* eight
ships wel fraught with French whores, which when her Maiesty
of *Cornwall* perceived, her was horn mad, especially for that her
French whores were almost naked, whereby her Maiesty knew
that her had gotten a great number of idle people into her Territories more then her had, though her Countrry was well provided before, as her own Countrey is to this day : But to proceed in her discourse, her Maiesty of *Cornwal* being willing to
cloath these French whores, and to set them to work, and there
being little store of cloath in *Cornwall*, because few good Hus-
wives dwelt there, her Maiesty of *Cornwal* writ a Letter to the
King of *Ireland* in the Cornish Tongue, to send him over as
many Irish Rugs as would cloath those French whores ; but
when her Majesty of *Ireland* had received her Letter, and not
well understanding the Cornish Tongue, her understood the
Rugs to be Rogues, of which *Ireland* was well stored ; whereupon her Majesty of *Ireland* mustered up as many Rogues as was
expressed in her Letter, and more too, because her would be rid
of

of them, and sent them over by shipping into *Cornwall*, which when her Majesty of *Cornwall* perceived, her was worse mad then before; whereupon her called her Councel together to consult what was fit to be done in such a case; whereupon, after much time spent in debate, some moving to hang them, others opposing that, alledged, that would make Hemp dear; and therefore in her judgment, it was best and the cheapest way to throw them all into the Sea, and drown them all: But against that was alledged, that that was the worst way that could be to dispose of them; for that was the way to breed a scarcity of fish in all the Nations round about, because the French whores and Irish rogues were such nasty stinking Cattel, that if her Majesty should throw them into the Sea, they would poyson all the Fishes in the Sea, and so not only bring famine into her own Territories, but also provoke all the Princes round about her to war against her Crown and Kingdom; and if her should hang them, it would not only make Hemp dear, but destroy all her loving Subiects with a pestilential air, or ill smell; and if her drown them, it would poyson all the fishes in the Sea, and bring famine upon all her Subiects, to her exceeding great detrement; wherefore there was a necessity to find out some other way, whereupon it was resolved, that forasmuch as *Wales* was not then inhabited, and that it was but a short cut from *Cornwall* to *Wales*, and that as there was many hils, there could not choose but be some Dales, and they being there, they could neither make hemp dear, nor poison the fish, but if they poisoned any body, they must poison one another; For these, and the like reasons it was unanimously agreed *Nemine contra dissente*, that they should be forthwith sent over, which was done accordingly, and of their Off-spring came her welsh cosen and countrey-men,

> *Who since by Procreation,*
> *Are now become a nasty Nation.*

Thus her hopes her have done her Countrey good service in freeing her Countrey-men from calumnies and aspersions, also humbly craving pardon for her prolixity, it being fery needfull to clear her self and her countreymen from such aspersions usually

ally caft upon her and her countreymen by prophane and ignorant Englifhmen; and as her have been long and large in fome things, fo her fhall be prief and fhort in fom other, and fo her comes to give her Iudgment to the gazing Star, or *Stella wovd*, feen in and neer London, about the 22 and 23 of *February*, 1654.

Her duz humbly conceive, that this Star duz portend (if any thing at all) either peace or war, or both, but which, hea do not fery wel know, becaufe her have not confulted with her Authors, becaufe her Library was burnt at the deftrution of *Sodom* and *Gomorah*, which neither her felf, nor any body els for her is ever like to recover; but her have borrowed one of the Modern Aftrologers books, which tells her, that Stars at that time of the day, fignifie only fair and dry weather, her duz confefs if there be no rain, it is like to be a dry fnmmer, but her can give no great credit to Modern Aftrologie, becaufe things new are not always true, but if her had her Library, before fpoken of, her would undertake to refolve her all her doubts, and fo hee bids her farewel.

F I N I S.

Sarah Ginnor's *The Womans Almanack: Or, Prognostication for ever* (Wing 1848) is reprinted from the copy in The British Library, Thomason Tracts Collection (Shelfmark E.2140 [1]). The text block of the British Library copy is 75 × 135 mm.

For passages that are blotched, please consult Appendix B, 'A Key to Difficult-to-Read Passages'.

The Womans Almanack:

OR,

Prognostication for ever : Shewing the nature of the Planets, with the Events that shall befall Women and children born under them. With several Predictions very useful for the Female Sex.

fig 1

By Sarah Ginnor *Student in Physick.*

London, Printed for J. J. **1659.**

MVSEVM
BRITAN
NICVM

COurtious Reader, The gift of learning being so little set by in these days amongst those of our Sex, is the chief invitation which hath caused me to publish this small Tract, thereby to stir up others, not to let their great worth with other learned Authors of our Sex ly in obscurity. I need not quote them for I think few of our Sex so ignorant but they have either read or heard of them, and though some of them have been abused by the quacksalving Mountibanks that would engrosse all knowledge into their own hands, yet have great & wonderful cures been done by our Sex, after these paper-scull Mongrels have left them. Why then should we suffer these Cater-pillers to eat up our vine ? Let me tell you, it is as lawful for us to be Judges & plead our own Causes in our own gowns as Lawyers to plead for others. Then lets rowse up our spirits, and show forth our Vertues, for the knowledg in this Art will animate our husbands to excel us, no doubt but we shall make them sencible where the sign lies; and make them be in our studies many times when they would be in an Alehouse; nay we shall find the nights will be more comfortable, and the days more pleasant. By this means we shall be counted instead of Mobs, maps of modesty, and for rattling Gossips, but Emblems of vertue, and patterns of civiliy to all the world.

Yours whilst S.G.

A 2   A

A

ROGNOSTICATION
for ever.

Astrological Observations.

FIrst, I shall begin with what concerns our own Sex *viz.* If we find *Mercury* in a feminine House with *Venus*, then we must allow *Mercury* a female, in a feminine Sign, and drawing to a conjunction with *Venus*, *Mercury* to a *Quartile* of *Mars* and *Pisces*, and *Gemini*, denotes some of our sex (not too much loaded with vertue) have a rare faculty in scolding, in other some sullenness and perversnesse.

Venus in the 12 house in exaltation, applying to combustion with the Sun, denoteth that women will be more free then usual in bestowing the P— on their Clients. But if *Luna* go to *Saturn* in the sixth house in *Libra*, it shews that old covetous fools will dote on young wenches, therefore beware of marrying, in the Spring, for if *Scorpio* be in the 7th house intercepted, it denotes unseemly wantonnesse, letchery and lightness in women.

If *Luna* be in the 7th house in *Pisces*, it denotes frequent marrying, and is a fortunate position for Oyster-women, Fish-women, & others who are under the sign *Pisces*.

If *Luna* and *Jupiter* be in reception, the Moon

in

in *Pisces* and Jupiter in Cancer, it is a fortunate time of marrying, many of our Sex shall obtain gallant matches, nay some better then they deserve. If Mercury and Venus be in Cancer, in conjunction in the eleventh house, to marry a Seaman is fortunate. If Venus be in Scorpio, the wantons of our Sex as well as the other sex will be pepper'd with the P — and then wo to your Noses, for its a fatal plague to the roof of your mouth besides the downfal of Narrow-bridge and the drying up your Fish-ponds by the opperation of malignant fireworks.

For this my Judgement, do not take distast ;
But as I am, I wish you all, be chast :
This is the only way, if you desire
To be preserved from the *Frenchmans* fire.

The Names of the Planets and the Dayes governd by each Planet.

As Saturn stands for Saturday so Luna *Sunday*,
Mars to *Tuesday* Sol stands up to Monday,
Jupiter boldly doth to *Thursday* fly,
To *Fryday* Venus, Wedensday Mercury.

The 12 signs ruling in the body are, Aries, *Taurus*, Gemini, Cancer, Leo, Virgo, Libra, *Scorpio*, *Sagitarius* Capricorn, Aquarius, Pisces.

Monthly

January. If it be on New-years day that the Clouds in the morning be red, it shall be an angry yeare with much War and great Tempests. If the Sun do shine on the 22. day of *January* there shall be much wind. If the Sun doth shine on Saint *Pauls* day, the 25 day of *January*, it shall be a fruitfull year, and if it do Rain or Snow, it shall be between both : If it be very misty it betokeneth great death : If thou hear it Thunder that day, it betokeneth great Winds, and great death and most especially among rich men that year.

February. On Shrove-Tuesday whosoever doth Plant or Sow, it shall remain alwayes green.

Item, how much the Sun did shine that day, so much he shall shine every day in Lent. And alwayes the next new Moon that falleth after Candlemas day, and after that the next Tuesday, shall be alwayes Shrove-Tuesday.

And when the Sun riseth and shineth early, then prospereth well all manner of Fruit : if you hear it Thunder, that it betokeneth great Wine and much Fruit.

Saint *Bede* saith there be three dayes, and three nights, that if a Child be born therein, the body abideth whole and shall not consume away untill the day of Judgment : that is in the last dayes of *January*; and the secrets thereof are full wondrous. And if a Tree be hewed at, on the same day, it shall never fall.

March.

March.

The more Mists that there be in *March*, the more good down it, and as many dayes as be in *March*, so many hoar frosts shall you have after Easter, and so many Mists in *August*. All manner of Trees that shall be cut down unto the two last Holy days in *March*, shall never fall.

Item, If on Palm Sunday be no fair weather, that betokeneth to goodness. If it do Thunder that day, then it signifieth a merry year, and death of great men.

April. If it rain never so little on the Ascension day, it betokeneth dearth of all manner of food for Cattel. But when it is fair weather it is prosperous, and there shall be plenty of Tallow and much Wooll.

May. If the Sun do shine on the 25 day of *May*, Wine shall prosper well; but if it doth rain, it doth much hurt. *Item*, if it rain on Whit-Sunday, it is not good. *Item* in the last of *May*, the Oak Trees begin to bear blossoms, if they blossom then, you shall have a good year of Tallow, and plenty of Fruit.

June. If it rain ne'r so little on Midsummer-day, that is the 24 day of *June*, then do not the Hasel Nuts prosper : If the holy Sacraments day of our Lord be fair, then it is good and causeth Fruit plenty, and the Lambs to dye.

July, If it Rain the second day of *July*, such weather shall be forty days after, day by day, yet some imputed it to *Swithin* the 15. *August.*

August. If the Sun do shine on the 15 day of *August*, that is a good token, and speciall for Wine.

September. If thou wilt see and know how it shall go that year, then take heed to the Oak Apples about Saint *Michaels* day, for by them you shall know how that year shall be : If the Apples of the Oak-Trees when they be cut, be within full of Spiders, then followeth a naughty year: If the Apples have within them Flies, that betokens a meetly good year. If they have Maggots in them, then followeth a good year: If there be nothing in them, then followeth great dearth : if the Apples be many and early ripe, so shall it be an early Winter, and very much Snow shall be afore Christmas, and after that it shall be cold.

If the inner part or kernall be fair, and clear, then shall the Summer be fair, and the Corne good also ; but if they be very moist then shall the Summer also be moist. If they be lean then shall there be a hot and dry Summer. If it Thunder in this moneth it presageth plenty of Wine and Corne that year.

October. When the leaves will not fall from the Trees, then followeth after a cold year, or else a great number of Caterpillars on the Trees.

November. Whether the Winter be cold or warm, go on *Alhollows* day to a Beech Tree, and cut a chip thereof ; and if it be dry then shall the Winter be warm : if thou wilt try on St. *Andrews* even,

even, whether, it shall be a moist or dry year that followeth, you shall know by a glass full of water: if the year shall be moist, and much Raine shall fall, then shall the Water in the Glass run over. And if there shall follow a dry year, then shall not the water arise to the brink thereof.

When there followeth a foggy Night, a good year after ensueth, that is, when it commeth on the Thursday Night, or on a flesh day at Night, and not on the Friday or Saturday, wherein some men will eat no other meat but Flesh: if there be Thundring, that betokeneth plenty of Fruit.

December. When Christmas day commeth while the Moon waxeth, it shall be a very good year, and the nearer it commeth to the New Moon, the better shall that year be.

If it come when the Moon decreaseth, it shall be a hard year, and the nearer the latter end thereof it commeth the worse and harder shall the year be. And if any Wood be cut off on the two last dayes of *December*, and on the first day of *January*, it shall not rot nor wither away, nor be full of Worms, but alwayes wax harder, and in his age as hard as a stone.

When Christmas Eve at midnight the wind waxeth high, it betokens a fruitful year; and when the Sun shines on Twelfth day in the morning, it betokeneth foul weather, if it be fair that day it is happy and fortunate.

To.

To find the time when the Sun shall be Eclipsed, and when not by his distance from these two sections called the head and tail of the Dragon.

If the apparent latitude of the Moon at the time of the visible Conjunction be lesse then 39. min. 49 seconds, there must be an Eclipse.

But if the apparent latitude of the Moon be more then 34 min. 51 seconds, there can be no Eclipse.

If the apparent latitude be more then 30 min. 40 seconds, and lesse then 34 min. 51 seconds, there may be a small Eclipse, as in this following Figure.

North

East   **West**

South

Of the Eclipse of the Moon.

If the Moon at the Noon at the time of her opposition to the Sun, shall be distant from either

cither of the two forementioned points, lesse then
10 degrees, 21 min. and 20 seconds, then must the
Moon suffer an Eclipse.

But if her distance be more then 13 degrees 5
min. and 13 seconds then the Moon cannot be
Eclipsed.

If her distance be more then 10 degrees 21 min.
& 20 seconds, then she may Happen to be Eclipsed, but not necessarily.

I shall not treat further on Eclipses, in regard
the happiness of our Sex doth appear in most splendour, when the Moon appears so clouded, as in
this following Figure, dark nights being to us as a
fountain, whence flows all our mirth, joy, pleasure,
sports, and melodious recreations.

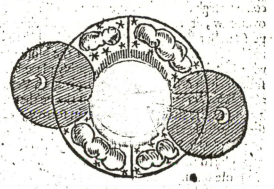

Expound you may the piece 'tis but a Riddle,
The pleasure of our Sex lies in the middle.

The

The signification of Moles in these of our sex.

If the Woman have a Mole on the left Breast, it denotes her undoubtedly wicked. If she have a Mole on her Belly, it denotes her a Glutton or great feeder. If a Mole right against the Spleen, it denotes she shall be often sick. If on the bottom of the Belly, it argues much debility and weakness. If near the privy Members it denotes unspeakable desires after Venery, and unsatiable in coacting. If a woman have a Mole on the right Knee, it denotes her honest, if on the left many Children. If on the Ankle of the foot, she shall take on her the mans part. Moles on the right side betokeneth honesty Riches, on the left side Calamity and Poverty. If on the Forhead, it denotes that she shall come to high dignity. If she have a Mole about the overbrow, it argues she shall marry a rich comely person. But if on the overbrow she shall have five Husbands. If she have a Mole on the Nose somewhat Ruddy, and another in the privy place, it doth shew such a person is over much given to Venerial acts. If a Woman have a Mole on the neither jaw, it denotes she shall lead her life in sorrow, which shall hinder her from bearing Children. If a Mole on any of the Lips, it doth portend that shees a great glutton. If on the Chin, it portends wealth. If a Mole on any of her Ears, it portends she shall be Rich and much reverenced, and hath the like Mole on her Thigh or Ham. If on the Neck, it likewise denotes Riches. If a Woman shall have a

Mole

Mole on her Loyns, it denotes poor Kindred, and always wanting. If on the shoulders, it denotes Imprisonment and sorrow. If she have a Mole on the Throat, it signifies she shall Marry a Wealthy and Comely man. If in the Hand a Mole shall appear, it denotes good Luck and Prosperous Children. If a Mole on the Breast, it denotes she shall be harmed by much poverty.

How to know whether a VVoman be with Child of Boy or Girl.

Write the proper names of the Father or Mother, and of the Moneth that she conceived with Child, and adding likewise all the numbers of those Letters together, divide them by seven, and if the remainder be even, it will be a Girle, if odd, it will be a Boy.

To know whether the VVife be Honest or no.

Write the name of the Wife, and of her Mother, and put all the number of those Letters together, and put to the totall sum 15, and divide it by 7, and if the remainder be un-even, she is honest, if even she is dishonest. Always write the proper names in Latine.

The same may be to know whether a Man or his Wife shall dye first, only add not the number 15, but divide by seven, if even the Woman shall dye, if odd the man.

A Prognostication.

What Thunder signifieth every Moneth.

Thunder in *January* signifieth the same year great Winds, plentifull of Corn and Cattel peradventure. Thunder in *February*, signifieth that same year many rich men shall dye in great sickness. Thunder in *March*, signifieth that same year great Winds, plenty of Corn, and debate amongst people. Thunder in *April* signifieth that same year to be fruitfull and merry, with the death of wicked men. Thunder in *May*, signifieth that year need, scarceneste and dearth of Corn, and great hunger. Thunder in *June*, signifieth that same year that Woods shall be overthrown with Winds, and great rageing shall be of Lyons and Wolves, and so like of other harmfull Beasts. Thunder in *July*, signifieth that same year shall be good Corn, and losse of Beasts, that is to say, their strength shall perish. Thunder in *August*, signifieth the same year sorrow, wailing of many, for many shall be sick. Thunder in *September*, signifieth the same year great Wind, plentifull of Corn, and much falling out between man and man. Thunder in *October* signifieth the same year great Wind, and scantness of Corn, Fruits and Trees. Thunder in *November* signifieth that same year to be fruitfull and merry, and cheapnes of Corn. Thunder in *December*, signifieth that same year cheapnesse of Corn, and Wheat, with peace and accord among the people.

Some.

Some memorable Accidents happened since 1639.

The Parliament began the 3 of *November*, 1639
and continued 12 years.

The Rebellion in *Ireland* began 23 *October*, 1641

Earl of *Strafford* beheaded 12 *May*, 1642

Earl of *Essex* made Gen. *July* 12 1642

Battel at *Edg-hill October.* 20. and at *Brainford* 12
November, 1642

Newbury fight 23 *Sept.* 1642

Scots enter into *England* Jan. 16. 1643

Bishop of *Cant.* beheaded Jan. 10 1644

Lord *Fairfax* made General *Decemb.* 31. 1644

Marstmore fight, *June* 14, 1644

House of Lords and King voted down, 1648

King *Charles* began his reign 27 *March* 1625 and
beheaded 30 *January*, 1648

Colchester taken, and *Lucas* and *Lisle* shot to
death, *Aug.* 28, 1648

Scots routed in *Lancashire Aug.* 7. 1648

Ormond beaten from *Dublin Aug* 2, 1649

The K. of *Scots* routed at *Worcester* 3 *Sep.* 1649

Scots routed at *Dunbar Sept.* 3. 1651

The long Parliament dissolved by the Lord Protector, *April* 20 1653

Victory against the *Dutch*, Jan. 23 1653

The Protector having Governed four years, three
months, and 5 days, departed his life the third
of Sept. 1658

Some

Some Signs of mirth for our sex.

When the Dragons head is in Scorpio, and he upon the Cusp of the 7 house, the Moon being in Cancer, and Venus applying to a Sextile of the Moon, there's hopes of abundance of satisfaction in the gallant recreation of night sport, by a stranger; which questionless will make the merry wantons of our age tittle, with laughter, at the tryal of the fundamentall Point of Mars, who shall venter to beat up their quarters to his own prejudice.

When Mars sits at home to wash the dishes and skim the Pot, and Venus walks the Exchange, it denotes great change in houshold government.

When men come sober home, and go to bed by day-light, our sex are in election to be merry at Candle-light.

When men grow blind and can't see to tell mony at home, then our sex may be merry abroad.

When husbands are jealous over night, it shews a fit time for our sex to go to St. Tantlins next morning.

If a man be fortified strongly with the Scepter of Mars, it denotes a fit time for Venus to lye down, that mirth may be produced by the Turks entrance into Constantinople.

Yet after mirth, I wish our Sex may mend,
And Vertue guide them whilst I make An End.

3 D 1

APPENDIX B: A KEY TO DIFFICULT-TO-READ PASSAGES

Page numbers refer to the modern pagination placed at the bottom of the text for the ease of the reader.

Sarah Jinner

An Almanack or Prognostication for the year of our Lord 1658

17.5–6	Wom/en
17.14–15	testimo-/ny
17.20	managed; Amazones
17.21	Semiramis
17.24	deny
17.30	business
17.31	old: and now of late
17.32	what a rare Poem; Mistris Kathe-
17.33	near
17.34–35	Cart-/wrightes Poetes; wit
17.37	many more
17.38	Countess of Kent; lastly, of
18.2	Cunetia
18.3	parts
18.4	to rust? Let us scowre the rust off, by ingenious endeavouring the
18.5	animate
18.8	to excell us: so by this means we should
18.15	at noon; Moon is in: the
18.16	remaining
18.17	Suns entering Ari-
18.18	handled according to
18.19	Medicines tending to the

18.20	could have inserted
18.21	most
18.23	or, the Feminine; profit and
18.24	use.); lastly,; Monthly; Astrological, and
18.25	other
18.26	advise
18.29–30	it is intended to be a collection of/Rarities, worth thy view and preserving.
19.6–7	In this figure and the figure of the preventional full/ Moon, and postventional new Moon, Saturn, Jupi-
22.3	I find Mars Lord of the ascendant in/
22.4	head it denoteth some
22.9	doth foretell many diseases in women. Well
22.13	neither can I pro-
22.14	mise you any riches: for Mars is in the second house next
22.16	house puts you a jogging to see your friends, and delight
22.17	in discourse, as gossipings.
22.19	but neither of them
22.20	the first the 22 day of
23.1	Physical observations
23.2–3	[Text obscured] ... Eringo roots, Conserves of Pioney and ... and Apple
23.4–9	[See Jinner, 1659, 26.18–23.]
23.10–16	An Electuary for the same. [See Jinner, 1659, 26.24–30.]
23.17–23	An Electuary for the same. [See Jinner, 1659, 26.31–37.]
23.24–30	Another Electuary to stay the terms. [See Jinner, 1659, 27.7–13.]
23.31–24.18	An Electuary to purge the Reins. [See Jinner, 1659, 27.28; 28.13.]
24.19–25	[See Jinner, 1659, 29.25–31.]
24.26–30	[See Jinner, 1659, 30.7–11.]
24.31–37	[See Jinner, 1659, 29.32–38.]
25.2–21	[See Jinner, 1664, 13.2–21.]

25.27	Rosemary
26.1	flowers and stecados, of each an ounce: six ounces of
26.2	boyl it into a syrup
26.10	currans, each
26.14–18	[See Jinner, 1659, 27.14–18.]
26.19–27	Another to move the Terms. [See Jinner, 1659, 27.19–27.]
26.28–33	Wines good to provoke the terms. [See Jinner, 1659, 26.8–13.]
27.2	let her abstain from strong wines and flesh meat, and all
27.3	such things as increase natural sperme.
27.4	And use letting blood, such meats and drinks as are
27.5	Cooling, and amongst the rest, this confection follow –
27.6	ing is very good.
27.7–28.3	[See Jinner, 1659, 31.5–35.]
28.3–30.20	[See Jinner, 1664, 16.2–18,17.]
30.22–33	Take eight ounces of honey, and two pints of water,/ boyl them well together, and scum it, and dip therein a/threefold cloth, and lay it on the Breasts, and when it is/cold renew it again./ Also for the same, take one dram of saffron, and eight/ounces of Malmsey, wet a cloth therein, and lay it on/the Breasts as aforesaid,/ Also, take Garden Mints, stamp them, and mix them/ with Oyl of Roses, and use it as the other./ For a Plaister to dry up the Milk, take Bean meal,/oyl of Roses, and red Vinegar, a sufficient quantity to/ make a Plaister, and apply it to the Breasts.
30.34–32.33	[See Jinner, 1664, 18.20–20.25.]
33.2	This season admitteth but of little action, therefore
33.3	the greater consultations are on foot: The Commo-
33.4	to pry into af-
34.2–3	your fruit trees from Moths, Cankers, and superfluous/ branches, plash hedges, lay your quicksets: Plant Rose;/
34.7	Some triumph; I am sure the

34.8	Discontents for
34.9	want of; they will expect better
34.10	times
34.11	Foreigners; bereave us
34.12	advantages therein
34.15	fewel
34.16	comfort
34.17	good earth, especially; Narcissus
34.18	Tuleps and Hyacinth; bore
34.20	uncovered; graft fruit
34.22	temperate
34.24–27	News of great transactions arrive of the affairs of Eu-/rope, the Marchant suffereth exceedingly, the Com-/mons of most Nations are discontented, the most devout/complain must. Flanders is much disturbed.
34.30–33	Sowe your hemp and flax, sowe and set all sorts of/hearbs, open your hives, and give your Bees their liber-/ty and let them labour for their living, cut your Oake
34.34	Scowre
34.35	your ditches, gather; heaps,
35.2–4	gather stones, repair high-waies, set Osiers and Wil-/lows, and cast up all decayed fences. For your health/use moderate exercise.
35.6	Seems to change. Mat-
35.7	ters of; the great
35.8	ones fear the lesse being more numerous, whose
35.9–10	Aspect speaks but little safety to them: Lawes and Cu-/stoms are much slighted,
35.14	fewel; winter, furnish your Dairy, let your
35.15	Mares go to horse, fat your dry kine, and away with
35.16	them: Sowe your tender seeds as Cucumbers
35.22	easing
35.23	wrung by heavy imposed
35.24	the sword is drawn, the wronged have the victory.
35.25	Fiet iustitia.
35.29–32	your rank Meadowes, fetch home fewell, carry forth/

Manure, Marle and Lime to mend your Land. Be sure/to be chast this Month, whatever you are the rest of the/year.

36.3	vexed, subjects not pleased: The
36.4	faction
36.5	suppresse that Sect
36.7	Reformation; subject to
36.8	great disasters.
36.12	run; seed; cut off the
36.13	cover
36.14	earth; fell; you intended for
36.15	Take no physick, or little in extraordinary cases, refrain
36.16	venery.
36.18–27	A hot and sickly season, about the latter end of this/ Moneth somewhat abated. The Austrian tamely/ endeavoureth to strengthen it self by Councell, and/ Arms. The French seem to be losers. Great abuses/of clipping and imbasing money; the watchful Magi-/strate ought to be more than ordinarily vigilant in pre-/venting so great and publick abuses. Ancient sports and/pastimes (heretofore suppressed) grow again in fashion./Great disputations and controversies to Divinity again/revived.
36.30–34	Follow diligently your Corn harvest, cut down your/ Wheat and Rye, mowe Barley and Oates, put off your/fat Sheep and Cattel, gather your Plums, Apples,/ and Pears; make your Summer Perry and Cyder, set/ your slips and scyons of all sorts of Gilly flowers and
37.3	Manure from your
37.4–6	Dove-coats put your swine to the early mast. Refraine/ all excesse in eating and drinking, drink that which is/cooling.
37.8	encouragements
37.9	the obstruction lyeth
37.10	misery.
37.11	success is not hereditary.
37.14	Beans, Pease; on

37.15	bestow the
37.16	and other commodities
37.17	Thatch your hive of Bees.
37.18	look that no Droans, Mice
37.19	them. Thrash your seed, Wheat and Rye. Use Physick
37.20	moderately, shun the eating of sweet or rotten fruit, avoid
37.21	[surfeiting?]
37.23	Men incline more than ordinary to cruelty, and
37.24	crossness, the conjunction of Saturn
37.25	not safe
37.26	let time speak the lan-
37.27	guage that the lines silenceth.
37.30–31	Finish with your Wheat seed, plash and lay your/ hedges and quicksets, scowre your Ditches, and ponds
38.2	transplant
38.3	Winter; and feed
38.4	upon your cornfields: draw in rows to drain;
38.5	keep by your new sowen Corn
38.8	not intend to winter, and separate Lambs
38.9–11	from Ewes you intend to keep. Recreate your/spirits by harmless sports, and take physick by good ad-/ vice if need be.
38.13	Marchant
38.15	Vexed
38.16	minds
38.17	irresistible. Fair words de-
38.18	ceive
38.21	Naves
38.22	Axeltrees, barrows, and other offices about husbundry,
38.23	Or housewifry; make the last return of grasse feed Cattel,
38.27	hot soyls
38.28	Use spices and wine, moderately.
38.40–45	The season admitted not of action, yet great consultati-/ ons are on foot; mony is wanted, foundations for great/attempts are laying against the season of action.

An Almanack and Prognostication for the year of our Lord 1659

An Almanack for the Year of our Lord God 1664

87.31	K. Charls I. Mar.
88.1	March XXXI Dayes; April XXX Dayes.
88.2	St. David.
88.4	Palm Sunday.
88.11	Easter Sunday
88.26	Mark Evang.
88.28	Term begins.
89.1	May XXXI Dayes; June XXX Dayes.
89.2	Phil, and Jacob
89.6	Trinity Sunday.
89.11	Term begins.
89.16	Rogation Sun.
89.20	Ascension day.
89.24	Term ends.
89.25	John Baptist.
89.30	Whitsunday
89.31	Term ends.
90.1	July XXXI Dayes.; August XXXI Dayes.
90.2	Lammas.
90.25	Bartholomew A.
90.26	James Apostle
91.1	September XXX Dayes.; October XXXI Dayes
91.19	Luke Evang.
91.22	Mathew Apostle.
91.29	Simon and Judas
91.30	Mich. Arch. Ang.
92.1	November XXX Days.; December XXXI Days.
92.2	All Saints.
92.6	Powder Treason
92.22	Thomas Apos
92.26	Christs Nativity
92.27	Steph
92.28	St. John Evang.
92.29	Term ends.; Innocents.
92.31	Andrew Apostle.
95.33	Since Charls the 2d. began to reign, 16 y
96.1	A Succinct Chronology

98.6–29	[See in this volume, Jinner 1659, 27–28.]
101.2	It is likewise good for
101.4	for any bruise, to draw out a Thorn
101.8–10	When the Woman with Childe be-/gins to draw near her time then let her use such/meats and drinks as nourish well, but use no excess
102.2	Plantain
102.8	ensue impostumes
102.9	distempers in the breasts
102.9–10	Re/medies .... use these prescriptions
102.13	superfluous
102.19	Breasts
102.21	keep
102.22	moyst meats that may engender subtle/milk
102.23	Saffron; Cinamon
102.25	Milk, and Oyl of Roses,
102.26	Seeth them together
102.29	ashes
103.4	Cuminth
103.7	make on Oyntment or Plaister hereof
103.20	then strain it, and mingle it with Wheaten meal
103.21	thickness of pap; to it Hens grease
103.22	Hogs Lard
104.28	flying ants
104.36	preventing
105.2	Mad-cap fellows.; Ingredient
105.3	Venery
105.8	same
105.9	under; when
105.18–20	A Turtles heart wrapped in a wolves skin he/that carrieth it about him shall be freed from immo-/derate Love, yea, from loving at all.
105.24	Frog; strew
105.26	discover
105.30	grind
105.31	them upon a Marble stone, as Painters do their Cou-
106.2	lours; put water

106.3–4	then take away the wa-/ter gently, and let the matter that stayeth behind dry
106.6	yellow skin as much
106.7	needful, lay it into distilled Vinegar the whole night/ untill it be dissolved; then strain it and add thereto
106.9–13	This hurteth not the/Face nor Teeth as other paints used by Ladies do, the/Face is no wise altered by the application of it and it is very beautiful to be old, the chiefest of the Venetian/Ladies use this sort of painting.
106.16	had in most Gardens, and rub the face
106.17	pale cheeks look red.
106.19	Gourd.
106.20–21	[bruise?] them and presse/them strongly, to draw forth an Oyly Liquor: with
106.22	touch the Car-
106.23–24	will be taken quite away, with red-/ness much abated.
106.29	they
106.34	Talcum, Salt
106.35	set them into
106.36	for fifteen or twenty dayes
107.3	that runneth
107.4	having first washed your face
107.10	thick to an Oyntment
107.11	morning and evening therewith
107.12	World
120.8	white

Mary Holden

The Womans Almanack for the Year of our Lord, 1688

128.1	The Vulgar Notes and Moveable Feasts for
128.13	The Anatomy of Man's Body.
129.2	Table of the Terms and Returns
129.21	term
129.24	glorious

149.6	them
149.10	colds
149.17	sorts
149.18	were
149.19	Moon
149.20	your
149.23	safely
149.24	Headache
149.28	land
149.29	manure; gather
149.30	plant Physical
149.34	tend
149.35	keep
149.36	about
149.37	sick moderately, shun
149.38	avoid surfeiting.
152.35	Seek the day on the side; and right against it in every month you have
152.36	the hour and minute of Sun-rising.
152.37	Look how many minutes the Sun rizes after 3, 4, 5, 6, 7, 8.
152.38	So many he sets before 9, 8, 7, 6, 5, 4.
154.29	the following Table is
154.30	Easter this present
154.32	look under
154.33	against the Golden Number 17 at the
154.34	common angle of meeting I find April 15
156.19–29	Fairs in March/The 1 day at Llangadog, at Llangavellah, at Madrin, 3 at/Bremwel-brakes in Norfolk, 4 at Bedford, Ockham, 8 at/Tragarton, 12 at Spiford, Stamford, Sudbury, Woodburn, Wrexam, Bodnam, Alsom in Norfolk, 13 at Wye, Bodwin/in Cornwal, Mountbowin, 17 at Patrington, 18 at Sturbridge,/20 at Alesbury, Durham, 24 at Llanercherith, 25 at St. Al-/bans, Ashwel in Hertfordshire, Burton, Cardigan, Carwalden,/in Essex, Huntington, St. Jones in Worcestershire, Malden,/

Malpas, Newcastle, Northampton, Oney in Buckinghamshire,/Woodstock, Whitland, Great Chart, 31 at Malmesbury.

157.23	Stansted; Stocknailand
157.25	Powlthelly
157.26	Bromyard
157.28	Denby
157.30	Tidnel
157.31	Montgomeryshire
157.32	Bath, Beverly, Hanslop
157.34	9 at
157.36	16
157.37	Odchil, Roche-
158.23	Tunbridge
158.24	Chester, Windsor, Wormester
158.25	Burton; Folkston
158.26	Merchenleth
158.27	Bennington, Biballance
158.28	ingford; Hodesdon, Holdsworth
158.29	Hadderfield; Knotsford, Lemspter, Lanorgan
158.30	der, Mansfield
158.31	Peterborough, Peterfield, Pontstephen
158.32	Southam; Stockworth, Sudbury, Therokgrais
158.33	Upton, Wem
158.34	hurst; 30 at Mansfield
158.35	Fairs in July
158.36–37	The 2 at Ashton under line, Congerton, Huntington, Rick-/minsworth, Smeath in Kent, Swansey, Wodburn, 3 at Haverson
159.2	5 at
160.10	de la Zouch; Brigstock
160.11	Farringdon; Kiddenminster
160.14	Walford
160.16	Colby in Lincolnshire, Kaerwis
160.17	after Barthol.
160.18	Fairs in September
160.24	Culver, Smeath, Snide

160.25	ter; Waltham
160.26	12 at Worseworth
160.27	in Kinwin, Powlthelly
160.28	Wocomb, Barsley, Church-Stretton
160.29	Hidom, Hersbury, Munston
160.30	Penhad, Rippon, Richmond
160.31	Stratford
160.32	15
160.33	Baldock
160.34	maiden
160.35	try, Eastrid.
160.36	hill
160.37	Mildnal
160.40	Malton; 26; Kaermarthen
161.5	Marketdeeping
161.6	Hull, Killingworth
161.9	Bedfordshire
161.16	Chicester, Hereford
161.18	Gainsborough, Harborough
161.19	Newport-Pagnel, Furnace
161.20	Creston
161.21	Hirchen
161.22	Taiton
161.24	Banbury
161.30	Cicester
161.31	22
161.38	Ruthin
164.2	Whitsun-Monday
164.3	Ryhil, Salisbury, Agmond-
164.4	Bromi-
164.7	Darrington
164.10	long Milford
164.12	Llandbedder
164.13	Pontstephen
164.16	Kendal
164.19	Abersrow
164.20	Eglesrew, Hallaron

| 164.21 | Llanimerchenith |
| 164.27 | Sanbich in Chesh. Monday after St. Michael at Fasely |

The Womans Almanack: Or, An Ephemerides For the Year of Our Lord, 1689

171.2	Last; the 3
171.3	New
171.5	Full Moon the 25 Day at 10
174.5	Full
201.31	a moist nature producing

Dorothy Partridge

The Womans Almanack, For the Year 1694

207.33	By Dorothy Partridge, Midwife, Student in Astrology.
207.34	London: Printed for J.S. in the Great Old-baily, 1694.
208.10	min
208.11	dens. A lusty
208.13	garden-herbs
208.14	[passages?]
208.21	etc.
209.9	Ply
211.9	Aris
211.10	Gemini
211.19	the 4, and 7. In July,
211.20	the 6, and 7. In Octo-
211.32	various and
211.33	Island, such as is Eng-
212.22	Lighten the day
212.23	a great wind
212.24	gapeth against the Sun in
212.25	Swarming of Bees
212.26	Droanes; Bettles
213.36	somewhat by the swiftness or

217.38	Balneo Mariae
218.3	Nape
218.5	Forehead; ano-
218.9	House-leek
218.12	roasted
218.14	her
218.15	die first,
218.16	Note,; there are
218.17	Stand for Numbers; 50
218.24	Love-powder.
218.27	them lie there 48 hours,
218.28	Powder very fine
218.29	Other, the breath-
218.30	ing the Basilick Veins, and distilling it after, is the best
218.32	Licensed according to Order.

Appendix A:

Mother Shipton

The Prophesie of Mother Shipton ... (1641)

221.11	Richard Lownds,
221.12	adjoyning to Ludgate
224.12	bur-
224.13	ned
224.18	doe well
224.18	Yorke pavement, and
224.25	Cawwood
224.29	shee
224.32	miles
224.33	ing sen
225.2	laske; Shipton's
225.5	hee
225.7	more of her

225.12–13	when the North shall rue it/wondrous sore, but the South shall rue it for evermore
225.14	Hares Kirle
225.18	Scots
225.21	Edinborough
225.25	bands, and when
225.26	let him beware of a stab.
225.27	the Castle yard, they shall never bee
225.28	after. When all Colton Hagge
225.29	there shall two; Mungate
226.4	well-away
226.9	Cadron
226.22	when they come to Bram-
226.23	mammore
226.24	Knavesmore
226.25	there will be a great
226.26	Scotland, at [Stoknmore?]; Then
226.27	and drink as much bloud
226.28	woe is me,
226.29	; Then there will
226.30	many
226.32	her; to him
227.2	she shall say, Goe with
227.3	for there are three Knights, and he will
227.4	there three dayes and three nights,
227.12	Castle six miles from Yorke, and he
227.13	shall choose there an Earle in
227.19	barre at a
228.2	St. James Church hill wee-
228.11–12	Unhappy he that lives to see these daies/But happy are the dead, Shiptons wife saies.

Shinkin ap Shone

The honest Welch-Cobler

231.17	[comro?]
231.24	Shiles
231.26	Harie
231.27	Shentlemen
231.29	Goat on
232.28	puisines:
232.33	under the feet of a Mountaine,
233.2–7	Taffie was fine, and her tranke of the wine,/the water out of the Fountaine:/Taffie eat Apple-Crabb, put her love was a Trabb,/for trinking the whey out of the firking,/Put all the long day of her Harpe her will play,/and make the lowse tance in her Sherking.
233.9	lick up cold, as
233.10–38	her countreymen use to lick up Welch. Flumrey: put neither wit/now nor honestie will pay anything in her Welsh Markets, her/must set her self flat and close to her Trade of Cobling, and first/I shall beekin with the createst piece of worke I have, though it may be worst payd for it, and that is Prince Ruperts Boots to sole,/and he useth to pay folkes with his Poleax. You may remember,/as I was informed by some of her owne Countreymen, and those/none of the pest qualitie, tat made a shift to save her selves by the/ nimble agilitie of her heeles at Marston fight, that Prince Rupert to/save her selfe, ran over the Beane field, and there her lost either, one/or both her soles, her stuck so fast in the Clay; & here her cannot put/ commend her for her wit, for her is sure her will never pe hangd/for her honestie, tat her would paralel her self with her Cossens of/Wales, tat when her see her could not overcome by fighting, to/save her selfe by flying; and for tat trick and one more that her/ canowes her will set her on a payre of the pest soles

tat her wore/in her life cratis, because her canow tat her lost all tere & at Naseby,/and never cot any good fortune since, except a purge and a broken/shyn at Abbington, and a little strong Beere at Bristol, and tere her/was forced to leave the createst part behind him, because he could/not stay to drink it, but upon these conditions, first, that her come/no more a plundring into her Welch territories, to carry away her/cood Welch Shees, that her should tost for her none selfe, her/wife and shildren, which though her sayt her selfe, is made as/cleanly as any Shees in all Wales, for her wife strained it through/the skirt of her foule smock, for feare there should be any hayres/of her Cow or Goat in her Shees to shoake her.

Secondly, tat if her ever shance to come againe into England/or Wales, and to have any of her countreymen under her command,/

234.10	knowes
234.12	her owne
234.13	plaister
234.16	her
234.24	her
234.25	from her heart
234.27	cust Queanes toungues,
234.30	upon her peds
234.31	unmoveable coods.
234.32	her whom
234.36	cood turne her tid tem seven years agoe, that is desperate debt.
235.2	and therefore
235.5	pestow a payre of soles upon him,
235.6	her would give
235.7	first,
235.8	measures tat her hath
235.9	houses; ministers and tivers
235.10	cave her no cause at all:
235.11	base a calling for one

235.12	Lyme-burner, if her remember
235.13	paines: when her went
235.16	little or pigg, to make
235.17	had done: and though her
235.18	yet it were put Titular;
235.19	in her shudgment it is not worth
235.20	when her wife makes
235.21	if her pee wise
235.22	for as her is a Prince of the
235.23	catcht, her can never be questioned:
235.24	her
235.26	growne men, have
235.27	tey were
235.29	warrant
235.30	yeare
235.32	her self as plack as a Tivell with
235.33	had peen; for
235.36	and her wives and shildren
235.37	life time, to get her some fire.
235.38	Welch Territories, her will make
235.39	when her run away beyond sea
236.6	cratis; tell
236.7	coasts; should
236.12	plood
236.16	te last
236.20	Tawsone
236.22	almost
236.29	ur
236.30	ship
236.31	apps; sheneologes; have
236.32	urship; entreat; Urship
236.33	poots; *Du Cat en*
236.34	*ergh*.
236.35	Cottington; more fami-
236.36	liaritie; keese
236.37	hatcht many; citie
236.38	Goosling

237.2	that her urship was
237.3	tall Cedar-like Honour
237.4	one infallible truth which
237.5	since her left her Urships creat House
237.6	more money told then all her Ho-
237.8	there pee shurch
237.9	Spaine
237.10	would with her urship
237.11	and
237.12	for her have put
237.13	nor Tucks, nor Hens
237.15	de-
237.16	devoure
237.17	Foxes never fare better than when
237.19	longer
237.20	rong her cood flanell shirt
237.21	her call
237.22	pone; shuse
237.24	said
237.25	expressions; her
237.30	turn Presby-
237.31	kinsman
237.32	become
237.35	as her sheese use to be full of Maggots
237.36	Cambridge, and made her
237.37	a payre of horning Spectacles
237.39	her was put to silence above threescore Mini-
238.2	Fisit; scandalous
238.3	as
238.4	fore-
238.5	trunke
238.6	covetous, tat her had put
238.9	mis-
238.10	do pray her
238.11	well to her, for her is put a
238.12	would pray
238.13	fly away: her

238.14	to
238.18	pasture makes; why not
238.21	that run away
238.24	because
238.25	take heed to her
238.26	pick-pocket petter
238.30	in such a quarrel
238.31	her a periwig of honour
238.34	but
238.35	with her; then

Sarah Ginnor

The Womans Almanack: Or, Prognostication for ever

257.3	more mists
257.4	doth
258.25	not fall from
258.26	[Lacuna]
258.27	the trees.
259.12	Flesh: if
259.22	first
259.25	a stone
259.26	[when? at?] christmas
259.27	[full? it?]
259.28	shines
260.17	true opposition
266.4	moon being
266.6	satisfaction in
266.8	wantons of
266.9	tryal of the
266.10	venter to
266.13	walks
266.28	vertue; whilst

3 5282 00570 6323